Learning in Motion

101+ Sensory Activities for the Classroom

2nd Edition

Patricia Angermeier, OTR
Joan Krzyzanowski, OTR
Kristina Keller Moir, OTR

Illustrated by Catherine Krzyzanowski

FUTURE HORIZONS INC.

Learning in Motion
101+ Sensory Activities for the Classroom

All marketing and publishing rights guaranteed to and reserved by

FUTURE HORIZONS INC.

721 W. Abram Street
Arlington, Texas 76013
800-489-0727
817-277-0727
817-277-2270 (fax)
E-mail: info@FHautism.com
www.FHautism.com

ISBN: 978-1-932565-90-4

Contents

Contents

Contents

Contents

Contents

Acknowledgments

We thank some very special people who helped us. First and foremost, we wish to thank our husbands and children for their patience and support. We would also like to thank some colleagues who provided suggestions, feedback, and encouragement: Alicia Marini, a special educator; Michele Wiley, a physical therapist; and Kathleen Kantruss Nerz, an occupational therapist. We want to thank the many teachers and children who helped us develop the activities. To our friend and editor, Dave Viggiano—thank you for your time and hard work in editing our manuscript. Thanks to Sensory Resources (and its editor, Polly McGlew) for bringing our book to larger audiences. A special thanks to Cathy Krzyzanowski, whose whimsical illustrations make this book more fun.

How to Use this Book

To help you use *Learning in Motion* effectively, the table of contents lists the theme-based activities by months. Following the table of contents, we provide a synopsis of motor development to help the reader understand the importance of the activities included in this book. The next section describes the educationally relevant sensorimotor goals addressed by the activities as those goals relate to child development and educational performance. It may be helpful to the reader to review this section prior to using the activities.

For each month, there is a table listing the educational goals for each activity during that month. This table is a valuable tool enabling quick identification of seasonally appropriate activities to enhance development of particular educational goals. For example, a teacher who wants to foster pre-writing skills can refer to the tables and easily select appropriate activities.

Each activity includes a detailed lesson plan that includes Activity Goals, estimated Time required to complete the activity, Objectives, Materials, Adaptations, and Multilevel Instruction. Adaptations are techniques to include children with various physical and learning needs. Multilevel Instruction offers ideas to make the activity simpler or more challenging.

Each activity is followed by a Letter to Parents that may be copied and sent home with the children. The Letter to Parents includes a brief description of the activity, the purpose and educational relevance of the activity, and suggestions for home activities to reinforce the activity goals and objectives.

In the appendix, the reader will find an alphabetical index of the activities so they may be used to reinforce letter recognition. The appendix also provides additional adaptations for children with special needs and recipes to use with the activities.

Theories of Motor Development

As an introduction to the reader, we will reference five common theories of normal motor development. These are important theories and some of the principles for development of our activities. In our eagerness to help children develop academic skills, we sometimes overlook significant areas of their development, such as large muscle strength or trunk stability, that result in poor outcomes in writing and other fine-motor tasks. Normal progression of motor skills needs to be followed and fostered.

Cephalocaudal—Motor control of the child's body occurs in a head-to-toe progression. The child first is able to gain head control, then trunk, and lastly control of limbs.

Proximal-Distal—Motor control also occurs from the spine outward. The child will first gain motor control over his trunk, shoulders, hips, and finally hands (fingers) and feet.

Automatic-Voluntary—For survival, the baby's beginning movement patterns are reflexive (automatic) in nature. Later, the child will gain voluntary control over his movements. For example, the baby first holds on to an object using a grasp reflex. Later, the child gains voluntary control over his hands and is able to grasp, release, and manipulate an object.

Stability-Mobility—In order to develop refined movements in our limbs, we require a stable base of support. For example, the baby needs to develop good sitting stability to be able to use his hands in this posture. Only when sitting balance is well-established is the ability to manipulate, reach, and play with toys while in this position possible.

Unrefined-Refined Movement Patterns—Unrefined movements are random motor patterns that infants typically use, such as swatting. Initially, the child swats at a cup. Later, the child develops refined control of that movement allowing him to reach out and pick up a cup to drink. The baby's first steps are awkward and poorly placed. Later, this same child is able to run and jump. This progression from unrefined to refined movements occurs as a result of practice and maturation of the nervous system.

Many of the activities in this book aid the development of posture, strength and stability, large motor patterns, refinement of movement, enhancement of sensory feedback during motor activities, and improvement of body awareness for better motor planning. Use of these activities provides the extensive practice needed to gain the strength, endurance, and level of skill necessary for school success. With this developmental, sensory-motor focus, the child will be better able to attend, practice, and succeed in gaining the refined and coordinated skills (for example, coloring, writing, and buttoning) that are necessary for academic success.

Educational Activity Goals

For each of the activities included in *Learning in Motion,* the reader will find two educational activity goals listed near the top of the page. This section contains detailed descriptions of how these activity goals relate to child development and educational performance. The goals are listed here in alphabetical order.

Attention Improvement

The ability to attend to a task is influenced by the child's internal body state, whether he is alert, calm, drowsy, irritable, etc. Parents, teachers, and therapists can help children to achieve the proper level of alertness through use of appropriate sensory input and/or motor activities.

In general, activities that require a lot of heavy muscle work (e.g., pushing objects, pulling objects, working with weights, etc.) will increase attention and readiness for focused academic work. Activities that may over stimulate a child include light touch experiences, such as tickling, using balloons, playing with feathers, and playing with Styrofoam®. Other potentially over-stimulating activities are loud noises, a lot of movement occurring in class, moving lights, and rotary movement (e.g., spinning on a tire swing). Activities that tend to calm an overexcited child include slow, gentle rocking; deep pressure for a sustained period of time; warm and quiet environments; dim lights; soothing music; and relaxation breathing.

Balance Improvement

Balance is the ability to maintain body alignment while engaged in either static (e.g., sitting or standing) or dynamic (e.g., climbing or jumping) activities. Balance serves a functional, protective nature, which is to keep the head and eyes aligned properly. Balance occurs when opposing groups of muscles, e.g., trunk flexors (benders) and trunk extensors (straighteners), act together so that a posture can be sustained. Throwing a ball, dressing ourselves and picking a piece of paper up from the floor while seated at a desk are examples of how our body needs to maintain alignment and balance.

Bilateral Coordination Development

Bilateral coordination means that both sides of the body are able to work together successfully. Development of bilateral coordination begins very early in life as a baby begins to roll. Learning to roll involves shifting weight to one side. Initially, the baby props himself on his elbows, shifts weight to the side, and rolls to his back. Weight shifting provides the mobility necessary for propulsion. For example, when a baby is crawling, he can stop, shift weight to one side, stabilize the other side, and reach for a toy with one hand. Following the principles of motor development, the ability to weight-shift occurs first in the trunk, then in the shoulders and hips, and lastly in the hands and feet. Once weight shifting is established, the baby can coordinate both sides of his body to accomplish more complex motor activities, such as sitting and reaching to either side, coordinating arm and leg movements for crawling, hopping on one foot, stair climbing, and using scissors.

Body-Scheme and Motor-Planning Improvement

During the first year of life, a baby begins to organize sensory experiences gained through vision, touch, smell, hearing, and movement. This internal picture, the body scheme, gives the baby the basis from which to perform coordinated movements when he attempts new tasks.

Motor planning is the ability to use sensory information and previous motor-learning experiences to successfully perform a novel activity. In the school setting, motor planning is an important component of imitation. For example, learning to handwrite involves the child watching the teacher form letters on the blackboard and the child subsequently copying them. As the child consistently practices making the letter, the movement becomes more automatic, indicating that he has developed motor memory. Children who have difficulty playing creatively may have motor planning problems because they are unable to vary the way in which they play with an object or the way that they play a game.

Cognitive Development

Cognitive development is the ability to respond to the world around us in a logical and knowledgable way. Cognitive development, such as matching, sequencing, sorting, and classifying objects by various characteristics, can be enhanced through motor activities. Stimulating motor activities can encourage use of imagination for creative play. Reasoning, judgment, sequential memory, and short- and long-term memory are all components of cognition. Motor activities can emphasize and reinforce academic concepts in a variety of ways. For example, hopping around the edges of a large shape will help the child learn to recognize and draw that shape. During a sensory-motor group, in which the children pretend to be in the grocery store, they can practice classifying foods according to "like" characteristics, matching foods to the pictures on coupons, counting coins to pay the cashier, and using visual-perceptual skills (as well as motor skills) to pack the grocery bag successfully. Recalling and sequencing the events of the activity add further cognitive elements to the experience.

Fine-Motor Skills Development

When a baby is born, vision is the leading sense in fine-motor development. The baby spends the first few months of life watching his environment and hands. He later uses vision, muscle feedback, and his sense of touch to coordinate reaching toward a target. His beginning arm movements are random and directed away from the center of his body. At approximately three months of age, the baby discovers his hands, bringing them together at his midline and playing with his hands together. The baby watches his hands work together and starts to transfer or pass objects from one hand to the other hand. Once the baby is able to hold a stable position or posture (prone, supine, or sitting) he will begin to reach to the opposite side of his body (crossing the midline) with either one or both hands.

Grasp and release patterns are strongly influenced by gross-motor skills that provide weight bearing through the child's trunk and arms. For example, the baby initially is able to grasp an object before being able to control the release of that object. As the baby crawls, he places more weight on his hands and this muscular feedback encourages the wrist strengthening and small muscle development needed for opening and closing the fingers with good control. This is the stage when the baby starts to have fun leaning over his high chair and dropping things.

By one year of age, the baby has good eye-hand coordination and finger feeds independently. From this point, refined finger movement, such as screwing and unscrewing objects, coloring, and cutting with scissors, continues (with practice) to develop.

Gross-Motor Skills Development

Gross-motor skills, such as running, climbing, and jumping, are movements that require the coordination of the large muscle groups in the body. Gross-motor skill development can be practiced directly; however, there are underlying motor components that facilitate this development. The underlying components include balance, body awareness, strength, endurance, bilateral coordination, eye-hand coordination, motor planning, and visual-perceptual skills. Many of the activities in this book address the development of gross-motor skills, such as standing on one foot, hopping, jumping, walking on a balance beam, and ball skills. The acquisition of rotational skills, such as rolling, is crucial to higher level gross-motor skill development.

Group Development

The child entering school has some of his first experiences with group learning. A child's development within a group occurs in stages. Initially, the child develops the ability to maintain his own space within the group and is able to sit within a group without bothering others. The child progresses, and is then able to attend to instruction within a group setting. Next, he begins to share materials with a partner who is in the group, and the skill of turn-taking begins to emerge. The child starts to perform tasks with a partner, for example, using a Hula Hoop to pull another child on the scooter board. Eventually, the child is able to function as an integral member of the group, contributing to the common goal of the group.

The use of environmental structure, such as carpet squares, chairs, a line of tape on the floor, and modeling by the teacher, encourages children to observe others and learn the initial, basic group rule of remaining in their own space. This structure also enhances the child's ability to attend to social cues given by the other members of the group and to develop social awareness. To move to the next step of group development, there needs to be a balance between attention to the group and the child's ability to attend to his task within the group. Once the child is able to attend to his own task as well as the group activity, he can then benefit from modeling and imitation within the group. When these skills are mastered, the child is able to participate in groups of multi-level cooperation, such as working with a partner, working toward a common goal, and cooperating with the members in the group to achieve mutually beneficial goals.

Hand-Dominance Development

During the second year of life, many children develop a hand preference. Hand preference means that the child most often chooses this hand for precision activities. For example, a child who uses his right hand to place raisins into a cup demonstrates a right-hand preference. Generally, as a child enters kindergarten age, he will show hand dominance, consistently choosing to use one hand for precision activities, regardless of the placement of the activity.

A child who does not show hand dominance by kindergarten age may begin to indicate which hand is going to become dominant. Some of these indicators are which hand is used for feeding, which hand is used to throw a small ball, or which hand is used to wind a toy. To gather information on hand dominance, place an object at the child's midline and observe which hand the child chooses for manipulation of that object. To obtain reliable information, dominance trials should occur over a period of days and a number of times throughout the day.

Development of hand dominance involves maturation, development of coordination, and awareness of both sides of the body, as well as strength. By the end of his fourth year, if a child is still having confusion regarding hand dominance or complaining of hand fatigue during fine-motor activities, he should be referred to an occupational therapist for further assessment.

Pre-Writing Skills Development

The skills necessary for successful handwriting are extensive. They include general balance, trunk and upper extremity strength, endurance, bilateral coordination, motor planning, visual perception, hand dominance, eye-hand coordination, visual and motor memory, tactile sense and attention. Many skills must be mastered before the child is able to handwrite.

The ability to imitate a stroke or shape precedes the ability to copy these same strokes or shapes. The first experience with pre-writing skills consists of contacting the paper with crayons to make dots. This is followed by random scribbling, and subsequently, by scribbling in a circular pattern. Pre-writing progresses through the imitation of vertical, then horizontal lines, followed by the production of a carefully drawn circle and a cross with two intersecting strokes. Next, the child is able to draw a square, with sharp corners, and then he is able to draw diagonal lines, in the direction of right to left, followed by left to right. The most difficult shape for the child to copy is the diamond, which most children can draw by the age of seven.

Scissor Skills Development

Cutting with scissors is a complex activity. To cut efficiently and accurately, children must use bilateral coordination, visual-perceptual skills, their fingers in isolation, and motor-planning skills. An important aspect of holding scissors is that the middle finger and thumb are placed in the loops with the index finger placed in front of the lower loop. Cues to be used during cutting are "Keep your cutting and helping hands in a thumbs up position;" "Let your helping hand win the race" (assist hand always in front of cutting hand) and "Point the way with your pointer finger" (index finger is not in loop, it stabilizes the scissors). Turning the chair toward the dominant side will allow the child to place his elbow on the table for additional stabilization, which will promote the use of wrist extension rather than wrist flexion. Children who are left-hand dominant need to reverse the direction of cutting. For example, left-handed children will cut a circle in a clockwise manner whereas right-handed children will cut it in a counter-clockwise way. Also, it is important that left-handed children use scissors designed specifically for them.

Typically, cutting skills progress in a certain way. Initially, children begin making short snips with scissors. They then progress to cutting straight, diagonal, and curved lines. Finally, children master cutting sharp corners. Materials to be cut vary in difficulty. The easiest paper to cut is thicker, stiffer paper such as oak tag, paper bags, and index cards. More difficult materials to cut include construction paper, copy paper, tissue paper, and string or yarn.

Self-Help Skills Development

Self-help skills are those skills that a child needs to complete his daily personal care. These include feeding, dressing, toileting, grooming, organizing, and caring for school supplies. Regarding the acquisition of dressing skills, children learn to undress before they learn to dress. By age four, children can generally dress and undress themselves independently, but they may need assistance manipulating clothing fasteners. Though many of these skills are taught in the child's home, activities in school can be used to emphasize self-care development and independence.

Sensory Processing Improvement

Response to auditory, visual, tactile, olfactory, and vestibular input varies from person to person. The physical, physiological, and emotional response to these types of input is the result of Sensory Processing Improvement—how our brain interprets and reacts to sensory input. Presented with the same stimuli, some people will be hyper-reactive, most will react appropriately, and some will be hypo-reactive. For example, if a smoke alarm goes off in the office or home, most people will react and deal with the matter appropriately. If a person is hyper-reactive, he might scream or hold his hands over his ears and fall to the floor. On the other hand, if a person is hypo-reactive, he might continue with his activity, seemingly oblivious to the warning sound of the fire alarm. Hypo-reactive or hyper-reactive responses can be made to a variety of stimuli, and sometimes a child can be hyper-reactive to one type of stimulus, such as sound, and hypo-reactive to another stimulus, such as movement.

A child learns to organize his environment through his senses and uses this information to perform daily activities. For example, the crawling child will move in, under, and around furniture in the house. This helps the child validate his sense of body size and helps him learn speed of movement and how to maneuver within his environment. At the same time that he is receiving feedback from his muscles and joints while crawling, he is using vision to compare, and memory to store this information. This stored information will later be integrated with other motor experiences to allow the child to successfully engage in future motor-planning activities.

Many of the activities in this book work on helping the child to organize sensory and motor experiences. These activities use the group setting to encourage children to participate in sensory-motor experiences and respond appropriately to the sensory input from these experiences. Young children learn best if materials are presented actively and in a multisensory environment. These activities reinforce learning while encouraging sensory exploration and motor experiences in order to help the child organize and respond appropriately to a group learning experience.

Strength and Endurance Improvement

Strength is the muscular force used to perform activities. Children develop strength through activities requiring resistance. Examples of activities that build strength are playing on playground equipment, riding a bike, shoveling sand, crawling, pulling apart pop-beads, and manipulating clay or dough. Sometimes a child who has poor strength can be seen attempting to complete tasks very quickly during classroom activities. For example, a child who can go across the balance beam rapidly, but is unable to stop or slow down his movement during the activity, may lack the muscle strength to perform this task in a controlled way.

Endurance is the ability to sustain and complete an age-appropriate activity, with good quality of performance, over time. This requires not only muscle strength, but also cardiovascular fitness. For example, a child with asthma could be very strong but have difficulty with pulmonary endurance. A child with Down syndrome could be strong but lack endurance, secondary to cardiac abnormalities.

Visual-Perceptual Development

Visual perception is the process of taking in sensory information through the eyes, organizing and interpreting this information in the brain, and giving an appropriate response to the visual stimuli. Visual-Perceptual Development involves visual discrimination, eye-hand coordination, and ocular-motor control. It includes areas such as shape discrimination, spatial discrimination, visual figure ground, and visual memory. While children are developing an intact body scheme and motor coordination, they are also developing visual perception through movement and sensory exploration. For example, as a baby places objects into containers, he is developing an awareness of spatial relationships, size concepts, and position in space that can be remembered and used during later learning and play.

Educational Goals by Activity

Attention Improvement	Balance Improvement	Bilateral Coordination Development	Body-Scheme and Motor-Planning Improvement	Cognitive Development	Fine-Motor Skills Development	Gross-Motor Skills Development	Group Development	Hand-Dominance Development	Pre-Writing Skills Development	Scissor Skills Development	Self-Help Skills Development	Sensory Processing Improvement	Strength and Endurance Improvement	Visual-Perceptual Development	Activity	Page
												✔			Apple Butter and People Sandwiches	8
										✔				✔	Apples on a Fence	10
			✔				✔								Balloons and Body Parts	12
			✔				✔								Body Tracings	14
				✔								✔			Guess Which Shape!	16
								✔				✔			Hide-and-Seek Apple Rubbings	18
✔													✔		Riding on the School Bus	20
			✔								✔				Scrub-a-Dub-Dub	22
				✔								✔			Sensory Stations	24
		✔		✔											Shapely Figures	26
									✔			✔			Textured Finger Paints	28
									✔					✔	We Go to School on a Bus	30
				✔								✔			Weather Ways	33

September

Apple Butter and People Sandwiches

Activity Goals: Self-Help Skills Development
Sensory Processing Improvement

Time: 30 minutes

Objectives: Upon successful completion of this activity, the child will be able to
1. Tolerate proprioceptive (deep pressure) input to his body
2. Spread jelly on a piece of bread using a plastic knife
3. Wipe his face with a napkin

Materials:
1. Two mats or large cushions
2. Jar of apple butter or other jelly
3. Loaf of bread
4. Plastic knife for each child
5. Napkin and paper plate for each child
6. Mirror (small or hand-held) if needed

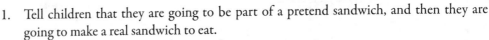

Procedure:
1. Tell children that they are going to be part of a pretend sandwich, and then they are going to make a real sandwich to eat.
2. Place mat or cushion on floor. This is one piece of bread.
3. Have two children at a time lie on mat on their stomachs, but with their heads sticking out. They are the filling.
4. Have the adult spreads pretend condiments (mayonnaise, mustard, ketchup) on each child by using both hands, applying pressure to the arms, legs, and backs of the children.
5. Place the other mat or cushion (bread slice) over the children.
6. One or two at a time, the other class members crawl over the top of the sandwich.
7. When all of the children have had turns being the sandwich filling and the sandwich pressers (crawlers), have the children wash their hands.
8. Seat the children at a table and give each child a plate, knife, piece of bread, and napkin.
9. Spoon one large spoonful of apple butter or other jelly on each child's plate.
10. Child uses knife to spread jelly/jam.
11. Child either folds bread over to make a sandwich or makes an open-face sandwich.
12. Child eats sandwich.
13. When finished, child wipes mouth and hands with napkin.

Adaptations:
1. For child who is afraid of being between two cushions, allow him to keep head and shoulders out from between mats.
2. For child who has poor grasp, build up handle of knife.
3. The child who has use of only one hand may stabilize bread against two sides of baking pan in order to spread jam. Bread will not slide as much.
4. If child is not able to locate mouth and wipe it successfully, he can use visual aids by viewing himself in a mirror.

Learning in Motion

Letter to Parents
Apple Butter and People Sandwiches

We made a "people" sandwich in group today. Using a mat or cushions as the "bread," we put one piece of bread on the floor, and then added a layer of children lying on their stomachs. The children were the "filling," and the adults added pretend "condiments" (ketchup, mustard, mayonnaise) using both hands to spread them all over the backs, arms, and legs of the filling. The last step was adding the top slice of "bread" (another mat.) One or two at a time, the class members not part of the filling crawled on top of the sandwich. As a snack today, the children made sandwiches by using a plastic knife to spread apple butter on a piece of bread. The best part, eating the sandwich, was last!

Purpose of the Activity

This activity allows children to really feel where their bodies are in space, because of all the deep pressure input that this activity provides. The body awareness that this promotes is an important basis for the development of movement skills. The children practiced using utensils while making their sandwiches, and they also used oral-motor control while eating.

Home Activities to Help Your Child Grow

You can replicate this activity at home using your child's bed. He or she can get under the covers, and you can use your hands to "spread the condiments" on him or her. Or, you can roll your child up in a blanket and pretend he or she is a hot dog. You can use your hands to apply deep pressure in order to spread the pretend mustard on the hot dog. Using heavy pressure that is slow and steady should be calming for your child. If this sensory input proves too stimulating for your child, you may have to play this game in the morning or afternoon rather than at bedtime.

Whenever possible, allow your child to practice spreading jelly on sandwiches, cutting apples, stirring pudding, etc. This will encourage him to become more adept at using utensils and become more independent in feeding skills.

September

Apples on a Fence

Activity Goals: Visual-Perceptual Development
Pre-Writing Skills Development

Time: 15-to-20 minutes

Objectives: Upon successful completion of this activity, the child will be able to
1. Discriminate long from short
2. Sequence long and short pieces of paper
3. Follow directions by copying an example
4. Demonstrate independence in self-help skills

Materials:
1. Long and short strips of paper, about 1" wide
2. Large sheets of paper
3. Red, yellow, and green paint
4. Apples cut in half
5. Glue
6. Examples of apples in three colors (e.g., red delicious, golden delicious, Granny Smith)

Procedure:
1. Before group, cover the table with newspaper and pour paint onto paper plates.
2. Show example of activity to children and demonstrate how to make a fence, alternating long and short strips of paper.
3. Let the children glue the strips onto large pieces of paper to make a fence.
4. Adult cuts the apples in half, and discusses what the apples look like inside (seeds, star form, white in the middle, etc.).
5. Children dip the apple halves in paint and press them onto the top of the fence.
6. Children make additional apple prints on newspaper that is covering table.
7. Children wash hands.

Adaptations:
1. For the child who has difficulty grasping, or for a young group, it is easier to hold the apple halves by sticking forks or wooden craft sticks in them. Show the children how to hold them with their thumbs turned up so that it is easier to press down firmly.
2. To lessen the chance of spilling dishes of paint, put the paint on top of sponges, which you have laid on paper plates.

Multilevel Instruction:
1. Draw lines on paper and have the children cut out their own paper strips to practice cutting skills.
2. Place the large papers on a chalkboard or wall so that the children are working on a vertical surface. This helps build shoulder, arm, and hand strength, which is necessary for developing writing skills, including a mature pencil grasp.
3. Add apple trees, birds, and pumpkins to the pictures using pre-cut figures or paper shapes cut from colored construction paper.
4. After the paint dries, encourage the children to draw pumpkins, grass, leaves, and birds on their picture.

September

Learning in Motion

Letter to Parents

Apples on a Fence

In group this week, the children made a picture of a fence with apples on top of it. First, the children glued strips of paper, both long and short, onto a piece of paper. They dipped apples that were cut in half in paint, and then "stamped" the apple prints on top of the fence. The children made additional apple prints on the newspaper covering the table.

Purpose of the Activity

The children used their visual discrimination skills to determine which paper strips were long and which were short. Visual discrimination is an important component in classroom activities, especially in reading and writing. Your child practiced looking at an example and listening to and following directions, which is frequently the way that concepts are taught in the classroom. Pressing the apples first into the paint and then onto the paper provided good feedback to your child's hands. Stamping emphasized the relationship of a three-dimensional object to a two-dimensional picture. Your child also had to use his or her perceptual skills to determine how many apple prints would fit across the fence.

Home Activities to Help Your Child Grow

Stamping is a wonderful activity for the young child. An extensive selection of stamps and stamp pads can be found in craft stores. Your child will have fun making cards, pictures, and books, and will get practice using his or her visual-perceptual skills in order to place the stamps in the correct orientation and amount of space. Look for stamps that will require the use of refined grasp patterns in order to be successful. As a general rule, smaller stamps require more precise and refined grasp patterns. Your child can even use the stamps to create and then recite a story about a series of events.

September

Balloons and Body Parts

Activity Goals: Body-Scheme and Motor-Planning Improvement
Group Development

Time: 20 minutes

Objectives: Upon successful completion of this activity, the child will be able to

1. Point to ten body parts
2. Name ten body parts
3. Accurately follow two-step directions

Materials:
1. A balloon for each child
2. Pictures of body parts

Procedure:
1. Review body parts with children. Depending on the level of the group, include body parts such as wrist, ankle, waist, neck, heel, etc.
2. Have children point to body parts when you show them the picture or call out the label for the part.
3. Point to a body part on yourself and have them call out the name.
4. Children get into pairs.
5. Each pair gets one balloon.
6. Adult leader calls out body part and together the partners hold balloon between that body part (e.g., leader names "ankle" and partners hold balloon between their ankles).

Adaptations:
1. Child who is tactilely sensitive can use harder ball rather than balloon.
2. Child with limited volitional movement may point to body part or tell another child or adult where the part is.
3. Child with limited movement could point to doll to show named body part.

Multilevel Instruction:
1. For lower-level group, adult can point to body part and children can imitate action.
2. Lower-level group can work individually. Each child gets a balloon, which he can hold on the body part that is named.
3. Group with beginning reading can use these skills to read cards that an adult is holding up. Simple words such as eye, nose, ear, arm, leg, etc., would be printed on cards.
4. Group can be given two-step directions, such as "touch your knee with your elbow," "touch your foot to your partner's knee," etc.

Letter to Parents

Balloons and Body Parts

This week, the children learned about body parts, including more complex parts such as wrist, elbow, ankle, neck, waist, etc. After pointing to a named body part, the children were given a balloon and used the balloon to touch the body part. Finally, the children got into pairs and played a game. When a body part was called, both children held the balloon with that body part. For example, if "ankle" was called out, the partners held the balloon between each of their ankles.

Purpose of the Activity

Being aware of our bodies and how each body part is related to other parts of the body is very important for developing an accurate mental picture of ourselves. Without a well-developed, internalized concept of our bodies, it is very difficult to perform skilled motor activities, learn new tasks, or successfully imitate postures and movements. An accurate mental picture of our body helps us to be successful in physical education classes, as well as in classroom tasks such as cutting and writing.

Home Activities to Help Your Child Grow

Playing games like "Simon Says" or "Twister," or dancing simple line dances or "The Hokey Pokey" will help develop your child's body awareness. You can review body parts while your child is bathing or drying off. For example, you can ask your child to "dry your wrist," "dry your neck," etc. You can play a game with your child and tell her that you are going to ask her to do silly things such as "touch your elbow to your ankle," "carry your doll with your knees," or "put your toys away with your feet." These games will also give your child opportunities to practice attending to and following verbal directions.

September

Body Tracings

Activity Goals: Group Development
Body-Scheme and Motor-Planning Improvement

Time: 30 minutes

Objectives: Upon successful completion of this activity, the child will be able to
1. Identify age-appropriate body parts
2. Look into a mirror to see what he is wearing, and transfer this information to the drawing
3. Accurately fill in facial features

Materials:
1. Large child-size pieces of paper
2. Crayons or markers
3. Full-length mirror

Procedure:
1. Children work with a partner.
2. First child lies on piece of paper, face-up. His partner traces around his body.
3. Children switch tasks.
4. When both drawings are finished, children take turns looking into mirror, noticing what they are wearing, hair, eye color, etc.
5. Children add details to their drawings, including clothing and facial features.
6. Children gather in circle, teacher holds up each child's drawing and asks class to identify who it is.

Adaptations:
1. For additional input, children can color over textured material, such as a plastic screen, short pile rug, cork board, etc.
2. Visually-impaired child could be assisted by adult (e.g., to fill in specific features). The child with visual impairment can add to body drawing using textured materials for hair, facial features, clothing, etc.
3. Partner can trace outline of child with visual impairment onto thin foam or cardboard so that child with visual impairment can work with this 3-dimensional figure.

Multilevel Instruction:
1. Children can cut drawing out. Make the paper double, stuff and seal the body tracing in order to make a doll.
2. Children draw clothes on body tracing that resembles clothing they're wearing that day.

September

Letter to Parents

Body Tracings

This week, we worked in pairs and took turns lying down and having our whole body outlined by our partner. When we stood up, we could see the outline of our bodies. We colored our images, adding facial features, hair, clothing, and other details. At the end of the group, an adult held up our masterpieces, and we identified whose body the drawing represented.

Purpose of the Activity

Making body tracings is a good way to improve a child's awareness of his or her own body and how it differs from the size and shape of a friend's body. A lot of fine-motor control and attention was required during this activity in order to accurately outline our partner's body. Your child was encouraged to hold the crayon/marker using a mature tripod grasp and to start and complete the outline using the same hand. When adding facial features, hair, and clothing to the drawings, it was necessary for your child to attend to details and to remember and translate these details onto paper. Attention and memory are building blocks of learning and must be well-developed to succeed in the classroom.

Home Activities to Help Your Child Grow

Your child can outline his or her hands and feet (or someone else's), and turn them into whimsical drawings. For example, hands placed around a circle or placed on top of stems look like flowers, and outlined feet can easily be turned into ghosts or monsters. Outlining common objects, such as jar lids, blocks, plastic containers, and kitchen gadgets, can yield some interesting drawings while giving your child good practice with crayon/marker control. To work on visual-perceptual skills, outline a few objects yourself and see if your child can guess what they are.

September

Guess Which Shape!

Activity Goals: Cognitive Development
Sensory Processing Improvement

Time: 20 minutes

Objectives: Upon successful completion of this activity, the child will be able to
1. Accurately name and describe simple shapes
2. Name shape that has been "drawn" on her back

Materials:
1. Common shapes, such as circle, triangle, square, etc.
2. Cloth bag large enough to hold the shapes

Procedure: Activity I
1. Children sit in a circle. Adult shows the shapes and asks children to name them.
2. Place shapes (pictures, blocks, etc.) into cloth bag.
3. Child chooses shape from bag and does not let the rest of the class see it.
4. Child describes the shape to the rest of the class.
5. Class members take turns guessing which shape it is, or, the first child to raise her hand and correctly guess the shape is the next teacher.
6. Repeat steps 2 to 5 until all of the children in the class have a chance to describe a shape.

Activity II
1. Children get into pairs with one child sitting behind the other.
2. Child sitting behind uses her index finger to "draw" a shape on her partner's back.
3. The partner attempts to guess the shape that has been drawn on her back.

Adaptations:
1. For children who have difficulty guessing shapes drawn on their back, draw the shapes on their hand - it may be easier for them.
2. To make the game easier, shape cards can be placed in front of the child and she can point to the shape that her partner has drawn of her back.

Multilevel Instruction:
1. A more challenging activity would be to let the children draw numbers, letters and/or short words on a partner's back.
2. Children can describe a letter or number and the other children can guess it.

Letter to Parents
Guess Which Shape!

This week, your child played guessing games that involved describing shapes. First, common shapes (circle, square, triangle, star, rectangle, oval, etc.) were placed in a bag, and the children took turns choosing one from the bag. Without letting the rest of the group see the shape, he or she described it. The first child to raise his hand and correctly guess the shape got to be the next "teacher." Then, the children formed pairs and used their index finger to "draw" shapes on their partner's back. The partner "felt" the drawing and guessed which shape it was.

Purpose of the Activity

We can mentally organize and recall characteristics of designs and objects without using our sense of vision. Sometimes, we use our sense of vision to further check and reinforce the information that we have obtained by using other senses, such as hearing, taste and touch. Both of the activities that we did this week helped your child to remember, discriminate among, and describe geometric shapes. They also enhanced your child's tactile discrimination skills by having him or her use the sense of touch to identify a shape. We use our sense of touch, without using visual cues, on a daily basis, as we write, button buttons near our neck, or identify coins in our pockets.

Home Activities to Help Your Child Grow

At home, you can play similar identification games with your child. You can draw shapes, numbers or letters on your child's back, or on the back of his or her hand (making sure the child doesn't peek). To make the game a little easier, you can have shape, number, or letter cards in front of your child. After you slowly draw the shape, number, or letter, ask your child to point to the card with the correct picture. You can also make a "feely" grab bag. Place small, common objects inside of the bag, and have your child reach into it and identify one object at a time, without using his or her sense of vision. If your child has beginning letter/number recognition skills, you can place small letters or numbers in the bag.

September

Hide-and-Seek Apple Rubbings

Activity Goals: Sensory Processing Improvement
Hand-Dominance Development

Time: 20-to-30 minutes

Objectives: Upon successful completion of this activity, the child will be able to
1. Draw vertical lines, horizontal lines, and circles using both hands at the same time
2. Cover a designated area with crayon strokes
3. Identify common objects outlined by crayon rubbings

Materials:
1. At least two large crayons per child
2. Newspaper - 4 to 5 sections
3. Large sheet of white paper
4. Cutouts made of cardboard or quick point. Cutouts should have apple theme (basket, worm, apple, tree)

Procedure: Activity I
1. Before group begins, cover large table with newspaper. Newspaper can be taped onto table so that it does not slide off during drawing.
2. Have children sit around table.
3. Explain that they are going to be drawing with both hands at the same time.
4. Give each child 2 large crayons and ask them to hold one in each hand.
5. Demonstrate how to draw 2 vertical lines at the same time and have the children imitate your actions.
6. Repeat step 5, drawing horizontal lines.
7. Repeat step 5, drawing 2 large circles.
8. Remove paper from tabletop.

Activity II
1. Children sit on the floor away from the table—tell them that you're going to play a hide-and-seek game using crayons and paper.
2. Adult places cutouts under a piece of white paper and tapes the top of the paper down.
3. Children sit at the table, and each child gets a large crayon and begins coloring so that the outline of object appears on paper.
4. Children identify objects that they've discovered.

Adaptations:
1. If child is having difficulty locating object under paper, circle the area in which object can be found.
2. Child with visual impairment can identify objects using touch rather than vision.
3. Child with visual impairment may have greater success if drawings and rubbings are made on paper that is affixed to a raised and slanted surface.

Multilevel Instruction:
1. Letter cutouts can be placed under the paper. If children are beginning readers, letters can be placed together so that the rubbings reveal a word.
2. More than one object can be placed under paper and children can identify the objects and the quantity.
3. For large line-and-circle drawings, newspaper can be hung on vertical surface to build strength and endurance.

September

Learning in Motion

Letter to Parents
Hide-and-Seek Apple Rubbings

This week, we made large, simple drawings using both hands at the same time. What a challenge that was! We also discovered what shapes were hiding under a large sheet of white paper by rubbing our crayons over the raised cutouts of the object. The children revealed items associated with apples, such as trees, seeds, baskets, and, of course, apples.

Purpose of the Activity

Using both hands at the same time to draw lines, circles, etc., works to improve bilateral coordination—this is important in overall gross- and fine-motor development. For example, walking, jumping, riding a bike, stringing beads, and cutting are all bilateral activities because they involve using both sides of the body together. Using crayons to find hidden objects allows children to work on control while coloring, without being concerned about staying in the lines. Grasping the crayon and pressing down on the paper also helps to build pinch and grip strength. Children need to use their sense of touch and vision to identify the "hidden" forms.

Home Activities to Help Your Child Grow

You can have your child do rubbings at home by placing small, flat objects under paper and encouraging your child to color over them. Some suggestions for objects are coins, feathers, leaves, shape cutouts, small shells, string, and bottle caps. Your child can also go outdoors with paper and crayons and make rubbings of different textures such as bricks, tree bark, sidewalks, hubcaps, car or bike tires, and playground balls. Then, try to guess what the rubbings were made from and have your child describe the texture of the surface (smooth, rough, hard, etc.) of the object.

September

Riding on the School Bus

Activity Goals: Strength and Endurance Improvement
Balance Improvement

Time: 15-to-20 minutes

Objectives: Upon successful completion of this activity, the child will be able to
1. Push box, with another child in it, a distance of 10 feet
2. Walk forward 6 steps on a balance beam

Materials:
1. Large, sturdy box
2. Balance beam
3. Stuffed animals (if desired)
4. Scooter boards

Procedure:
1. Discuss buses with the group. How many ride on a bus? Is it big or small? What color is it? Explain that each child is going to walk down the sidewalk (balance beam) and drive or ride a school bus across the floor.
2. Children get into pairs.
3. First pair gets up. One child goes across the balance beam.
4. First child across climbs into big box and sits down in it.
5. Second child in pair walks across balance beam and steps off.
6. Second child pushes first child (in box) across floor (about 10 feet).
7. Both children sit down.
8. Each pair of children takes a turn.
9. Reverse the order in the pairs so that the children who rode get to push and the children that pushed get to ride.
10. Repeat steps 4 through 8.
11. Activity can be repeated, placing a stuffed animal on a scooter board and pushing it across the room.
12. Gather children in a circle and conclude group by singing "The Wheels on the Bus."

Adaptations:
1. The child in a wheelchair can steer along a pathway made of 2 pieces of masking tape approximately 8 feet long and 3.5 feet wide. His partner can push him across the room. Rather than pushing his partner in a box, he can push a toy bus across the table.
2. For the child with visual impairment, outline the balance beam in a bright fluorescent color. If blind, the child can hold someone's hand while crossing the beam.

Multilevel Instruction:
1. Children can walk heel-to-toe, backwards or sideways on the balance beam.
2. Children can push boxes shorter or greater distances.

Learning in Motion

Letter to Parents

Riding on the School Bus

This week in our group, we talked about school buses, their size, what color they are, who rides on the bus, etc. Working with partners, one person sat in a big box and pretended to steer while his or her partner pushed the box (bus) across the floor. Then, we switched roles. For added fun, we also put stuffed animals on scooter boards and pushed them across the floor, pretending that they were passengers in a bus.

Purpose of the Activity

Working on activities like carrying or pushing heavy items across the floor helps a child build up strength and endurance. Using his or her body for heavy work also helps to make a child more aware of where his or her body is in space and reinforces how a child can use his or her body to perform a task successfully. Doing heavy work can also have the benefit of being a calming and organizing type of activity for a child to be successful. Strength, endurance, and awareness of one's own body are important qualities for the child in school. By doing a similar activity later in the group, the children learned that they can apply previously learned information to a new task. In order to learn new activities, it is often necessary to remember and apply previously learned skills.

Home Activities to Help Your Child Grow

You can have your child perform heavy-work activities at home. Encourage him or her to help you carry a child-sized bag of groceries in from the car, or vacuum a small section of the rug. Your child will enjoy helping with these grown-up tasks and will be building his or her strength and endurance at the same time. Your child can give stuffed animals rides by placing them in boxes and pushing the boxes along the floor. You could set up some obstacles and tell your child to push the animals around them, which will help develop motor-planning skills.

September

Scrub-a-Dub-Dub

Activity Goals: Body Scheme and Motor-Planning Improvement
Self-Help Skills Development

Time: 20-to-30 minutes

Objectives: Upon successful completion of this activity, the child will be able to
1. Name and identify 10 body parts
2. Tolerate touch input to her body

Materials:
1. Wash cloth for each child
2. Lotion

Procedure:
1. Explain to the group, "we're going to pretend to take a bath today, but since we're in school and it's pretend, we're not going to get wet or take off any of our clothes, except for shoes and socks."
2. Each child removes her shoes and socks.
3. Each child is given a washcloth.
4. Adult names body part and begins pretending to wash it. Children imitate adult.
5. After group is finished washing, it is time to put on lotion.
6. Each child is given a small dollop of lotion to rub on her face, hands, feet and arms and legs if they're exposed. As the child rubs in the lotion, have her name the body part.

Adaptations: For child who is sensitive to touch, have her wash a doll and name the body parts. Or, have the child rub herself briskly with the wash cloth to desensitize herself.

Multilevel Instruction:
1. Children can be asked to name and scrub less commonly known body parts, such as forehead, chin, chest, shoulders, wrists, hips, ankles, heels, etc.
2. "Dot Spot" game can be played—child closes her eyes and adult touches a spot on her. Child opens her eyes and points to the spot that has been touched.

September

Letter to Parents
Scrub-a-Dub-Dub

This week, we pretended to take a bath, but since we were in school, we didn't get wet or take off any of our clothes except shoes and socks. We used washcloths to "wash" the body part that was named, and then we rubbed our hands, faces, arms and feet with lotion.

Purpose of the Activity

Children who are young are still developing a good sense of their bodies and how they work. Body awareness is necessary for learning motor skills, including those used in school. Rubbing a body part while it is being named combines sensory (touch) information with verbal information. Teaching information is generally more effective when multiple sensory channels are used. For example, it is usually easier to assemble products if you are given written directions as well as drawings to follow. It is even simpler if you are actually shown what to do on a model. Children learn best when teaching involves a multisensory approach. For children who have a difficult time accepting touch, rubbing themselves with a wash cloth and lotion can help them become less sensitive to tactile input.

Home Activities to Help Your Child Grow

You can try a game called "Dot Spot" with your child to further help with developing body awareness. Have your child close his or her eyes, and then touch a spot on him or her. To make this game easy in the beginning, you can dip your finger in some powder or flour first so that the dot is visible when you touch your child. Your child then opens his or her eyes and "rubs off the spot." Let your child put a "spot" on you when he or she is successful. You'll have a good time trying to trick each other with hard spots, such as your back. You might find that your child doesn't like this game if he or she is sensitive to touch. If so, make sure you use firm pressure when you touch your child, as firm touch is less difficult to tolerate than light touch, which may seem irritating to your child.

September

Sensory Stations

Activity Goal: Sensory Processing Improvement
Cognitive Development

Time: 20-to-30 minutes

Objectives: Upon successful completion of this activity, the child will be able to
1. Determine which container is the heaviest and which is the lightest
2. Identify three common smells
3. Identify, through touch, the textures or shapes that are the same

Materials:
1. Three containers with a different weight in each
2. Five film canisters
3. Five materials with different smells (e.g., vanilla, lemon, cinnamon, coffee)
4. Small bag
5. Blocks of different shapes or textures (2 of each)

Procedure:
1. Before group begins, set up three sensory stations: 1. weight; 2. smell; 3. touch.
    1. Weight Station: place a different amount of weight in each of 3 containers. Containers should look the same on the outside.
    2. Smell Station: place a small amount of scent in each of 5 containers. Scents should be very different (e.g., coffee and mint).
    3. Touch Station: place 4 or 5 shapes in bag. Set aside corresponding shape.
2. Have adult supervise each station.
3. Explain to group that you are going to use your senses to identify things today. What are your 5 senses? Today you're going to use your senses of smell and touch. Point out the three different stations.
4. Divide children into 3 groups:
    Weight Station: At the weight station, the child determines, by holding each container, which is the heaviest and which is the lightest.
    Smell Station: At the smell station, the child identifies each of the common smells.
    Touch Station: At the touch station, the adult shows the child a shape. The child then reaches into the bag, feels the shapes, and without looking, identifies (by touch) which shape matches the one that the adult is holding up.
5. Each child takes a turn going through each station.

Multilevel Instruction:
1. Charts can be made for each station. Children can place colored star sticker next to their choice. For example: canister #1 is mint, canister #2 is vanilla, etc. Provide several of each choice and see if children can sort accurately.
2. The touch station can be made easier or more difficult by adding or subtracting shapes from the bag, or shapes that are similar (oval and circle) can be used. Also, pictures (2-dimensional) of shapes, rather than three-dimensional shapes, can be used as prompts.

September

Letter to Parents

Sensory Stations

In group this week, the children participated in a few activities to learn more about the senses. They played with and compared three different weights inside three canisters. They smelled five different smells such as vinegar, cinnamon, orange, coffee, and vanilla. We placed several differently shaped blocks in a bag and matched the correct one to the corresponding picture without looking. They also reached into a bag and used their sense of touch to identify which shape they were feeling.

Purpose of the Activity

Activities we did in group this week will heighten awareness of sensory clues in our environment. These clues help us to remember and distinguish among the objects surrounding us. By improving the sense of touch without vision, we increase the awareness of how our hands functions in space. This is an important skill, especially in the areas of handwriting and dressing. As your child gets older, he or she will be expected to manipulate clothing fasteners and write without looking at his or her hands.

Home Activities to Help Your Child Grow

Help your child become more aware of the different scents that objects have. Expose him or her to a variety of tactile (touch), gustatory (taste), and olfactory (smell) experiences around the house, at the mall, in the garden, and while cooking. To improve your child's sense of touch discrimination, place two or three common objects (coins, safety pin, block, crayon, marble, small figurine) into a tube sock. Ask your child to pull out a specific item and leave the rest in the sock. You can make this activity more difficult by placing more objects in the sock and/or by placing objects that are similar in size and shape in the sock.

September

Shapely Figures

Activity Goals: Cognitive Development
Bilateral Coordination Development

Time: 30 minutes

Objectives: Upon successful completion of this activity, the child will be able to
1. Identify common shapes (e.g., circle, square, rectangle, and triangle)
2. Place toothpicks into foam to create simple shapes

Materials:
1. Shapes or pictures of shapes
2. Box of toothpicks (colored)
3. Styrofoam® packing peanuts
4. Glue
5. Construction paper

Procedure: Hold up shapes or pictures of shapes and have children identify them.

Activity I
1. Choose three children. Have them make a triangle by lying down on the ground with each child's body being one side of the triangle.
2. Choose four children. Have them make a square on the ground.
3. Choose six children. Have them make a rectangle on the ground.
4. Choose four or five children. Have them make a circle on the ground.

Activity II
1. Children sit at a table.
2. Each child is given three toothpicks and three small pieces of foam and asked to make a triangle.
3. Give each child four toothpicks and four pieces of Styrofoam and ask the child to make a square.
4. Give each child six toothpicks and six pieces of Styrofoam and ask the child to make a rectangle. The shape will have two toothpicks on each long side.
5. Children can glue toothpick shapes onto construction paper, if desired.

Adaptations:
1. Child in wheelchair will probably require assistance to be a part of "floor shapes." If she is unable to get out of wheelchair, she could hold up sign telling children what kind of shape to make. Or, she could hold the end of a streamer and her partners could make the sides.
2. Children with limited fine-motor control can use straws placed on construction paper to make shapes.
3. Children with visual impairment may benefit from using brightly colored toothpicks or straws in order to construct their shapes.

Multilevel Instruction:
1. Children can make free-form designs using toothpicks and Styrofoam.
2. Children can look around the room and take turns pointing out different shapes.

September

Letter to Parents

Shapely Figures

This week in group, we reinforced the concept of shapes. The children lie down on the floor and let their bodies be the boundaries of the shapes. For example, four children made the shape of a square by lying head-to-toe. The group made triangles, squares, rectangles and even attempted a circle. During the next group activity, the children sat at the table and made a variety of simple shapes by joining Styrofoam pieces together with toothpicks. For example, they used three toothpicks and three Styrofoam peanuts to make a triangle. Then, they glued the shape constructions to a piece of colorful paper.

Purpose of the Activity

Using as many of our senses as possible while learning a skill reinforces that concept. Building shapes using toothpicks and Styrofoam and making shapes using their bodies helped the children really learn, understand, and remember what shapes are. Generally, the more senses involved in learning, the more ingrained the information becomes. Active learning, where the child participates directly in the process, is a very effective tool for teaching everyone, especially the young child.

Home Activities to Help Your Child Grow

Reinforcement of shape or color concepts can come from multiple senses. You can have your child engage in a number of activities to reinforce shape and color learning. Have your child look through magazines and find pictures of different shapes or colors. He or she can cut the pictures out and glue them to a large piece of construction paper to make a shape/color collage. Instruct your child to go on a shape or color hunt. Your child can go through the house gathering objects that are a specific shape or color. Another idea is to place salt or sand in a cookie sheet and have your child use his or her index finger to draw simple shapes in the salt/sand.

September

Textured Finger Paints

Activity Goals: Sensory Processing Improvement
Pre-Writing Skills Development

Time: 20 minutes

Objectives: Upon successful completion of this activity, the child will be able to
1. Isolate each finger to draw a line in the shaving cream
2. Tolerate working with the textured shaving cream finger paint
3. Use index finger of preferred or dominant hand to draw these shapes: —, |, O, +

Materials:
1. One large can of shaving cream
2. Uncooked rice (about 2 cups)

Procedure:
1. Children sit at a table with a non-porous top.
2. Adult squirts 4-inch circle of shaving cream directly on table, in front of each child.
3. Children spread shaving cream using their hands.
4. Children practice drawing lines, shapes, and faces in the shaving cream, using each finger individually.
5. If the shaving cream is drying up, squirt more on the table.
6. Have child sprinkle some rice on top of the shaving cream.
7. Mix rice into shaving cream.
8. Repeat steps 4 and 5.
9. Children clean off tabletop using wet paper towel.
10. Children wash hands.

Adaptations:
1. Child who has difficulty tolerating the texture of the finger paint can use a paintbrush or tongue depressor to draw lines, shapes, letters, etc.
2. Child with visual impairment can spread shaving cream on laminated piece of paper or chalkboard that is in great contrast to the white shaving cream.
3. Child who has difficulty isolating her index finger for drawing can be encouraged to hold small sponge with the little, ring, and middle fingers of their drawing hand while she is using her index finger to draw.
4. Food-coloring can be added to the shaving cream to provide a better visual contrast.

Multilevel Instruction:
1. Children can be asked to draw letters, numbers, first names, etc. in the shaving cream finger paint.
2. Children can imitate or copy lines and/or shapes that the teacher draws on the board.
3. Lower-level groups can draw faces inside a circle that has been drawn for them.

Letter to Parents
Textured Finger Paints

This week we used our fingers to draw lines and shapes into textured finger paint. The finger paint was made of shaving cream, and the texture came from adding uncooked rice to it.

Purpose of the Activity

We used shaving cream with rice as finger paint because feeling the texture of the paint helped to increase touch awareness through the entire hand. It also promoted tolerance of different tactile input to the hands and fingers. By using different fingers to draw lines and shapes, finger awareness and dexterity were improved. Improving finger awareness, dexterity, and the tolerance of a variety of textures will help to improve manipulation skills in the classroom. Also, using your finger to draw simple lines and shapes helps to reinforce pre-writing and visual-perceptual motor skills.

Home Activities to Help Your Child Grow

You can replicate this activity at home by squirting a three-to-four-inch dollop of shaving cream onto a non-porous tabletop or place mat in front of your child. To increase texture, your child can then add uncooked rice or beans to the shaving cream. Have your child practice writing lines, shapes, letters, numbers, and drawing faces. You can fill a shoebox with materials of different textures such as sandpaper, silk, wood, felt, and cotton. Have your child close his or her eyes and identify the material or match identical materials by using his or her sense of touch.

September

We Go to School on a Bus

Activity Goals: Visual-Perceptual Development
                          Pre-Writing Skills Development

Time: 30-to-40 minutes

Objectives: Upon successful completion of this activity, the child will be able to
1. Draw two parallel horizontal lines across paper
2. Place buses on roadway after looking at model
3. "Connect the dots" to draw simple shapes
4. Color in a vertical plane
5. Visually discriminate shapes within a drawing

Materials:
1. Large piece of paper for each child
2. Black crayon or marker for each child
3. Small bus cut-outs (using Ellison machine) approximately 4 per child
4. Glue sticks
5. Large sheet of mural paper with bus drawn on it using dotted lines

Procedure: Before group begins: a. make sample of Activity I; b. draw large school bus on mural paper and hang vertically at children's eye level.

Activity I
1. Children sit at table.
2. Discuss school buses. Who takes the bus to school? Who takes the bus home? Is it big? Does it have windows? What color is it?
3. Show picture of school bus.
4. Give each child a large piece of construction paper.
5. Give each child a dark crayon and have him draw two horizontal lines across paper. Make lines 3-to-4 inches apart.
6. Give each child a black crayon and ask him to color in the "road" (area between two lines).
7. Each child gets 3 or 4 small bus cutouts and a glue stick.
8. Child opens glue stick, applies glue, and places buses on road.

Activity II
1. Hang large piece of mural paper on wall. On paper, draw simple outline of bus. Include squares as windows, circles as wheels, triangles as lights, and straight lines to trace. Lines should be dotted so that the children can trace over them.
2. Children sit in front of mural. Adult discusses buses and has children point out shapes. As child indicates shape, the teacher calls him up to the mural.
3. Child gets a crayon from the teacher and connects the dots to complete the shape he has pointed out.
4. Child sits down. Children take turns repeating steps 2 and 3 until all shapes on bus are identified.
5. Children sing "The Wheels on the Bus."

September

Adaptations:

1. If children are unable to draw horizontal lines on paper, they can trace a previously drawn line or connect a row of horizontal dots.

2. Children with visual impairments can use their crayon to follow a raised glue line, a ruler, or a piece of yarn.

3. To help child draw horizontal lines, adult can draw green dot on left edge of paper and red dot on right edge of paper so that starting and stopping points are clearly indicated.

4. Children who are unable to grasp crayon can use bingo markers to dab paint on mural bus shapes.

Multilevel Instruction:

1. Children can color in mural shapes and bus.

2. On individual pictures, children can add details such as clouds, trees, sky, birds, school buildings, etc.

September

Letter to Parents
We Go to School on a Bus

We discussed buses in group this week. We talked about the color and size of buses, how the ride was slightly bumpy, and who rode on buses. We also talked about some of the rules that the bus driver has so that everyone who rides on the bus is safe. Then we made two pictures: one was a drawing of a road with buses on it, and the other was a mural of a bus that was made of different shapes.

Purpose of the Activity

This week's activities focused on practicing pre-writing skills, using common classroom tools that build strength and endurance in your child's hands and arms, and Visual-Perceptual Development. Your child was asked to draw two horizontal lines on the paper to represent the road. The ability to copy horizontal lines is an early pre-writing skill that most children demonstrate by the age of three years. The ability to imitate and then copy designs is extremely important in the classroom, as it correlates with the development of handwriting skills. Your child used visual-perceptual skills when placing the school buses on the road, drawing the horizontal lines on the road, and tracing the shapes on the large school bus mural. Since the bus mural was placed on the wall, a vertical orientation, your child was required to use hand and arm strength to trace the shapes that were a part of the bus.

Home Activities to Help Your Child Grow

Many children enjoy using chalkboards to practice pre-writing and writing skills. It would be fun for them to pretend to be the teacher, a figure with whom they are familiar, and for you to pretend to be the student. Your child could use white or colored chalk to draw pictures, shapes, letters, or numbers. If you break the chalk into small pieces (about 1½ inches in length), he or she will have a tendency to use a more refined, tripod type of grasp. To reinforce the lines, shapes, letters, or numbers that your child has drawn, have him or her erase the drawings by tracing over the lines with an eraser, tissue or wet sponge. It is also great fun to use a paintbrush and water to draw shapes on the chalkboard. Another chalkboard activity is to write in shaving cream on the board. Spray a small amount on the board, have your child spread it out evenly, and then use his or her index finger to draw or write in the shaving cream.

Weather Ways

Activity Goals: Sensory Processing Improvement
Body-Scheme and Motor-Planning Improvement

Time: 30-to-40 minutes

Objectives: Upon successful completion of this activity, the child will be able to

1. Discriminate temperatures by touch
2. For five seconds, maintain an "arms up, feet off the ground" posture while on stomach on the ground
3. Catch a paper ball with both hands thrown from a distance of eight feet
4. Hit a one-foot target with the paper ball thrown from a distance of five feet

Materials:
1. Container filled with hot water
2. Container filled with warm water
3. Container filled with ice
4. A towel for each child
5. Two sections of newspaper or newsprint
6. Masking tape
7. Target–a snowman about one-foot tall

Procedure:
1. Before group beings:
   a. Fill one container with ice, one with hot water and one with warm water.
   b. Hang snowman target on wall at children's eye level. Make masking tape line directly in front of it, about five feet from wall.
2. Discuss warm and cold weather and what activities the children might do in each type of weather. Tell the children that they're going to pretend to do some of these activities.

Activity I—Hot, Warm, Cold
Have each child take turns feeling the three containers and describing whether they are cold, warm, or hot.

Activity II—Swimming
1. Children engage in pretend swimming by lying on rug and moving their arms and legs like they're doing freestyle.
2. Breaststroke is demonstrated and children pretend to swim this way.
3. Children pretend to "dive" by lying on their stomachs, holding their arms in front of them (hands together) and their straight legs off the ground.
4. Children sit or stand up and pretend to towel themselves dry.

Activity III—Snowball Throwing
1. Have children sit on floor close to target.
2. Give each child a double page of the newspaper or newsprint.
3. Have each child crumple the newspaper into a ball using both hands.
4. Wrap masking tape around the "snowball" to ensure that it does not "melt" (become loose).

September

5. Children line up behind target line.
6. The first child throws the ball at the snowman target. Each child gets a turn (or a few) to hit the target.

Activity IV

1. Children get into pairs. One child in pair keeps her snowball.
2. Children stand approximately 8 feet apart.
3. Children practice throwing and catching with their partners.

Adaptations:

1. Children in wheelchairs can pretend to swim using their arms only. They can pretend to do a "cannon ball" jump by using their hands on the wheelchair arms to lift their bottoms off the wheelchair seat (wheelchair pushups). The other children could also try this using chairs with arms on them or sitting on the floor, putting their hands on blocks placed beside them, and raising themselves off the floor.
2. For children with visual impairment, the snowman target should be made in white and placed on a black background.
3. A child with visual impairment can throw a "snowball" that has bell in or on it.

Multilevel Instruction:

1. Children can crumple paper using only one hand.
2. Children can "swim" using scooter boards, by propelling themselves along with their hands and feet.
3. Children can make a chart, using pictures or stickers of which activities are done in warm weather and which are done in cold weather.

Letter to Parents
Weather Ways

This week in group, we learned about the weather. We tried some activities to help us learn about different temperatures. We took three containers and compared the temperatures (hot, warm, and cold) of each without using our eyes. Then, we pretended that we were going to the beach by swimming on the rug and drying off with a towel. After we dried off, we laid on our rug square in the sun. Our next activity reminded us of winter because we made snow balls out of paper and threw them at a snowman target.

Purpose of the Activity

These tasks help the child associate temperature with certain activities. Learning to feel differences in temperature gives the child another way to explore and learn the meaning of hot, warm, and cold. By pretending to play on the beach, we worked on combining motor planning and tactile sensations to improve coordination and awareness of body parts and their movements. While making snowballs, we worked on improving hand strength and finger coordination—two skills needed for success in fine-motor activities.

Home Activities to Help Your Child Grow

You can feel and talk about different temperatures at home when you're making and eating meals. For example, the soup may be hot, the bread warm, and the ice cream cold. Also, as you are getting ready to go outside, you may say to your child, "It's cold out today. What do you need to wear?" Practicing different motor patterns helps the child gain an awareness of where his or her body is in space. You can pretend you are swimming in the pool by doing free-style, backstroke, breaststroke, and sidestroke, and having your child imitate the motor patterns. You can also imitate his or her made-up movement sequences. It's always fun for children to teach grown-ups! To improve hand strength and eye-hand coordination skills, your child can crumple up newspaper and practice throwing it into a trash can, a box, or through a hoop.

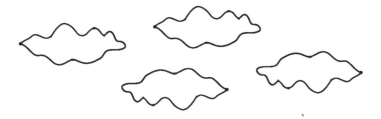

September

Educational Goals by Activity

Attention Improvement	Balance Improvement	Bilateral Coordination Development	Body-Scheme and Motor-Planning Improvement	Cognitive Development	Fine-Motor Skills Development	Gross-Motor Skills Development	Group Development	Hand-Dominance Development	Pre-Writing Skills Development	Scissor Skills Development	Self-Help Skills Development	Sensory Processing Improvement	Strength and Endurance Improvement	Visual-Perceptual Development	Activity	Page
							✔				✔				Creepy, Wiggly Spiders	38
✔													✔		Crow, Crow, Scarecrow!	40
									✔			✔			Dalmatians	42
					✔						✔				Fall Leaves	44
✔														✔	Flying Bats and Ghosts	46
						✔	✔								Flying Ghosts	48
												✔		✔	Ghost, Ghost, Witch!	50
													✔	✔	Jack o'Lanterns	52
					✔							✔			October Party	54
				✔										✔	Pumpkin Hide-and-Seek	56
		✔											✔		Rolling Pumpkins	58
							✔				✔				Scarecrows	60
		✔		✔											Stop, Drop, and Roll	62

October

Creepy, Wiggly Spiders

Activity Goals: Self-Help Skills Development
Group Development

Time: 30 minutes

Objectives: Upon successful completion of this activity, the child will be able to
1. Dress self with fabric tubes
2. Demonstrate adequate strength to perform animal walks
3. Demonstrate imitative skills for animal walks and finger plays
4. Show awareness of personal space and cooperation with others during motor activity

Materials:
1. Fabric tubes made from sock cuffs, tights
2. Spider rings
3. Stuffed animal spiders or yarn balls
4. Round plastic tablecloth made to look like a web with masking tape. Cut hole in center for parachute play.
5. Scooter boards

Procedure:
1. Pass out fabric tubes, which you have made from colored socks with the ends cut off, the ends of old sweaters, tights, and leg warmers. Encourage the children to take off their shoes so that they can cover their legs as well as their arms to make colorful costumes.
2. Lay the "spider web" down on the floor. Have the children pretend to be spiders creeping around the web using the scooter boards. Demonstrate "bear-walking," where they keep their arms and legs straight while they walk on all fours. Try "crab-walking," where they sit, put their arms behind them, and then push up on their hands and feet to walk. Let the children try jumping from one section of the spider web to another.
3. Have the children pick up the spider web. Put the stuffed spiders or yarn balls on the web. Ask the children to try to shake the web so that the spiders stay on the web and then to shake so the spiders fly off.
4. Using the spider rings, play "Eensie Weensie Spider" and other October fingerplays. If you have both black and orange rings, ask them to put one color on their left hands and the other on their right.

Adaptations:
1. Some children may have difficulty wearing a lot of unfamiliar "clothes." Encourage them to try putting them on during free play times to build up their comfort level.
2. If a child has limited mobility, have the spiders roll as well as bear walk, crabwalk, and jump. If the child needs to stay in a wheelchair or use a walker, let the other children try sitting on the scooter boards and pushing with their feet to imitate spiders while he uses his wheelchair or walker.
3. Give hand-over-hand assistance or a defined space for movement if a student has low vision. Provide a partner to help him stay oriented when moving.

Multilevel Instruction: To make the activity less stimulating and/or easier, break this up into several days of activities. Use "Flying Bats and Ghosts" to help the children calm and focus themselves.

Learning in Motion

Letter to Parents
Creepy Wiggly Spiders

We dressed up and pretended to be spiders this week in our motor group. First we slid different colored tubes of fabric made from old socks and tights on our arms and legs. Then we practiced walking like spiders on a pretend "web." We played with the web like a parachute, making toy spiders bounce. Then we put on some spider rings and played "Eensie, Weensie Spider."

Purpose of the Activity

Our activity this week focused on helping the children improve their dressing skills and their ability to cooperate as a group. Tubes of fabric instead of real clothes were used in order for the children to practice putting a smaller, less-complicated piece of clothing over their arms and legs. Each child was encouraged to put several tubes on each of his arms and legs so he would get lots of practice developing the coordination he need to dress himself. The children were encouraged to take off their shoes in order to put the tubes on over their feet. Those children who could put their own shoes back on by themselves were praised. We also wanted to help the children learn to cooperate as a group during this activity. Our spider web was made with a piece of plastic that had a hole cut in the middle so it would be like a parachute. Then the children had fun not only shaking the spiders off, but also shaking the web so the spiders would stay on. That was a lot harder, and required more awareness of what everyone else was doing.

Of course, this activity helped with other important skills that the children need to develop: their strength, their ability to imitate gross-motor skills such as "bear walking" and "crab walking," and their ability to imitate fingerplays such as the well known favorite, "Eensie Weensie Spider."

Home Activities to Help Your Child Grow

See if you can find some old clothes to let your child use for "dress up." Besides your own clothes, check out thrift stores for some wonderful, creative bargains! Look for clothes that have large buttons and easily manipulated zippers and snaps to help your child develop skill with clothing fasteners.

October

Crow, Crow, Scarecrow!

Activity Goals: Strength and Endurance Improvement
Attention Improvement

Time: 15 minutes

Objectives: Upon successful completion of this activity, the child will be able to

1. Walk in a squatting position
2. Start and stop walking at appropriate time
3. Hold arms stretched outward while turning from back to front

Materials:
1. Plaid shirt and straw hat for a "scarecrow"

Procedure:
1. Explain to the children that they will take turns being a "scarecrow" and "crows." Demonstrate how the crows will move, squatting down and walking like a duck. Demonstrate how the scarecrow will stand with his arms stretched out, facing backwards while the crows creep up and then turning around to "chase" them away.
2. Have the children practice both walking like crows and standing and turning with their arms stretched out wide.
3. Let the children take turns being a scarecrow. The crows will start at a line and walk in a squatting position as quietly as they can toward the scarecrow until he turns around. When the scarecrow turns toward them, the crows are to stop and freeze. When the scarecrow turns away, they can start again. The crows will try to get all the way to the scarecrow without being seen moving. If the scarecrow sees them move, they have to fly back to their nests at the beginning line.

Adaptations:
1. Refer to the Appendix for lighting suggestions for a child with a visual impairment. Using contrast or adjusting lighting may facilitate the child's ability to see.
2. Provide a pullover shirt for children who have not mastered buttoning yet.

Multilevel Instruction:
1. Provide plaid shirts with buttons for all the children to practice buttoning.
2. Give the children a picture of a scarecrow to color or cut out, staple to a straw, and then try twirling between their thumbs and first two fingers to turn backwards and forwards.

Letter to Parents

Crow, Crow, Scarecrow!

The children had fun today playing a game called "Crow, Crow, Scarecrow!" One child played the scarecrow and wore a plaid shirt and hat. He or she had to stand with arms outstretched facing away from the crows. The crows walked as quietly as possible toward the scarecrow as long as he or she was facing away from them. When the scarecrow turned, the crows froze. If the scarecrow saw anyone moving, that crow had to fly back to the "nest."

Purpose of the Activity

Today's activity worked on helping your child build strength and endurance in his or her arms and legs while improving your child's attention span. To walk like a crow, the children were instructed to squat down and waddle like ducks. This took quite a lot of effort, but helped give all the muscles in your child's legs a good workout. Your child also had to pay close attention to the scarecrow, freezing whenever the scarecrow turned. This develops the children's ability to monitor what a "leader" is doing, even when they were busy, preparing them to perform tasks at their desks while listening to the teacher's directions.

Home Activities to Help Your Child Grow

Your child had some practice with buttoning today, putting on and taking off the shirt. If your child is having difficulty with this task, he or she may first need to build up more strength in his or her fingers for pinching. You can make up some simple games for him or her. Save a coffee can or other can with a plastic lid. Cut a slit in the top with a knife, keeping it very narrow. Give your child either coins or poker chips to push through the slot. If you have used a metal can, the objects make a nice noise when they hit the bottom, which makes this fun. Another activity is to squeeze large plastic packaging bubbles to make them pop. You can make a matching game with clothespins, too. Write numbers or letters, or place small stickers along the edge of a shoebox. Make duplicate ones on clothespins. Have your child match them by squeezing the clothespin to attach it to the shoebox. You also can make a lacing activity with your child using the picture side of a colorful card. Let your child cut off the other half first. Then help him or her punch holes around the edge of the picture. Show him how to lace through the holes. Try using yarn with a wide diameter to add a little resistance in order to build up pinch strength.

October

Dalmatians

Activity Goals: Pre-Writing Skills Development
Sensory Processing Improvement

Time: 30 minutes

Objectives: Upon successful completion of this activity, the child will be able to

1. Coordinate to paint a Dalmatian, staying within outline
2. Use index finger to make black spots, with other fingers curled underneath
3. Identify various textures by touch alone

Materials:
1. Large outline of Dalmatian
2. Small pieces of sponge
3. Dishes of white and black paint
4. Large sock or "feely box"
5. Fur and other textures of cloth, two of each type

Procedure:
1. Have the children use sponges and white paint to paint their Dalmatians white.
2. While the paint is drying, let the children feel the fur pieces and other textures. Place one of each in the sock or feely box. Let each child take a turn finding a piece of textured fabric and identifying it, either verbally or by pointing at one in front of her, before taking it out.
3. Returning to the Dalmatians, have the children put spots on them by dipping their index finger in the black paint and then dotting it on their Dalmatian.

Adaptations:
1. Refer to the appendix for adaptations for a child with a visual impairment in order to facilitate painting her Dalmatian.
2. If a child has difficulty extending just her index finger, try hanging the Dalmatian on a vertical surface such as an easel to promote a more mature hand position.

Multilevel Instruction:
1. Let the more skilled child cut out dog bones for the Dalmatians.
2. Enhance the activity with a gross-motor activity. Have the children pretend to be puppies, either playing ball or pretending to carry bones by placing them under their chins.

Learning in Motion

Letter to Parents
Dalmatians

This week we had fun talking about dogs. We painted a Dalmatian, putting on the spots with our index fingers. We felt objects with different textures, including fur. Then we played a guessing game with objects hidden in a fuzzy sock.

Purpose of the Activity

Painting is a good activity for developing pre-writing skills. Our painting activity helped the children work on improving their eye-hand coordination, which they will need for coloring and writing. Being able to use just one finger while curling the other fingers out of the way to make the spots on their dogs helped the children learn to control each finger individually. The children will need good finger control for coloring, writing, and cutting with scissors.

Identifying textures without looking at them helps the children improve their sense of touch. When they are older, the children will write faster and easier if they have a good sense of touch, as they will not have to look at their hands to know how they are moving them as they form letters.

Home Activities to Help Your Child Grow

Painting is lots of fun for most children. Your child can paint both inside and outside. Did you ever "paint the house" with a large brush and a bucket of water? This activity will keep your child busy while you work on outside chores and will help him or her develop good arm and hand strength for writing, too.

You can also help your child grow if you vary the position in which he or she is painting, the painting tool, and materials. Try hanging paper on the wall or place it on the floor, rather than flat on a table. Let your child paint with his or her finger, a cotton swab, or a cosmetic sponge. You can make "paint" using pudding, shaving cream, or a frozen ice cube tinted with food color.

Try our sock game at home, hiding small toys or plastic letters for him or her to guess. Perhaps your child will get dressed faster if you put a "surprise" in his socks every morning!

October

Fall Leaves

Activity Goals: Self-Help Skills Development
Cognitive Development

Time: 45 minutes

Objectives: Upon successful completion of this activity, the child will be able to
1. Dress self in outdoor clothing, including fasteners
2. Identify colors, matching like colors and shapes of leaves
3. Find hidden objects by touch alone

Materials:
1. Fall leaves
2. Crayons
3. Newsprint paper
4. Tape
5. Paste
6. Plastic grocery bags

Procedure:
1. Choose a cool day for the children to practice putting on their jackets or sweaters for a walk outside to gather leaves. Give each child a plastic grocery bag to hold her leaves.
2. Back inside, help the children choose a few leaves and tape a piece of newsprint over them. Have them use different colors of crayon pieces held sideways to rub over the paper until they can see the shapes. Encourage them to find the leaves by rubbing on top of the paper with their hands first.
3. When done rubbing their papers, let them rub some paste on the leaves and glue them on another piece. You could help them group all the same types of leaves or colors of leaves together.

Adaptations:
1. No-roll crayons with the paper peeled off are the easiest kind to hold and help develop good finger strength for holding crayons in a tripod grasp.
2. Use a heavier weight of paper if the child rubs too hard and tears the newsprint.
3. Use paste from a jar rather than a glue stick to help the children develop better finger control while pasting the leaves.

Multilevel Instruction:
1. You can make textured leaf shapes by cutting out plastic embroidery canvas. Try covering them with a large sheet of paper. Ask the children how many they can find just by feeling with their hands. You can ask them to draw a circle or another shape around each one that they find.
2. Have the children draw a circle around a leaf they have rubbed and cut it out with scissors.

October

Learning in Motion

Letter to Parents

Fall Leaves

We did a fine-motor activity today. The children put on their outerwear and went outside to gather fall leaves. We came back and made leaf rubbings by placing paper on top of the leaves and rubbing over it with crayons. The children used their thinking skills by helping to sort the leaves by color and type.

Purpose of the Activity

One of our goals today was to get extra practice putting on and taking off jackets and other outerwear. The children also practiced staying together as a group as we walked outside. They enjoyed picking up leaves and other "treasures" and putting them into their bags.

Making leaf rubbings helped the children develop hand strength and skill using a crayon. It also helped the children develop their sense of touch, as they had to feel the leaf through the paper in order to know where to rub. Sorting out the leaves (and other treasures) also helped the children learn to classify objects by their characteristics. Learning to group like objects helped your child learn that things can be organized. This helped your child strengthen his or her ability to make things orderly, designate "spaces" to put things, and organize himself/herself to get jobs done.

Home Activities to Help Your Child Grow

You can have fun making rubbings at home with objects such as coins, paper clips, and other fairly flat objects. If you have some plastic canvas, cut it into shapes or letters for surprise pictures. Let your child rub on paper with the crayon held sideways, so he or she has to pinch it with the ends of his or her fingers. This will build up a lot of strength in his or her fingers for holding crayons in a tripod grasp.

A simple task to reinforce the idea of sorting objects would be to have your child sort the eating utensils after you wash the dishes. Giving your child a daily chore like this will help him learn to be independent and feel that he is an important contributor to the family, too.

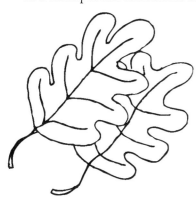

October

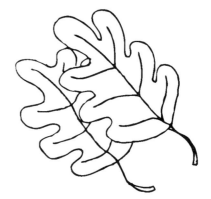

Flying Bats and Ghosts

Activity Goals: Visual-Perceptual Development
Attention Improvement

Time: 10 minutes

Objectives: Upon successful completion of this activity, the child will be able to
1. Demonstrate improved attention at end of activity
2. Fold square into a triangle after demonstration
3. Coordinate eyes with hands to blow squares off finger

Materials:
1. Squares of stretchy rubber exercise band or Lycra® fabric
2. Facial tissues

Procedure:
1. Give each child a square of the stretchy material. Show him how to hold it to look like a square, and then move one hand so that he is holding opposite corners to turn it into a triangle "bat." Let the children have fun pulling the bat's wings to make it "fly." Have them try blowing on the bat to make it flutter.
2. Show them how to put the square on the end of their index finger to make a ghost and blow on it to make the ghost fly. Let them try to blow the ghost off their fingers, or give them a tissue to blow the ghost away.
3. To close the activity, have the children hide the ghosts and bats in their hands by squeezing them into a ball. A box or wastebasket can be the "cave" they fly into.

Adaptations:
1. Monitor children with asthma to make sure that rapid or forceful blowing doesn't trigger bronchospasm. Ghosts made of facial tissue would be easier to blow.
2. Latex-free Thera-Band' is available to use if a child has a latex allergy.
3. Some young children have a hard time learning to motor plan to blow but will learn in a group because they are more motivated. Try providing a mirror so the children can see how they purse their lips.

Multilevel Instruction:
1. Use this activity to transition from a stimulating gross-motor activity or a circle time, where the children might have been sitting for some time, to begin a fine-motor activity at the table (See "Ghost, Ghost, Witch!" on next page for a fine-motor idea).
2. Use small squares of white fabric instead of tissues for the ghosts. To finish the activity, have the children put their squares over a lollipop and secure it with a piece of pipe cleaner or bow.

Letter to Parents

Flying Bats and Ghosts

This week we pretended to make bats and ghosts fly. We used squares of stretchy material and learned how to fold them into triangles to make a bat. We also pulled on the corners to flap the bats' wings and blew on the bats and ghosts to make them fly.

Purpose of the Activity

Our activities this week worked on the concepts of squares and triangles, which require visual perception. Since young children understand concepts better using a "hands-on" approach, they are given these types of experiences many times in school. Other types of visual-perceptual "hands-on" activities include using puzzles made with shapes and paper projects where they cut out and color shapes.

Stretching, squeezing, and blowing on the bats and ghosts worked on another goal, helping to improve attention. Using an activity that requires pressure, force, and taking a few deep breaths can help children (and adults) become physically ready to be alert and focused. Comparable activities many adults find useful in becoming mentally alert and focused are yoga, weight lifting, and working out on exercise equipment. Using this activity can help your child become ready to listen to a story or do a fine-motor activity with better concentration.

Home Activities to Help Your Child Grow

You can use activities to help your child focus at home, too. For example, if your child has a hard time sitting still for a story, even though he or she seems to enjoy it, try giving him or her a "job" to do first that involves using some force, such as helping you carry bundles of groceries, sweeping, or raking. You can use the "blowing" idea by spending some time blowing bubbles. Another thing to try would be serving your child a thick shake to drink through a straw. If you find this helpful, try freezing bananas or another fruit when they are ripe and keeping them handy in the freezer. Then you can make a quick shake with juice or milk any time you want to help your child prepare to settle down.

October

Flying Ghosts

Activity Goals: Gross-Motor Skills Development
Group Development

Time: 15 minutes

Objectives: Upon successful completion of this activity, the child will be able to
1. Throw a ball accurately to a target
2. Catch a ball thrown to him by a partner
3. Cooperate in a throwing and catching game with one partner

Materials:
1. White plastic trash bags
2. Balls: playground, beach balls, and tennis balls
3. Targets: Hula Hoop, large box, or trash can

Procedure:
1. Make ghosts by placing each ball inside a plastic trash bag and closing the bag with a rubber band.
2. Direct the children to try throwing their ghosts at the targets. They will discover that the ghosts "fly" a little slower and are a little easier to visually track than a regular ball.
3. Pair up the children with a partner, and have them practice catching and throwing to each other.
4. End the activity by having the "ghosts fly back home to hide" in a box or trash can.

Adaptations:
1. Some children with physical disabilities may find it hard to throw a large ball because they cannot use both hands together easily. Let them try "flying" a smaller ghost, made with a tennis ball, using one hand.
2. Put beans inside a ball or use a ball with an auditory signal for the child with low vision. Tie on colored streamers or use a colored bag if he has trouble seeing a white one.
3. Play this game outside on a grassy surface to slow down the balls when they hit the ground. A fenced-in area will help keep the group more organized.

Multilevel Instruction:
1. To increase the structure of this activity, lay down two lines with a rope or streamers. Divide the group and have them stand behind the lines. Use only one ball and ask each child to say the name of the child before he throws the ghost to him.
2. For children who are doing well catching and throwing to a partner, teach them to take one giant step backward every time they catch the ghost. If they miss, take one step closer.

October

Learning in Motion

Letter to Parents

Flying Ghosts

The children had a great time this week making "ghosts fly." We used a white plastic trash bag with a ball inside, put a rubber band around the "neck" to close it, and drew eyes and a mouth for features. The children practiced throwing their ghosts at targets and back and forth to each other.

Purpose of the Activity

Our motor group activity this week worked on helping the children develop skills for throwing and catching balls. We used balls of different sizes, both playground size and tennis ball size, so the children would have a chance to practice catching both. Using the plastic trash bags made the balls travel more slowly and also provided a bigger surface for the children to grab on to, making it easier to catch and throw accurately.

Using pairs of children for throwing and catching also gave the children a chance to work on their social skill development. Young children sometimes need practice in order to develop the ability to maintain eye contact with another person when they are interacting with him or her. They also need to learn how to get another person's attention and cooperate in a pleasant way. Since a great deal of communication is non-verbal, setting up motor games in pairs helps the children learn to read body language and practice these important social cues.

Home Activities to Help Your Child Grow

Working on ball skills with young children can be fun and can help build good coordination at an early age. Be aware that children learn to throw faster than they learn to catch. If your child is having some trouble with these skills, build up his or her eye-hand coordination by letting him or her swing at a balloon suspended from a string. Your child can use her hands or a piece of foam pipe insulation for a bat.

You can help your child with social development by making sure that you take the time to get eye contact when speaking to her. This can be hard nowadays when we are so busy, so try to set a time, such as mealtime, when the family talks to one another. Reduce distractions by turning off the TV!

October

Ghost, Ghost, Witch!

Activity Goals: Sensory Processing Improvement
Visual-Perceptual Development

Time: 30 minutes

Objectives: Upon successful completion of this activity, the child will be able to

1. Locate objects hidden around the classroom
2. Follow rules for a circle game
3. Demonstrate good tolerance for touch by tolerating touch from other children and the touch from cotton and glue
4. Demonstrate agility and strength during circle game

Materials:

1. Figures of ghosts and witches' hats
2. Large ghost figure for each child, drawn on a piece of black paper or cut out
3. Cotton balls and glue

Procedure:

1. Place the figures of the ghosts and witches' hats around the classroom while the children are out.
2. Show the children examples of the figures they will be looking for. Let them hunt for and bring back the figures.
3. Have the children sit in a circle on the floor and play "Ghost, Ghost, Witch!" which is the same as "Duck, Duck, Goose."
4. Make ghosts by gluing the cotton balls on the black paper ghost figures.

Adaptations:

1. If there are children who have mobility impairments, set the limits on how many figures each child can find. Ask the other children to walk backwards, hop, or perform some other type of movement to allow the child who cannot move quickly more time to catch them and to run away from them when playing "Ghost, Ghost, Witch."
2. A child with a visual impairment is more likely to see objects that are in contrast to one another. Some children see better with bright light or when the light comes from behind them.
3. If a child is sensitive to being touched by others and seems to dislike touching certain textures such as cotton or glue, you can help her get ready by starting with a weight bearing activity. Try having the children crawl, bear walk, or crab walk to find the ghosts in witches' hats.

Multilevel Instruction:

1. Enhance this activity by asking the children to perform motor skills such as hopping or walking backwards as they move back and forth playing the games.
2. Have the children cut out the ghost shapes. Ask them to pull the cotton balls into small pieces or stretch them out like "spooky Halloween fog."

October

Letter to Parents

Ghost, Ghost, Witch!

The children had fun playing some games this week for our motor group. They hunted around the classroom looking for figures of "ghosts" and "witches' hats." Then they played a game we called, "Ghost, Ghost, Witch," just like "Duck, Duck, Goose." The children sat in a circle. One child walked around the circle touching the heads of the other children saying the word, "ghost" to each child. When he or she said the word "witch," the child whose head he or she touched jumped up and chased him or her around the circle. The first child tried to sit in the second child's place before he or she was tagged. For our last activity, the children were given ghost shapes made from black paper. They glued on white cotton balls, leaving space for their ghosts' eyes and mouth.

Purpose of the Activity

Our first game today, where the children hunted for figures, worked on their ability to discriminate objects, which is a visual-perceptual task. Our circle game helped the children learn a beginning group game and also helped them learn to accept light touch from their classmates. In school, children can be distracted easily when other children brush up against them. Since this is often accidental, the children need to learn that this is something to be ignored. Our last activity, making the "ghosts," combined using sensory and visual-perceptual processing. The children handled soft cotton balls, which help them develop their "touch" sense. They also had to leave spaces for eyes and a mouth when they glued the cotton balls on the black paper, which worked on being able to arrange the cotton correctly, another visual-perceptual task.

Home Activities to Help Your Child Grow

You can help your child sharpen his ability to find "hidden" objects at home by asking him to help you look for objects around the house. Try sending your child to the refrigerator for a small food item that he can bring you. Let him help you look for a misplaced shoe! There are lots of books available from the library which have hidden picture games, for example, the "Where's Waldo" series.

October

Jack-o'-Lanterns

Activity Goals: Strength and Endurance Improvement
Visual-Perceptual Development

Time: 20 minutes

Objectives: Upon successful completion of this activity, the child will be able to
1. Demonstrate sufficient hand strength to make at least 6 paper balls
2. Match similar pumpkins
3. Group the pumpkins by attributes

Materials:
1. Large pumpkin leaf bag
2. Sheets of newspaper
3. Pictures of jack-o'-lanterns with varied expressions, colors, or sizes; two or more of each

Procedure:
1. Demonstrate how to make a paper ball to the children, stressing that they need to "squeeze the paper ball." Try to have them make at least a half dozen each.
2. Let them fill up the leaf bag. If you wish, you can make this a target game.
3. After you have finished making the large jack-o'-lantern, show the children the smaller ones, lining them up. See if they can help you match them.
4. Lay all the pumpkins down. Have the children take turns finding "all the happy ones," "all the large ones," "all the yellow ones," etc.

Adaptations:
1. Try to include groups of jack-o'-lanterns of various textures for students with visual impairments.
2. Some children may demonstrate sensitivity to manipulating the paper and refuse to make paper balls. Try having the group do a gross-motor activity that involves putting weight on the palms of the hands first, such as crawling. You may have to start the balls and then let the child squeeze them. Consult your occupational therapist for additional suggestions.

Multilevel Instruction:
1. Let the children each have two pumpkin shapes to make their own pairs by drawing on the faces. Combine them to make a new class game.
2. Provide paper clips or clothespins to place on matched pairs of jack-o'-lanterns.

October

Letter to Parents
Jack-o'-Lanterns

We had fun with jack-o'-lanterns this week in our motor group. First, we made lots of paper balls by squeezing sheets of newspapers. Then we threw them into a big pumpkin leaf bag. Last, we played a matching game with smaller pictures of jack-o'-lanterns, finding the ones which looked the same.

Purpose of the Activity

Crumpling up paper to make balls helps the children improve their hand strength, which they need to develop a good grasp for coloring, writing, and cutting with scissors.

Matching the jack-o'-lanterns worked on learning to recognize things that look the same. The jack-o'-lanterns were different colors and also had different expressions so the children could group them in different ways.

Home Activities to Help Your Child Grow

You can use pairs of playing cards or even grocery coupons from the newspapers to make a matching game for your child. To make the activity more challenging, try setting up the game like "Concentration." Using three or four pairs at first, lay the pairs of cards face down and take turns turning two of them face up to see if they match. If they match, you get to keep the pair. If they don't match, you have to turn them back face down and let the other person take a turn. A simpler way to play the game would be to give your child one from each pair of the "cards." Put the other ones face down, with some pictures mixed in which she doesn't have. As your child turns the hidden pictures over, she must look her cards over and match them to make the pairs. These games will help your child develop visual discrimination and visual memory, the ability to see forms and remember them. Your child will need this in order to learn to read and write.

October

October Party

Activity Goals: Gross-Motor Skills Development
Sensory Processing Improvement

Time: 20 minutes

Objectives: Upon successful completion of this activity, the child will be able to
1. Throw objects into a target
2. Demonstrate good sense of body position by finding the location of the pumpkin's nose
3. Demonstrate good sense of touch in finding objects hidden in rice without looking

Materials:
1. Beanbags
2. Large pot or kettle
3. Large picture of pumpkin
4. Blindfold (hat)
5. Triangle "noses"
6. Small wrapped treats
7. Rice table or large box of rice

Procedure:
1. Set up three stations for the games:
   a. Tossing a beanbag into the witch's cauldron: use beanbags and a kettle.
   b. Pin the nose on the jack-o'-lantern: use large picture of a pumpkin with a space left for the triangle nose to be pinned on
   c. Find a hidden treat: bury wrapped treats in rice
2. Demonstrate each game to the children. If you have enough adults to have one at each station, divide the class so that the children can rotate around the stations in small groups.
3. To close, try having each child take one more turn throwing a beanbag into the cauldron before sitting in an area you have designated for the next activity.

Adaptations:
1. To make pinning the nose on the jack-o'-lantern easier let the child stand within arm's length of the picture. Practice reaching with eyes open. Then let him see if he can reproduce the same movement with his eyes closed, hitting the target.
2. Have the children find the treats hidden in the rice box with their eyes closed. Use a hat pulled down over the eyes if the child cannot keep his eyes closed.

Multilevel Instruction:
1. Children love to find hidden objects. Try the "Pumpkin Hide & Seek" game (on page 56) for another activity for your party.
2. For very young children, try moving them through the three stations singly or in pairs during playtime in order to keep the "party" low-key.
3. For a more challenging activity, try putting spider rings in the cauldron and having the children pick them out with tongs or tweezers. This will help develop and strengthen pinch muscles for using scissors and crayons.

Letter to Parents

October Party

We had a party this week in our group and played some games. We threw beanbags into a pot ("cauldron"), we played "Pin the Nose on the Jack-O'-Lantern," and, with our eyes closed, used our hands to find treats hidden in rice.

Purpose of the Activities

We're working on a gross-motor skill this week, throwing objects at a target. Another important goal we worked on is developing the sense of touch and position in the children's arms and hands. Being able to judge what position his or her arm is in without looking helps your child with writing and other fine-motor tasks like cutting with scissors, because he or she needs to be looking at other things— the material he is copying, the spaces between lines, or whether he or she is cutting accurately along a line. If your child doesn't develop accurate position sense, he or she will use a lot more effort for fine-motor tasks and might do them slowly or awkwardly. The sense of touch in the hands is important for fine-motor tasks as well. A child who has not developed an accurate sense of touch may hold a pencil too tightly when writing and complain that his or her hand is "tired." He or she also may press down too hard when writing or erasing and tear the paper. You can get a feel for what it might be like to have reduced sensation in your hands by trying a fine-motor task, such as keyboarding, with gloves on.

Home Activities to Help Your Child Grow

Target games are fun and easy to set up at home. Inside, try using a balloon, nerf ball, or Koosh® ball, and outside, try using a basketball or large plastic ball. Set up some stuffed animals to knock off a table inside. Outside, try knocking down plastic soda bottles.

You can help your child improve his or her sense of touch by burying a ball or toy in a leaf pile or sandbox and then having your child find it. For an inside game, try putting rice or macaroni in a shoebox and hiding small objects in it. If you choose objects with different qualities, such as something smooth, something rough, something heavy, etc., you can teach your child how to describe them when he or she finds them.

Pumpkin Hide-and-Seek

Activity Goals: Visual-Perceptual Development
Cognitive Development

Time: 20 minutes

Objectives: Upon successful completion of this activity, the child will be able to
1. Visually locate two partially visible pumpkins hidden around the room
2. Follow two- to three-step verbal directions with visual cues
3. Wait for turn during the activity

Materials:
1. Two paper pumpkins per child, made with Ellison machine
2. Large pumpkin for class discussion
3. Basket to hold paper pumpkins after they are picked

Procedure:
1. Hide pumpkins around the room so that a small section is visible to the children.
2. Have them sit on rug squares in a semi-circle around the teacher.
3. Show them the large pumpkin and relate it to the Fall/Halloween theme.
4. Explain that the children will be taking turns finding a pumpkin and bringing it back to the basket.
5. Allow one child at a time to find a pumpkin, bring it back to the basket, and sit down.
6. Let each child find two pumpkins.

Adaptations:
1. For the child in a wheelchair or with limited physical mobility, allow her to go first with a partner to help her pick her pumpkin when she finds it.
2. Make sure the pumpkins are placed at an accessible height, especially for a child in a wheelchair; for example, on a tabletop, a chair, or a bookshelf.
3. For a child with a visual impairment, use high contrast behind the pumpkin. In a dark room, highlight a pumpkin using a flashlight to illuminate it.
4. For a child who is blind or one who has a cognitive disability, try using three-dimensional pumpkins, such as small plastic ones. Try placing two objects in the child's hand, one the same as the pumpkins and one different to help the child learn to discriminate differences and match.

Multilevel Instruction:
1. For a higher-level group, make cutouts of pumpkins and bats with the Ellison machine. Have each child find one of each.
2. To incorporate fine-motor and body awareness into the task, have the children add the eyes, nose, and mouth on their pumpkins.

Learning in Motion

Letter to Parents
Pumpkin Hide-and-Seek

This week in our motor group we pretended to be hunting for hidden pumpkins in a pumpkin patch. The pumpkins were hidden so that we could see only a little bit of them. Once we found the pumpkins, we put them in the pumpkin basket. We had fun bringing our pumpkins back using "giant steps," walking backwards, and trying out other motor movements.

Purpose of the Activity

Visual discrimination and the ability to visually find or locate an object are important skills for school and home activities. In school, your child will need to find his or her place in a book, find information on a chalkboard, and locate objects in the classroom. Being able to visually discriminate differences is also important so that your child can recognize letters, numbers, and words.

This activity also required your child to be able to wait for his or her turn and to follow directions. Being attentive in the group is important because most instruction in school occurs in a group.

Home Activities to Help Your Child Grow

To help your child practice finding things, you can try hiding objects about the room at home, too. Try hiding a familiar toy or a common object, such as a spoon. To make it easy, place the object in full view. Then, to make the activity harder, partially hide a number of objects so your child can only see part of them. If your child does really well with this activity, you can try harder games. Use same-size pictures, such as photos, and ask your child to find a specific one in the pile. Try playing card games, such as "Old Maid" or "Go Fish," which involve matching cards to make sets.

October

Rolling Pumpkins

Activity Goals: Strength and Endurance Improvement
Bilateral Coordination Development

Time: 20 minutes

Objectives: Upon successful completion of this activity, the child will be able to

1. Demonstrate sufficient large muscle strength to roll up and down an inclined wedge and push a ball with both hands or feet
2. Coordinate both sides of the body to roll sequentially
3. Roll a ball to a partner accurately
4. Demonstrate tolerance to movement without a behavioral over-reaction

Materials:
1. Mats, large inclined wedge
2. Large orange gymnastics ball
3. Screw-top soda bottles, partially filled with rice or beans and covered with a square of white plastic with ghost features drawn on

Procedure:
1. Set wedge on mats. Show the children how a pumpkin (orange ball) can roll down. Help the children roll down, encouraging them to roll straight and stay on the mats. Have them try rolling up the wedge, too.
2. Have the children lie down along the edge of the mats, holding their arms out. Let them take turns pushing the orange ball to knock down the soda bottle "ghosts."
3. Have the children sit on the edge of the mats with their arms behind them and feet held off the floor. Let them try to push the orange ball with their feet together to knock down the ghosts.

Adaptations:
1. If a child has difficulty rolling, give him hands-on assistance at the lower part of his legs. Starting on his back, cross one leg over the other quickly. See if he can complete the movement by turning his upper body over. When he's on his stomach, help by pushing his hip over as you cross the leg. Encourage him to push with his hands to finish the movement.
2. Some children will get easily stimulated with rolling. If you find that the child is getting over-stimulated rolling down the wedge, have him roll up the wedge too. Usually an activity that requires a lot of effort helps children calm down.
3. Provide a low wedge or a towel roll to help children hold up their arms or legs if they are not strong enough to do so independently during the bowling part of the activity.

Multilevel Instruction:
1. Let the children make newspaper balls or use yarn balls and throw them to knock the ghosts down. Demonstrate how they can throw a ball either overhand or underhand.
2. Let an older group lie on their stomachs or lean back on their arms to push the ball to each other. Put a few "ghosts" in the middle of the circle to use as targets.

October

Letter to Parents
Rolling Pumpkins

We pretended a big orange ball was a pumpkin this week. First, we watched it roll down a mat, and tried to imitate rolling, too. Then we lay on our stomachs and rolled the ball with our hands to knock down "ghosts" made from soda bottles. We tried sitting up and rolling the ball with our feet, too.

Purpose of the Activity

This week's motor group activities worked on helping your child build up strength and endurance in his or her neck, stomach, back, and arm muscles, and bilateral coordination, which is using both sides of the body together. Lying on the stomach and raising the arms is a type of position that we sometimes call "airplaning." You might have seen your child do it when he was a baby, before he learned to sit and to crawl. He was building up the back muscles. On his back while you were changing his diaper, you may remember your child trying to sit up. This, too, was a natural developmental step in which your child was building up his "flexor" muscles so he would be strong enough to sit up and crawl. Although babies seem to naturally "exercise," we often find that school-age children need to engage in motor activities to increase their strength in order to be able to sit comfortably in a stable position, listen, and do fine-motor activities. Children who have strong muscles often find it easier to pay attention, too.

Home Activities to Help Your Child Grow

Try our games at home by making some bowling pin "ghosts." We used 12- ounce plastic bottles. Put some rice or dried pasta in to weight them and screw on the tops. Then, cut out squares of white plastic from trash bags or white cotton sheets and fasten them over the tops of the bottles with a rubber band. Add eyes and a mouth with a black marker. You can use a playground-size ball to roll with your hands or feet at the "ghosts." Try this with your child, and you'll both get a great workout! Outside, have fun knocking the "ghosts" off a ledge with tennis-size balls. Teach your child to throw underhand as well as overhand.

October

Scarecrows

Activity Goals: Self-Help Skills Development
 Group Development

Time: 30 minutes

Objectives: Upon successful completion of this activity, the child will be able to
1. Demonstrate sufficient hand strength to make paper balls
2. Help straighten and arrange clothing and manipulate clothing fasteners
3. Take turns during a group activity

Materials:
1. Newspapers, torn in half or quarter pages, 10 sheets or more per child.
2. Plastic bag or pillowcase
3. Button front shirt, jeans, hat, socks, gloves, and high top sneakers.
4. Yardstick
5. Rubber bands
6. Masking tape
7. Picture or model of a scarecrow

Procedure:
1. Show the children a picture or model of a scarecrow. Give them two or three pieces of newspaper and ask them to make a ball with each one.
2. Put rubber bands around the ends of the legs on the pants. Let the children help you fill the legs with newspapers. Have them help zip and snap the pants and fill with newspaper balls.
3. Put rubber bands around the ends of the sleeves. Let the children help fill the sleeves with more paper balls.
4. Let the children help button up the shirt, tuck it into the pants, and fill with paper balls or a pillow. Slide the yardstick down into the shirt and pants for a "backbone" and "neck."
5. Fill up the pillowcase "head" and socks and put them on the scarecrow, using rubber bands as needed to secure them. Let the children help you put the "feet" into the sneakers and pull the laces. Perhaps one of the children can tie a knot and bow. Use gloves for hands and put a hat on the scarecrow.

Adaptations:
1. Try to find a shirt with the largest buttons to make it easier to button for young children. You might even find a shirt that snaps at a local thrift store.
2. If some of the children have a short attention span, try dividing the group and making two scarecrows; or try keeping some children busy either balling up paper or tearing it up for the group while others take turns filling the scarecrow.

Multilevel Instruction:
1. Collect plaid shirts. Let each child put one on, button it up, and pretend to be a scarecrow using a song or fingerplay (see, "Crow, Crow, Scarecrow).
2. Provide a picture of a scarecrow to color. Let the children cut it out, staple it to a plastic straw and pretend to make it dance. You can encourage the children to blow on the paper scarecrows "to make them dance" as a way to calm and focus the group.
3. Follow up this activity by tracing around each child on a large piece of paper. Help them identify the parts of their bodies, add facial features and hair. You could even make the body by tracing two layers and let them stuff it to make their own "scarecrow."

October

Learning in Motion

Letter to Parents
Scarecrows

We made scarecrows this week in our group. We made balls of newspapers with our hands to stuff a shirt, pants, socks, and gloves. Our group worked together to fill up the clothes and put the scarecrow together, fastening the buttons, zipper and snaps and tying the shoelaces. We decided that a scarecrow is like a big doll.

Purpose of the Activity

Our activity this week worked on helping the children build strength in their hands and their skill in manipulating clothing fasteners. We worked together as a group in order to build the children's social development, learning to take turns. and to acknowledge each other's achievements. It's very motivating to children to see that they are recognized for having skill, such as being able to show the group how to button up a shirt or zipper and snap pants. Children learn from each other, too, so observing their classmates helping with clothing fasteners will help motivate and teach the other children how to do these tasks.

Another purpose of the activity was to give the children a chance to see close up how scarecrows are made. This time of year, many people decorate the outsides of their homes with fall decorations. Since stuffed figures can look frightening to young children, making a scarecrow themselves can help the children learn that the figures are not real.

Home Activities to Help Your Child Grow

You can make a scarecrow at home with your child like we did at school using an old shirt, pants, socks, gloves, and shoes. We used a white plastic bag for the head and added the features with markers. We closed the ends of the shirt and pants with rubber bands and then stuffed them. If you don't have any old clothes to use, you can find some inexpensive ones at thrift stores. Also, you can make your scarecrow sit up straight using a yardstick for a "backbone."

October

Stop, Drop, and Roll

Activity Goals: Bilateral Coordination Development
Cognitive Development

Time: 30 minutes

Objectives: Upon successful completion of this activity, the child will be able to
1. Sequence stepping patterns and rolling patterns, moving through a multi-step task
2. Coordinate body to step in between markers and roll smoothly
3. Demonstrate sufficient hand strength and bilateral coordination to pull apart "Rapper Snappers"

Materials:
1. Rolled up newspapers, secured with a rubber band
2. Play house made with a white sheet thrown over a table
3. Mats or rug squares to make a pathway to roll along
4. "Rapper Snappers" (see Appendix)
5. Scooter boards

Procedure:
1. Have the children use the scooter boards as "fire trucks" and pretend to race to the fire. You can use a musical accompaniment if you wish (see Appendix).
2. Set up the play area so that the children can pretend to be firemen. Lay the newspaper rolls first, so they look like steps of a ladder. Then place the table with a sheet on it so the children can crawl under it. Next, line up some mats or rug squares so that the children can roll back to where they will be starting, the "fire station."
3. Explain and demonstrate to the children how they will pretend to be firemen. They will "climb up the ladder" by stepping over the newspaper rolls and then crawl under the "smoke" which is the white sheet. Last, they will roll back to the start, which is getting away from the fire. Let the children practice this several times.
4. To close the activity, use some Rapper Snappers and have the children pull them apart to make a fire hose. Have the children work together as a group to join the "Rapper Snappers" and carry the hose to the fire.

Adaptations:
1. If stepping over the newspaper rolls poses a problem for the group, try making it easier by using rug squares to step on or wooden sticks to step over.
2. If you have a student who uses a walker or wheelchair and would have a problem crawling under the "smoke," try hanging the sheet from a line and raise the line for him or her.
3. Use high-contrast materials for the ladder and pathway to help the child with low vision participate independently.

Multilevel Instruction:
1. Enhance motor skill development by having the children go through the obstacle course backwards or jump over the newspaper rolls.
2. Follow up this activity by teaching the children a fingerplay or having them cut out their own firemen hats.
3. Make "Sparky," a Dalmatian fire dog, using foam cups and paper ears, nose, and eyes.

Learning in Motion

Letter to Parents

Stop, Drop, and Roll

The children pretended to be firemen this week in our motor group. They raced to the fire on their scooter boards. Then, they climbed up the "ladder," which was made of a series of newspaper rolls. Next, they crawled through the "smoke," a sheet over a table. Last, they practiced rolling down the mats, another important safety technique that the firemen talk about with them. We also had some fun using "Rapper Snappers," which are plastic accordion pipe toys. The children stretched them out and snapped them together to make a long hose to pretend to put out a fire.

Purpose of the Activity

We used fire safety activities this week in order to practice motor skills and thinking skills, too. Stepping over rolls of newspaper, crawling and then standing up, followed by rolling helped build the children's agility and motor sequencing skills. Crawling, rolling, and pulling apart the Rapper Snappers helps build body strength and bilateral coordination.

To "stop, drop, and roll," the children had to remember a sequence of three motor tasks in a row. Some of the children may have needed to be told at first what to do step by step as they didn't always remember all three steps; however, after a little practice, they could do them without much prompting.

Home Activities to Help Your Child Grow

You can have fun with your child practicing two- and three-step directions at home. For example, next time you have to take your child somewhere in the car, try making a game of it: "Walk backwards to the door, jump outside, and then make giant steps to the car." This type of game will help your child increase his or her memory for following verbal directions. He or she needs to be able to do this in school when the teacher gives directions, such as, "Throw your trash away, put on your coat, and line up by the door." Later, when your child is older, he or she will be following even more complicated directions for seat work in school, so helping him or her learn to listen carefully now and follow verbal directions is important.

October

Educational Goals by Activity

Attention Improvement	Balance Improvement	Bilateral Coordination Development	Body-Scheme and Motor-Planning Improvement	Cognitive Development	Fine-Motor Skills Development	Gross-Motor Skills Development	Group Development	Hand-Dominance Development	Pre-Writing Skills Development	Scissor Skills Development	Self-Help Skills Development	Sensory Processing Improvement	Strength and Endurance Improvement	Visual-Perceptual Development	Activity	Page
										✔	✔				Celebrating Corn	66
						✔		✔							Corn and Popcorn Play I	69
						✔		✔							Corn and Popcorn Play II	72
		✔						✔							Drums and Turkey Hunt	75
			✔			✔									Football Workout	78
			✔					✔							Friends Sandwich and Dance	81
	✔	✔													Jumping Over the Creek	83
									✔			✔			Making Pottery	85
									✔	✔					Native American Jewelry	87
									✔			✔			Pudding Painting	89
✔	✔														Story of Thanksgiving	91
				✔					✔						Turkey Day	94
									✔			✔			Turkey Finger Painting	96

November

Celebrating Corn

Activity Goals: Scissor Skills Development

Self-Help Skills Development

Time: 40-to-45 minutes

Objectives: Upon successful completion of this activity, the child will be able to
1. Pour wet or dry materials into a container
2. Stir with a spoon
3. Spread with a spoon
4. Place small objects accurately
5. Cut with scissors along a slightly curved line

Materials:
1. One box of corn muffin mix per 5-6 children
2. Ingredients as stated on the corn muffin box
3. Muffin tins and potholder
4. Large mixing bowl, measuring cups and large spoons
5. Jelly and plastic spoons
6. Dry Indian corn kernels or pop corn kernels
7. Brown paper bag or wrapping paper
8. Dark marker
9. Indian corn

Procedure:
1. Seat children at a table and explain the relationship between corn and Thanksgiving.
2. Show the children Indian corn and corn kernels.
3. Explain the relationship between corn and corn muffins and show the children the box.
4. Have the children identify the ingredients as you show them.
5. With your assistance, allow each child to measure ingredients or pour them into the bowl.
6. Use a large spoon or a small ladle to let children stir and spoon the batter into muffin tins.
7. Place in oven to bake according to recipe on box.
8. While waiting for the muffins to bake and cool, start the children on the corn picture.
9. Give the corncob outline and a small bowl or cup containing corn kernels to each child.
10. Show the children how to glue these onto paper. Elmer's School Glue Gel® works best.
11. Use pieces of brown paper and give each child a piece approximately one foot square.
12. Have the child squeeze this paper into a ball and then gently flatten out this paper to give the paper the look of a corn husk.
13. Either now or before the children wrinkle the paper, draw 3-4 corn husks on each paper in a dark marker or crayon.
14. Supply children with scissors and have them cut out husks.
15. Then glue on the corn husks.
16. Serve muffins and give each child a spoon.
17. Demonstrate how to spread jelly with spoon on the muffin.

November

Learning in Motion

18. Allow each child a turn to spread jelly on his or her muffin.

19. Enjoy this treat.

Adaptations:

1. If your children are small or have problems with strength, try stabilizing the bowl with Dycem¨, or a non-slip material or wet pad. Enlarge the spoon handle with a sponge wrapped around it. Have the children stand up while stirring.

2. If you have a child who can use only one hand or has a visual impairment, use this adaptation for spreading the jelly: place the muffin in the corner of a small shallow container, e.g., a plastic sandwich holder. It will contain and stabilize the muffin for the child.

Multilevel Instruction:

1. Try using popped corn instead of corn kernels to glue on the corn husks.

2. Give children stencils or templates of the corn husks and allow them to trace and cut out the husks.

3. Make corn prints with the corncobs by placing them in paint and rolling them on a large piece of paper.

November

Letter to Parents
Celebrating Corn

This week we talked about corn and the Thanksgiving celebration. Our first activity was to prepare a special treat, corn muffins. After we measured, mixed and placed our muffins in the oven to cook, we made a corncob. After finishing our hard work, we enjoyed eating our corn muffins. We spread some jelly on them to make them taste even better.

Purpose of the Activity

This activity required the use of our hand strength to open packages, pour and measure ingredients, stir corn muffin mix, place corn kernels on a picture and cut out corn husks. Hand strength is needed for pre-writing/coloring activities and for self-care. Your child will need finger and hand strength to button or zipper his or her clothes and open food packages for school lunches or snacks. We also worked on the self-help skills of cooking and spreading with a spoon.

Home Activities to Help Your Child Grow

You can help your child develop hand strength at home. Let your child help you with some cooking activities. Children really love to cook and bake and take great pride in their accomplishments. Letting your child help mix or stir is a great way to increase hand strength. Encouraging your child to open small packages, such as individually wrapped cookies, cakes, fruit snacks, and juice containers, will help with independence during lunch or snacks. The bathtub is a good place to practice pouring into containers. Have several different size containers in the bathtub and have your child pretend to be measuring or cooking while in the tub.

Corn and Popcorn Play I

Activity Goals: Gross-Motor Skills Development
Hand-Dominance Development

Time: 30 minutes

Objectives: Upon successful completion of this activity, the child will be able to
1. Jump 5-10 times with even foot strike
2. Pinch with either hand
3. Use a tripod grasp to pinch 10 or more small objects

Materials:
1. Small trampoline or a 36-x-36 inch foam rubber pad 4-to-5 inches thick
2. Small clear-plastic bottles, 1 per child, partially filled with dry rice or beans
3. Large or small bubble wrap, approximately one foot square per child
4. Popcorn kernels or miniature Indian corn cobs that can be popped in a microwave oven
5. Indian corn

Procedure:
1. Gather children in a circle to talk about the relationship between corn and the Thanksgiving celebration. Show children the Indian corn, corn kernels, and popcorn. Explain the relationship of these foods to each other.
2. Sing a rhyme or play music and demonstrate jumping while the children shake their plastic bottles. For added safety, tape the screw-on tops closed and have the children shake the bottles with tops turned towards the floor. Explain to the children how their shaker bottles sound just like the noise of popping corn.
3. Have each child take a turn at jumping. To make this activity less noisy and stimulating, only one bottle should be used by the child who is jumping; although, if the entire group shakes the bottles, they will get lots of exercise! After each child is finished jumping, have her pass the bottle to the next child.
4. While sitting either in the circle or at the table, give each child a square of bubble wrap and show her how to squeeze the wrap between her thumb and index and middle finger to pop it. If you are using the wrap with large bubbles, encourage the children to search the bubbles feeling with their fingers to find the ones that haven't been popped yet. When their fingers get tired, show them how to "wring" the bubble wrap, or even jump on it, to get all the bubbles popped.
5. Next, get some popcorn ready to be popped in a microwave. Have the children quietly watch and listen for the sound as the popcorn or Indian corn begins to pop. Let them help you decide when the sound stops, and you should open the oven.
6. Taste the popcorn and enjoy it!

Adaptations:
1. For the child who is using a wheelchair or is unable to stand and jump, have her sit and bounce on a therapy ball to give her the jumping sensation.
2. For the child with visual impairment, hold the child's hands while she jumps.
3. For the child with decreased strength, use a hammer to pop bubble wrap on a hard surface such as a tabletop or floor.
4. For the child with use of only one hand, use a smaller bottle (e.g., spice bottle) for the shaking experience while jumping.

November

Multilevel Instruction:

1. With your assistance, have the children hold your hands and try to jump on one foot and then the other on the trampoline or foam pad.

2. Using popped corn or kernels of corn or Indian corn, have the children make a picture, fill in the outline of a corncob, or trace their names.

3. Have each child fill a plastic bottle one-third full of dried rice or beans using her fingers to pick up and place the materials through the narrow mouth of the bottle. This will help develop finger awareness, control and pinch strength, needed for coloring, writing, and self-help skills. Use this activity while the class listens to Native American music or as part of your Native American celebration.

4. Use popped corn instead of sand or rice in a large container for tactile play; although the children should be asked not to eat it. Provide them with small shovels, scoops, and sandwich bags so they can pretend to make movie snacks.

November

Learning in Motion

Letter to Parents

Corn and Popcorn Play I

This week in our group, we did several activities to learn about corn and popcorn. We jumped and shook a popcorn-sounding instrument. Then we used our fingers to pop bubble wrap, which sounded like popping corn. Our teacher let us watch, listen, and smell while she/he made popcorn for a yummy snack.

Purpose of the Activity

We practiced jumping and shaking while on a trampoline or foam rubber mat. These activities help your child develop leg and arm strength, as well as balance. Balance and strength are important for both gross and fine-motor skill development. Good sitting posture and stability are needed for your child to use his fine-motor skills such as coloring, writing, scissor skills, blocks, etc. This activity helps your child build arm and hand strength. As your child was shaking the popcorn bottle and pinching the bubble wrap, she was using muscles that are responsible for grasping small objects like pencils, crayons, or buttons.

Home Activities to Help Your Child Grow

Children need lots of practice to learn new or challenging motor skills. You can make a game out of hopping with feet together at home. If you have an old sofa or chair cushion in a playroom, allow your child to practice jumping on it. Some children really need this opportunity to jump and bounce to let off steam in order to be able to then play calmly. You can also make going from one room to another an opportunity to practice jumping. Have your child come to the kitchen by hopping with feet together. If this is easy for your child, try having your child hop on one foot and then the other. If you are in the car or during the trip to grandmother's for Thanksgiving, take some bubble wrap with you and give it to your children to pop during the ride. This is a great way to make the time pass more quickly for the children while working on finger strength at the same time. Enjoy your holiday!

Corn and Popcorn Play II

Activity Goals: Gross-Motor Skills Development
Hand-Dominance Development

Time: 30-to-40 minutes

Objectives: Upon successful completion of this activity, the child will be able to

1. Jump forward with feet together 5-10 times, demonstrating an even foot strike
2. Pinch and pop plastic bubbles with either hand
3. Hold on with both hands and move parachute up and down for three-to-five minutes
4. Demonstrate Hand-Dominance Development while hammering using predominantly one hand

Materials:

1. Large bubble wrap, one piece approximately 36-by-24 inches for every five children
2. Small bubble wrap, approximately one foot square per child
3. Plastic or wooden toy hammers
4. Rug squares or padding for hammering
5. Parachute and yarn, nerf or Koosh™ balls or beanbags (10)
6. Popcorn kernels and popper
7. Indian corn

Procedure:

1. Start with children in a circle. Explain the relationship between corn and Thanksgiving. Show the children the Indian corn and corn kernels.
2. Demonstrate jumping forward with feet together to do a "bunny hop."
3. Have each child jump forward on the large bubble wrap to create a popping sound.
4. After each child has had a turn, he returns to the circle.
5. Next, have children hold on to the edges of the parachute.
6. Demonstrate up-and-down arm movements to shake the parachute to make the balls pop up in the air. Encourage the children to hold and shake with both hands. Explain to the children that they are going to pretend to make corn kernels pop. Let them practice making small waves first, with nothing on the parachute; you can tell them "the oil in the pot is getting hot." Then, add the "popcorn kernels" (balls, etc.). At first, caution the children not to "pop the kernels too hard or they will jump out of the pot." Then, give them a signal to shake the parachute hard so the popcorn flies "out of the pot"!
7. After 5 minutes of play, return to the table.
8. Give each child a square of small bubble wrap and allow him to hammer it to pop the bubbles, (use a rug square or padding under the bubble wrap to decrease the noise). Let him try popping bubbles with his fingers, too, to practice a refined pinch.
9. Then have the children watch, listen, and smell as you pop the corn.
10. Enjoy this special treat.

Adaptations:

1. For the child using a wheelchair or a mobility device, allow her to use it or give hands-on assistance to the child to walk or jump on the bubble wrap.
2. Give hands-on assistance to a child with a visual impairment or poor balance.
3. To enable a child with weak grasp or poor hand/finger closure to hold a hammer easily, wrap a sponge around the handle and hold it in place with several rubber bands.

November

Learning in Motion

4. For the child with limited arm or hand movement, have him press on a rolling pin to pop bubble wrap.

5. You may need to assist a child with weak grasp by holding on to the parachute with him hand over hand.

Multilevel Instruction:

1. To assist with turn-taking while hopping on the bubble wrap, help the children count the times the group hears the bubbles being popped. For example, "After you hear five bubbles pop, it's the next child's turn."

2. Play a song while the children are using the parachute. Use the music to play a stop-and-go game with the parachute. Keep the parachute moving until the music stops.

3. Create a popcorn or corn kernel picture.

November

Letter to Parents
Corn and Popcorn Play II

This week we talked about corn and Thanksgiving. We hopped on bubble wrap to make popping sounds like popcorn. Then we played with a large parachute with colorful balls on it. As we held the parachute and moved it up and down, the balls on it popped into the air looking like popcorn. Then we got another chance to make popping noises. We used a hammer and small bubble wrap and hit it to make it pop. We practiced pinching the bubbles, too. Finally, after all our hard work, we watched popcorn being popped by our teacher and enjoyed eating it.

Purpose of the Activity

This activity used a lot of big muscles to jump, hold, move a parachute, and hammer the bubble wrap. Strong muscles in the large joints of the body are important for balance, maintaining a posture, and developing dominance (hand and foot). Young children will, at times, change the hand or foot they are using during motor tasks, not because they haven't established their dominant hand and foot, but because of decreased strength. By building up strength and endurance in the large muscles around their arms and legs, children will be able to use their more skilled hand and foot most of the time and develop refined use of them in activities such as kicking, coloring, and even for feeding themselves, such as mastering using a knife and fork.

Home Activities to Help Your Child Grow

You can help your child build strength in his or her legs at home by working on the following gross-motor skills. Start practicing jumping with both feet together. Have your child try to coordinate multiple jumps to get across the room. Then try some different types of jumping such as sideways, backwards, hopping from one area on the rug to another, and then hopping on one foot. You can work on one-foot balance by having your child practice kicking skills outside. Line up empty soda bottles and give your child a ball. See how many bottles your child can knock down while standing on one foot. Then make it more challenging by setting up soda bottles and having your child hop on one foot first to reach the bottle, and then kicking it. Start with the soda bottles close together (one hop away); and, then, increase the distance as your child improves at this skill.

November

Drums and Turkey Hunt

Activity Goals: Bilateral Coordination Development
Hand-Dominance Development

Time: 30-to-40 minutes

Objectives: Upon successful completion of this activity, the child will be able to
1. Perform a reciprocal pattern with both hands; propelling a scooter board, pulling self along with a rope, and drumming
2. Imitate patterns of movement using visual and auditory feedback
3. Wait turn to participate in activity

Materials:
1. Cardboard boxes, oatmeal containers, or cookie tins for drums
2. Drumsticks or rolled-up newspapers
3. Scooter boards
4. Chairs, tables, or traffic cones to make an obstacle course
5. Rope, 1-to-2 inches in diameter and 10-to-15 feet long
6. Balance beam

Procedure:
1. Set up a pretend hunt for a turkey by making an obstacle course:
   a. Set up a group of chairs or tables arranged to allow a scooter board through
   b. Set up a 10-to-15 feet long rope tied to a stable object at one end
   c. Place the balance beam at the end.
2. Bring the children together to discuss the Native Americans' use of drums and music for celebrations like Thanksgiving. Also talk about how turkeys were hunted for the first Thanksgiving. You may want to explain that the Pilgrims invited the Native American Indians as their guests to the celebration, and they, in turn, brought food as a sign of friendship. They made music and danced together.
3. Have the children sit or kneel in a circle with their drums (boxes, cans, oatmeal containers, play drums, etc.). Tell them they are going to make some music before they hunt for the turkey.
4. Start with a simple hand sequence for drumming, such as alternating hands. Do a series of three or four motions and let the children attempt to imitate.
5. Increase the complexity and change the timing of the beats as children become successful; for example, cross the arms, hit the sticks together, and tap on opposite shoulders as you drum.
6. Next, start the obstacle course. Pretend that the scooter boards are "canoes." Have the children lie on their stomachs and use their arms to move forward through the course. Warn them to do this quietly so they will not frighten the turkey!
7. Once through the chair/table course, have the children sit on the scooter boards to pull themselves (using the rope) across the river on their "canoes." Encourage the children to use a hand-over-hand approach with thumbs on top of the rope.
8. End the course with a walk across the balance beam (bridge). Have the children stop in the middle of the bridge to place one hand above their eyebrows and "search for the turkey" turning side to side to "look up and down the river." Then they can resume the walk across the bridge, back to their friends, to "tell them where the turkey is hiding."

Adaptations:

1. For the child with functional use of one hand or decreased hand use, try using drum sticks or large wooden spoons with built-up handles to hit a box (larger surface area).

2. For the child with decreased vision, use the bottom of a cookie tin as a drum. It will reflect light and give good auditory feedback.

3. For the child with motor planning problems, try to practice the sequence several times before moving to a new sequence. Add hand-over-hand assistance and have the child concentrate on one method (visual or auditory) of instruction or feedback at a time.

Multilevel Instruction:

1. For the child unable to imitate reciprocal movements, have him or her shake a rattle or container filled with rice. The child can do this with one or both hands.

2. Increase the length of the sequences in the drumming or in the obstacle course.

3. To work more on listening skills, perform a drumming sequence; then have the children wait to the count of 10 before imitating the sequence.

4. Have the children dance while holding and playing their drums.

5. To conclude, hold a large piece of exercise band (or rubber bicycle inner tube) at both ends and let each child try to stretch it out to "shoot a bow and arrow."

November

Learning in Motion

Letter to Parents

Drums and Turkey Hunt

This week we pretended to be Native Americans getting ready for our turkey hunt and celebration. We made music with our drums and then went on a pretend turkey hunt. We quietly went through the woods, across the lakes and rivers, and over a bridge in search of a turkey.

Purpose of the Activity

Most of the activities involved using two hands together in a coordinated manner. While drumming, we used our hands reciprocally in a pattern. Then, we pushed ourselves along on the scooter board on our stomachs. Next, while sitting on a scooter board, we pulled ourselves forward using a hand-over-hand pattern along a long rope. These types of activities help to build arm and hand strength that the children need to develop stronger hand dominance, hand coordination, and visual attention to their hands. All of these skills are important for learning to write, color, and use scissors successfully.

Home Activities to Help Your Child Grow

Playing musical instruments at home is fun for the young child. Often, musical toys are around the house or can be easily fabricated. You can make a drum using wooden mixing spoons and a cardboard box. You can take an empty plastic seasoning or cheese container and fill it one-third of the way with dry rice or beans to make a maraca. Making a wrist or ankle cuff with bells sewn on it is another way to encourage your child to move to music. Try having your child play these instruments while listening to some children's music. In addition, you can have your child imitate your rhythm pattern with the instrument. For example, set up a shaking pattern where you shake three times, stop, and then shake one more time. Make the patterns more difficult as the child easily succeeds. See if your child can make up a pattern that you must imitate!

November

Football Workout

Activity Goals: Body-Scheme and Motor-Planning Improvement
Gross-Motor Skills Development

Time: 30 minutes

Objectives: Upon successful completion of this activity, the child will be able to
1. Run and change directions without falling
2. Run and change speed without falling
3. Use arms to push body from the floor
4. Perform a sit up
5. Throw a ball a distance of five feet at a three-foot target

Materials:
1. Sponge or soft football
2. Hula hoop
3. Cones or large plastic or cardboard blocks
4. Picture of a football player or video of a football game.

Procedure:
1. Gather children in a circle. You can either show a picture or video of football players. Explain that football is a game played in the fall. It is a game that requires speed, fast and accurate movements, and the ability to throw a ball. Also explain that the players spend a great deal of time getting their bodies ready for the game by practicing skills. Let the children know that today we a going to have a football workout or practice.
2. If you have more than one adult present you can begin this as a station procedure. Stations would be:
   a. First station should be a stretching station or whole class station. Have the children imitate you on the following stretches. Try to reach up as high as possible, then down toward their toes. Have the children reach out to either side as far a possible. Try to have them place their feet far apart and reach to the opposite foot with their hand. Then try this with both hands together reaching for one foot.
   b. Children run in place, then get down on the floor and try to get up as quickly as possible. Repeat this segment for five repetitions.
   c. Running around cones and over large blocks on the floor.
   d. Throwing the soft football or yarn ball through a suspended Hula Hoop—suspend the hoop at approximately the child's waist height.
   e. Instruct the children in knee push-ups and bent knees sit-ups.
   f. Have the whole class shake out their bodies and do the same stretches again.

Adaptations:
1. For the child with limited physical abilities to navigate the obstacle course, use a scooter board, wheelchair, or walker; or, crawl through or partner with a physically able individual to push the child through the obstacle course.
2. Have the child with visual impairment follow the obstacle course either by using a rope or holding on to the arm of an adult giving verbal cues, e.g., "obstacle off to the right side."
3. For the child with motor planning problems, try using a bright tape to show the direction of movement through the obstacle course.

4. For the child who is using a wheelchair or is unable to perform traditional pushups, have him sit either in the wheelchair or a child's size chair with arms, place his hands on the arm rests, and attempt to lift his buttocks off the seat and hold this position for two-to-five seconds.

5. For the child who is too weak to do a push up on the floor, try a wall push up. Stand arm's length from the wall and bend and straighten his elbows while keeping his feet in the original position.

6. For the child who is too weak to perform a sit up with knees bent, place several pillows under the child's head and back to see if raising the child to a semi-reclining position will help him perform situps. If the child is very weak, have him hold your hands and pull up while in the bent-knee position.

Multilevel Instruction:

1. Obstacle courses can be made more difficult by adding additional items, changing directions, or adding timing to the course.

2. Change the distance of the target or make the target smaller. Also add throwing and catching to the practice.

3. Add more involved warm-up exercises, like jumping jacks, lunges, and more imitation activities for an older group.

4. For young children, change to a midget-size football for throwing at the target.

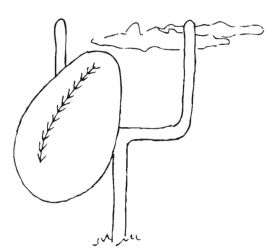

November

Letter to Parents
Football Workout

This week in our group we had a football practice session. We started with stretching exercises, then went on to some running, pushups and sit-ups, agility trials in our obstacle course, and then threw the football at a target. We had time to finish our activity with a cool-down stretch at the end.

Purpose of the Activity

This activity involves a variety of gross-motor skills and motor planning or motor coordination skills needed to participate in most play and self-help skills. During the early years, children spend a lot of time involved in gross-motor games with their peers. Playing tag, hide-and-seek, dodge ball, jump rope, and ball games all involve the ability to change positions, move in different speeds and directions, and plan a course of movement quickly. By playing some of these games in our football practice and working on general strength and agility, your child will feel more comfortable participating in these childhood activities.

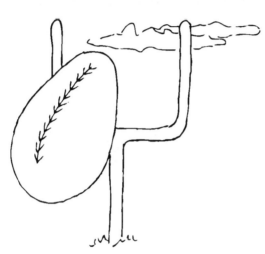

Home Activities to Help Your Child Grow

At home or in the backyard, you can play or set up similar obstacle courses. Try having your child play a relay type game by going to a target, picking it up, and returning it to you as quickly as possible. This type of activity works on movement speed, changing direction, and the ability to stop quickly. Set up a tire or target in the backyard to encourage your child to throw a ball with accuracy. Start with the target close and then move it away to increase the throwing distance as your child's aim becomes more accurate. Later, work on throw and catch skills with your child. Start with a slow moving ball like a beach ball, and then increase the speed and direction of the ball as your child's skill improves. Encourage your child to look at the ball by prompting, "keep your eyes on the ball."

Friends Sandwich and Dance

Activity Goals: Body-Scheme and Motor-Planning Improvement
Group Development

Time: 20-to-30 minutes

Objectives: Upon successful completion of this activity, the child will be able to

1. Roll five-to-seven times consecutively across a mat
2. Imitate a motor sequence of two or three steps
3. Follow simple directional commands with visual cues; (top, under, over, next to, across, backwards, sideways)

Materials:
1. Two large mats
2. A radio, tape player, or CD player with children's music

Procedure:
1. Gather children in a circle and explain to them the relationship between friends and Thanksgiving.
2. Have a child demonstrate rolling on the mat. Explain to the children that they will be divided into two groups and that each group will get an opportunity to be the sandwich while the other is a condiment (mustard, ketchup, etc.) Ask the children what condiments they like to put on their sandwiches, hamburgers, and hot dogs.
3. Take half of the group and have them lay face down on the first large mat, then place the second mat on top of them.
4. Take the children in the other half of the group and ask the children "What are you going to put on the sandwich?" After they tell you a condiment, have the children roll on the top mat with the other children under it.
5. After half the group has rolled over the other half, exchange roles.
6. Next, have the children make pairs by holding hands.
7. Before putting on the music demonstrate different paired movement patterns such as moving together side to side or backward and forward.
8. Have the children follow the commands and practice pair moving patterns with verbal commands and visual demonstration.
9. Turn on the music softly and call out the motor patterns, move side to side, backwards, forward, etc.
10. Allow children the opportunity to call out the motor patterns and make up their own. See if the child's partner can imitate their dance.

Adaptations:
1. For the child with motor impairments, choose a child or be her dance partner.
2. For the child who is fearful, start by placing only her body between the mats. Instead of a child rolling over, try giving firm pressure with your hands over the top mat.
3. For the child with visual impairment take her through the motor sequence with physical prompts and guidance.
4. For the child who is resistant to holding hands with other children, allow the partner to hold on to a scarf instead of holding hands. This also may help a child with a weak grasp.

Multilevel Instruction: During the dance activity, make up a sequence of motor patterns like a line dance.

November

Letter to Parents
Friends Sandwich and Dance

This week we became a pretend giant sandwich while we took turns rolling over our friends who were between the "bread" (large gym mats). Then we had fun dancing to music in pairs. During this season, family and friendship are an important part of our celebrations.

Purpose of the Activity

While we were pretending to be sandwich filling and rolling over the sandwich, the children were getting a lot of deep pressure input, which helps improve their body awareness. The children rolling on top of the mat were getting vestibular or movement sensation at the same time. These types of sensory input help the child develop motor coordination and planning skills for learning new or different motor tasks. By imitating each other's movements, and following verbal directions, the children are able to perform dances together. Motor coordination, imitation, and planning skills are important in the classroom in order to stay on task, learn new motor activities, and follow the teacher's instructions.

Home Activities to Help Your Child Grow

Activities that involve movement (e.g., rolling, jumping, bouncing, swinging, and running) tend to stimulate the child. The sensory input they get from movement is called "vestibular input." Vestibular input has been found to be helpful in stimulating speech. Activities that provide deep pressure to the body, especially for a sustained period of time (e.g., swaddling or lying under a heavy cover, bean bag chair or mat), tend to calm the child.

When you choose toys or activities for your child, think about balancing your choices of activities with those that provide movement stimulation and deep pressure. For example, if you want your child to be playful or if his or her activity level is low, you may want to try to stimulate the child with movement activities such as riding a bike, playing "Ring Around the Rosy," or jumping on a trampoline or a thick foam cushion. If your child is excited and is having difficulty calming down or needs to focus his or her attention towards an activity, you may want to try some deep pressure activities such as rolling your child up firmly inside a mat or blanket or having your child lay on the floor under a large cushion or a bean bag chair for a few minutes. Of course, you would monitor these activities carefully to make sure that your child is comfortable and not overly calmed or overly stimulated. If you have questions about using activities such as these, consult with your school's occupational therapist.

November

Jumping Over the Creek

Activity Goals: Bilateral Coordination Development
Balance Improvement

Objectives: Upon successful completion of this activity, the child will be able to

1. Jump forward twenty-four to thirty inches with feet together
2. Lying on his stomach push self forward ten feet on scooter board
3. Walk forward six steps on a four-inch-wide balance beam
4. Recognize or verbalize his address
5. Follow two-step verbal commands with visual demonstration

Materials:
1. Scooter board
2. Masking tape
3. Cards with the child's address
4. Balance beam

Procedure:
1. Set up balance beam and use masking tape to make a trapezoid with one end 10 inches between the two long sides and the other end 30 inches between the two long ends. These long ends should be approximately 6 feet in length. This is the jumping creek.
2. Place scooter boards at one end of the room at least 10 feet from the creek.
3. Have children gather in the circle. Explain that they are going to play a game pretending to find their way home.
4. Review the children's home address information and introduce the card with the address written on it. Place the cards at the far side of the obstacle course.
5. Have a child perform the motor activities in sequence starting with the scooter board ride, then jumping over the creek, walking the balance beam (bridge), and finding her address card.
6. Place the address card on a flannel board, easel, chalkboard, bulletin board, or the floor.
7. Each child rejoins the circle waiting for her turn.

Adaptations:
1. For the child unable to push the scooter board on her stomach, have the child lie or sit on the scooter board and pull her with a Hula Hoop or rope.
2. For the child with very poor balance or mobility, instead of a balance beam, tape masking tape on the floor and have the child walk or ride her wheelchair on the taped trail.
3. For the child with visual impairment, have him say his name and address at the end of the obstacle course.
4. If the child has a communication impairment, have him hand you his card when finished with the obstacle course. If the child has a communication device, preprogram the address. Have the child press the proper icon for his address.

Multilevel Instruction:
1. Break the activity into three separate tasks rather than a multi-step obstacle course: scooter board, balance beam and broad jumping.
2. For the young child, have him hop with both feet together for a distance of 10 feet instead of broad jumping.
3. Change methods of walking the balance beam to make it easier or more difficult.
4. Have the children copy their address from the board when finished.

November

Letter to Parents

Jumping Over the Creek

This week we made a pretend trip through the forest to our house. First, we took our raft (scooter board) down the river and then we jumped across the creek. After jumping the creek, we crossed the bridge (balance beam) to find our home address. We worked hard on our expedition and tried to remember our home address.

Purpose of the Activity

This activity worked on learning a sequence, working with both sides of our body in a coordinated way, and using visual skills to discriminate and remember our address. The way that this activity was presented involved learning with our whole body. This is called a "multisensory approach."

Learning to perform a series of movements in a specific sequence involves visual and auditory attention, memory, and motor planning skills. Motor planning is important for the young learner in the classroom, during physical education, art, music and athletic activities, such as gymnastics, jump rope, baseball, dance, and karate. Most of these activities also build strength and stability of the large muscles and the trunk. These muscles need to be strong in order to help the child hold a stable posture in sitting and standing in the classroom. The child who has difficulty sitting up in his or her chair will have more difficulty working on fine-motor control in his or her hands during writing, coloring, cutting, and other fine-motor tasks.

Home Activities to Help Your Child Grow

Many toys are available to help to develop strength and stability while working with both sides of the body together (bilateral coordination). Some examples of these toys are Sit 'n Spin, bicycles, skates, snow disks and sleds, rocking toys, ZoomBalls, and basketballs. You can find climbing and balancing experiences at your local playground. Try to give your child opportunities every week to build his or her strength and practice important gross-motor skills.

November

Making Pottery

Activity Goals: Pre-Writing Skills Development
Sensory Processing Improvement

Time: 20 minutes

Objectives: Upon successful completion of this activity, the child will be able to
1. Work with hands together
2. Visually attend to an activity for 5 minutes
3. Tolerate wet and sticky textures on hands

Materials:
1. Flour, salt, and water (see recipes for Play Clay on page 346)
2. Piece of pottery
3. Tempera paints

Procedure:
1. Gather the children on rug squares or at a table.
2. Show the children a piece of pottery and describe how the Pilgrims and Native Americans created their own plates, bowls, cups, etc.
3. Have each child help measure and pour parts of the ingredients to make the clay.
4. Have all the children take turns holding the bowl with one hand and stirring the mixture with the other. The children may be more successful stirring this mixture if they stand at the table to stir rather than sit.
5. Once mixed, place each child at the table with a piece of clay the size of a squash ball. Show the children how to form the clay into a ball by rolling it between their hands.
6. Demonstrate to the children how to use their pointer finger to press down in the middle of the clay ball to make a small hole (the beginning of the bowl).
7. Then have children model your demonstration.
8. Using both hands together, model for the children how to pinch along the walls of the clay ball to create a bowl/pinch pot.
9. Let pinch pot dry for a few days and then paint or decorate it.

Adaptations:
1. For the child with poor coordination or strength, allow him to pull off small pieces of the clay and press it inside a plastic bowl. Try to fill in the entire bowl. Allow clay to dry for a few days inside the bowl until it pulls away from the bowl. Remove and let dry completely.
2. For a child with either one functional hand or poor coordination, stabilize the pinch pot with Dycem®, a wet paper towel, or other non-slip materials.

Multilevel Instruction:
1. Instead of a pinch pot, have the children make a pot using a coil method of construction. Prepare the clay the same but have the children make long snakes with the clay. Coil the snakes into a bowl shape and gently press the coils to each other to remain stable.
2. Have the children complete the pot and then add texture or designs on the wet clay with a clay tool, orange peeler, toothpick or small sharpened dowel.

November

Making Pottery

This week we made a pinch pot. We made our clay with flour, salt, and water. Then we took a small ball of the clay and worked with our fingers to create a bowl. Our bowl needs to dry and then it can be decorated and brought home to find a special place to show off this work of art.

Purpose of the Activity

Increasing hand strength, fine-motor control, and following directions are all parts of this task. Your child also helped to mix and measure the ingredients used in making this clay. While stirring the mixture, your child needed to use one hand to stabilize the bowl and the other to stir. The ability to use both hands together in a dominant-assist pattern is important for later academic skills. For example, when your child colors, he or she uses one hand to stabilize the paper while the other colors. Your child will need to use this hand pattern in higher level skills such as writing and cutting. This pattern needs to be automatic so that your child can put more effort into mastering his or her dominant hand control to write letters on lined paper and cut around complicated shapes with scissors.

Home Activities to Help Your Child Grow

Young children enjoy playing with clay and putty. They like to roll it out with a rolling pin and cut out shapes with cookie cutters. Often, this activity is done using an academic theme to reinforce learning shapes, numbers, and letters. Other times, the children use tools in the clay to make pictures, letters, numbers, or shapes. This resistive drawing and writing in clay not only help reinforce beginning letter, number or shapes formation—it also builds hand and finger strength.

November

Learning in Motion

Native American Jewelry

Activity Goals: Pre-Writing Skills Development
Scissor Skills Development

Time: 20-to-30 minutes

Objectives: Upon successful completion of this activity, the child will be able to
1.   Use both hands to coordinate stringing fruit Os and straws
2.   Visually attend to this activity for two-to-three minutes
3.   Hold small objects with a pincer grasp
4.   Snip with scissors

Materials:
1.   Large box of fruit Os
2.   Colorful plastic straws (three or four per child)
3.   Yarn or string
4.   Masking tape
5.   Scissors
6.   Picture of Native Americans in costume

Procedure:
1.   Gather children in a circle and show them a picture of a Native American in costume. Point out the fact that both men and women wore jewelry.
2.   Explain the purpose of the jewelry: how it was given as gifts (signs of friendship) and used as money.
3.   Give each child scissors and a straw.
4.   Show the children how to cut the straws into 1½" lengths and place in a cup in front of them. Repeat with two to three more straws.
5.   Give each child a string approximately 28-to-30 inches in length. Tie a large knot at one end and reinforce the other end with masking tape to make a "needle."
6.   Demonstrate stringing procedure.
7.   Have the children string the fruit Os and straws.
8.   Encourage the children to complete this project.

Adaptations:
1.   For the child who is unable to coordinate or hold the string, you can use a pipe cleaner and make a bracelet or join several pipe cleaners together to make a necklace.
2.   For the child with a visual or motor impairment, try stringing large objects such as rigatoni, wagon wheel pasta, or cut pieces of toilet paper rolls.
3.   For the child who is confused about which end to start with, tape down the knotted end with masking tape.
4.   For the child with use of only one hand, try using a pipe cleaner and place pasta in a small shallow container. Have the child put the pipe cleaner through the rigatoni or wagon wheel pasta using his one hand.

Multilevel Instruction:
1.   Hands-on assistance may be needed for the young or inattentive child.
2.   Set up a sequence to complete this activity: for example, string 5 fruit Os, then one straw piece.

November

Letter to Parents
Native American Jewelry

This week we learned about the importance of jewelry to the Native Americans. We made some jewelry in preparation for the Thanksgiving holiday. Our jewelry was made from cut up straws and fruit Os.

Purpose of the Activity

This activity involves the use of visual attention, refined eye-hand coordination, cutting skills, and coordination of both hands working together. These are the same skills we need to be able to cut along a curved line, hold our paper down as we write, and manage clothing fasteners such as snaps, buttons, and zippers.

Home Activities to Help Your Child Grow

Stringing beads, Cheerios™, macaroni, and other small foods is a fun activity to do at home. It has a purpose to the child if he or she makes it for a grandparent, for a decoration for the holiday, or for something to wear. Some other toys that develop eye-hand coordination are commonly available in toy stores. These toys are pop beads. Tinker Toys®, Lite-Brite, lacing cards, leather lacing kits, and dolls or toys with snaps and buttons. There is a new activity called Perler® beads that would be fun for your child. This activity uses tiny beads and a small pegboard. Follow the model (or let children use their own design) to create a bead picture that can be set with an iron. Use caution in giving your child small objects to play with if your child still tends to mouth things. The suggested activities will help to develop your child's pinch and grip strength, as well as his or her ability to work with both hands together.

November

Learning in Motion

Pudding Painting

Activity Goals: Sensory Processing Improvement
Pre-Writing Skills Development

Time: 20-to-30 minutes

Objectives: Upon successful completion of this activity, the child will be able to
1. Identify or name each finger
2. Point with the index finger
3. Tolerate touching wet and sticky materials without behavioral problems

Materials:
1. ½ cup of cold pudding per child
2. Scented hand lotion (be careful of children's allergies)

Procedure:
1. Start in a circle and talk about hands and fingers.
2. Give each child a small amount of hand cream and instruct or demonstrate how to rub the cream into her hands.
3. After rubbing in the cream, have the children imitate you rubbing your thumb with the opposite hand, and progress slowly through all fingers. Name the fingers as you go. "Now I'm rubbing my pointer finger, let me see everybody rubbing their pointer finger." Go slowly and give lots of verbal feedback and hands-on assistance if needed.
4. Wash or wipe off the cream with either a washcloth or paper towel and water. Encourage the children to rub firmly as they do this.
5. Place some pudding on the table in order to demonstrate the activity. Show the children how to use their hands to spread out the pudding and then use their index fingers to draw shapes and pictures.
6. Place about one-half cup of cold pudding in front of each child and let her begin to experiment.
7. Demonstrate how to make a smiley face or other shapes or letters.
8. Show the children how to draw a person in their pudding paint and then work on having them draw their family.

Adaptations:
1. For the child who is extremely resistant to touching wet materials, try a Popsicle® stick or dowel.
2. For the child who has a visual impairment, place a stencil on top of the pudding and have the child trace inside it.
3. For the child who is unable to extend her fingers or open her hand, try to gently shake her hands to open them. Encourage this and other sensory play and involve her fingers and palms in the play.

**Multilevel
Instruction:**
1. Make this activity a two-step process. Have the children make the instant pudding, and after it thickens, start painting.
2. Have the children practice letters, numbers, their names, brothers' and sisters' names, etc.
3. For the child who is unable to isolate her fingers, use the whole hand for this activity. Try to get the child's hand to open during this task.

November

Letter to Parents

Pudding Painting

This week we talked about families and Thanksgiving. First we massaged our hands with hand lotion, and then we massaged each of our fingers individually. While we were doing this, we learned our finger names. Then we painted with cold pudding. We made shapes and drew pictures of ourselves and family members.

Purpose of the Activity

Many activities that we perform daily involve using the sense of touch and fine-motor coordination of our fingers. For example, we can write, button, and type without looking at our fingers. This type of finger awareness requires a well developed sense of touch that is learned by practice and attention to tactile input. The better our awareness and sense of touch are, the more efficient and precise our movements will be.

Home Activities to Help Your Child Grow

Our first activity involved identifying our fingers individually and naming them. Finger plays help to develop fine-motor coordination: for example, you can help your child practice songs with fingerplays such as "Where is Thumbkin (pointer, tall man, ring man, and pinkie)?" 'Ten Little Indians," and "Three Little Monkeys," and to follow your commands such as "Hold up ring man" or "Make your fingers look like mine" (holding up just your pointer finger or thumb). Activities to increase finger awareness include drawing with materials such as finger paints, shaving cream, sand, snow, rice, salt and flour. Using individual fingers while performing these activities will help your child improve his or her fine-motor coordination, finger awareness, and finger strength, too.

November

Learning in Motion

Story of Thanksgiving

Activity Goals: Balance Improvement
Attention Improvement

Time: 30-to-40 minutes

Objectives: Upon successful completion of this activity, the child will be able to
1. Walk with both feet on the balance beam for 5-6 steps
2. Squat and return to standing without assistance
3. Use forearm rotation to turn over an object

Materials:
1. Balance beam
2. Step bridge
3. Enough for half the group:
    a. Food flippers and frying pans (or rug squares to pretend)
    b. Long-handled grabbers, tongs, or magnetic fishing poles
    c. Magnetic fish, 4-to-6 inches long, or 2 or 3 beanbags per child
    d. Small pompoms and wooden beads, 5 or 6 per child
    e. Small tongs and baskets
    f. Large bowls and spoons

Procedure:
1. Gather children in a circle and explain the story of the Pilgrims and Native Americans. Start with the Pilgrims coming in boats and then foraging for berries and nuts for a feast with their new friends (Native Americans). Explain how fishing was an important way to get food for the feast. Then explain that these friends got together to prepare a feast.
2. After explaining the story, show the children the representation of the story using the activity sequence.
3. First activity: To represent the Native Americans, who used canoes, and the Pilgrims, who sailed over the ocean, half of the group will be the bridges (non-moving bridge or crab-walking position) and the other half will be the boats. Encourage the "bridges" to stay still and keep their stomachs up high. As boats, the children will lie on their stomachs and commando crawl across the ocean and under the bridges.
4. Have the groups reverse roles: boats become bridges.
5. Second activity:
    One group will be the Pilgrims, who will be using the grabbers or small tongs and baskets to gather berries (pompoms) and nuts (beads) hidden around the room. The other group will be the Native Americans who go fishing. They will stand on the balance beam and attempt to pick up the fish with the magnetic fishing poles, long tongs, or grabbers.
6. Third activity:
    Pilgrims go back and prepare the berries by placing them with the tongs or grabbers in a bowl and stirring. Native Americans prepare the fish by pretending to cook them, turning them with the flippers.
7. Reverse roles if you have time.

Adaptations:
1. For the child with poor balance, have him stand on a 2-inch wide piece of masking tape while fishing.

November

2. For the child with poor balance, allow him to walk across the balance beam with one foot on and one foot off.

3. For the child using a wheelchair, place 2 pieces of masking tape 18-to-24 inches apart and 6 feet long as his bridge/balance beam.

Multilevel Instruction:

1. Use scooter boards to represent the Pilgrims crossing the ocean on the Mayflower. Hang blue streamers between chairs or traffic cones to be the "ocean waves."

2. For the group with good balance, have them walk across the balance beam backwards or heel to toe.

3. For the child who is unable to perform activities with tools such as grabbers, have him use his hands to grab and turn the play food.

4. Give specific instructions to each child to retrieve a particular number of items, i.e., give me four berries, two fish and five nuts.

November

Letter to Parents
Story of Thanksgiving

This week we learned about the story of Thanksgiving by pretending to be the Pilgrims and Native Americans on that first celebration. First, our teacher told us the story and then we acted out the story. We pretended to be the boats coming across the ocean. After we arrived in this New World, we met the Native Americans who helped us find food. We had a pretend hunt for berries, nuts, and fish, and prepared them for our feast.

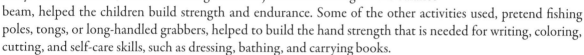

Purpose of the Activity

For the young learner, the more senses and active learning involved, the better re-call and understanding of the material. We not only talked about the Thanksgiving story, we used both gross- and fine-motor activities and real objects to reinforce the story. These activities, such as crawling under objects and walking on the balance beam, helped the children build strength and endurance. Some of the other activities used, pretend fishing poles, tongs, or long-handled grabbers, helped to build the hand strength that is needed for writing, coloring, cutting, and self-care skills, such as dressing, bathing, and carrying books.

Home Activities to Help Your Child Grow

Talk again with your child about the Thanksgiving story. See what they can recall and help them remember by sharing some of the activities above. Plan your own pretend Thanksgiving feast to reinforce the story.

Perhaps your child could assist in the preparation of your actual Thanksgiving feast. Allowing your child to scrub the potatoes or other vegetables with a brush, tear apart lettuce for a salad, take the paper off the butter, and fill the sugar or salt containers are safe activities that will help build his or her coordination. These activities will teach your child some self-help skills and allow him or her to help you and contribute to the holiday meal.

November

Turkey Day

Activity Goals: Cognitive Development
Pre-Writing Skills Development

Time: 20-to-30 minutes

Objectives: Upon successful completion of this activity, the child will be able to

1. Open and close scissors to snip edge of paper
2. Place scissors properly on fingers for cutting
3. Hold paper with assistive hand while snipping paper
4. Color a large area staying within edges
5. Work independently on a fine-motor activity for 3-5 minutes
6. Attend to 1-2 step verbal directions

Materials:

1. Pre-cut feather shapes in 5-6 different colors for each child
2. Brown crayon for each child
3. Glue
4. Scissors
5. Pre-cut turkey finger puppets
6. Words to "The Turkey Is a Silly Bird" or another song
7. A large picture of a turkey or a completed turkey project

Procedure:

1. Gather children in a circle and explain the significance of eating turkey on Thanksgiving.
2. Teach the children the song, "The Turkey is a Silly Bird," and try out the finger puppets.
3. Have the children move to a worktable to make their turkeys.
4. Give each child a turkey body and a brown crayon to color it. Set aside when completed.
5. Instruct the children how to snip the edge of a feather with scissors. Emphasize how to cut by using cues like "open and close the scissors" or "cut and stop" to increase control of the scissors.
6. Hand out feathers and have the children make small cuts along the edge of each feather.
7. After the feathers are snipped, show the children how to place and glue the tail feathers on the turkey bodies.
8. Allow the turkeys to dry and add to the children's Thanksgiving projects.

Adaptations:

1. For the child who is unable to snip with scissors, you can pre-cut her feathers.
2. For the child just learning to cut, use a heavier weight paper such as card stock; and avoid using construction or copy paper.
3. Use a glue stick instead of a glue bottle for a child who has poor motor control.
4. For a child who has difficulty with coordination or reduced hand strength, substitute using a marker or sponge painting the turkey's body for coloring with a crayon.
5. For a child with a visual impairment, use a dried glue line around the edge of the turkey body or provide a turkey stencil to help her stay within the lines when coloring.

Multilevel Instruction:

1. Have the children trace and cut out the feathers in addition to snipping the edges.
2. Have the children follow a color sequence for the placement of the feathers.
3. Simplify the activity by having the children place the feathers on a turkey without cutting the edges.

Learning in Motion

Letter to Parents
Turkey Day

This week we colored and made our own turkey picture. We practiced snipping with scissors to make the feathers. We also played with finger puppets and learned a new song, "The Turkey Is a Silly Bird."

Purpose of the Activity

We had an opportunity to practice many school skills today in our activity. We used crayons for coloring, scissors for snipping, and glue to stick the paper together. Young children are often involved with using "school tools" in the classroom. This week's activities helped your child become more proficient in tool use and increase his or her hand and finger coordination that will be needed for writing. Learning songs in class and using fingers to gesture is also a way for your child to build his or her attention span, fine-motor coordination, and memory.

Home Activities to Help Your Child Grow

Scissor skills are something that, with your supervision, are important to develop in your child. For beginning scissor users, it is important to choose the correct type of paper and type of line to cut. Initially, the paper should be more the size of an index card than a whole piece of paper. The easiest line to cut is straight and short. For extra cutting practice at home, try having your child help you by cutting junk mail in half. Place a thick dark line across any of the heavier-weight paper and ask your child to cut it in half for recycling. As this gets easier for your child, change the line to a diagonal one, next, a slight curve, then a moderate curve, and, finally, a half circle. Keeping crayons readily available and coloring with your child will help to encourage him or her to develop his or her coloring skills. In addition, providing a chalkboard or a Magna Doodle™ toy at home will encourage your child to practice drawing and writing.

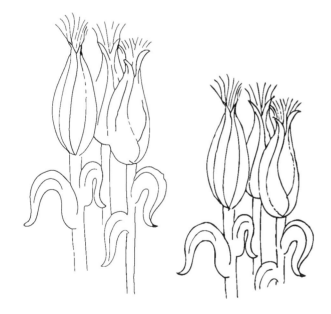

November

Turkey Finger Painting

Activity Goals: Sensory Processing Improvement
Pre-Writing Skills Development

Time: 20-to-30 minutes

Objectives: Upon successful completion of this activity, the child will be able to
1. Paint with finger paints
2. Follow two-step verbal commands
3. Wait his turn in a group
4. Name the color of the feather he painted
5. Work within a group

Materials:
1. Picture of a turkey body
2. Finger paints; yellow, red, orange, green, and purple
3. Glue
4. Finger paint paper cut into large feathers, one per child
5. Large picture of a turkey

Procedure:
1. Gather children in a circle and explain the significance of the turkey to the Thanksgiving holiday. Show a picture of a turkey to the children.
2. Have children get out of their chairs and imitate a turkey walk and warble "gobble, gobble."
3. Explain that the turkey has very colorful tail feathers and point to the turkey body you have at the front of the class.
4. Have the children tell you what is missing from your turkey body.
5. After they identify the missing feathers, give each child a large pre-cut feather.
6. Using finger paint, have each child paint his pre-cut feather with one color-name the color to the child and class when he chooses it.
7. After each child finishes, start the next child painting with a different color for his feather.
8. Returning to the first child, have him paste the feather onto the class turkey.
9. After the feathers are attached, enjoy your class turkey. Practice turkey songs and finger plays.

Adaptations:
1. For the child with severe motor impairment, let him hold the turkey picture and say "gobble, gobble," while the other children practice their turkey movement imitation.
2. For the child with visual impairments bring in a real feather and let the child and classmates feel it. This will help the child understand the concept of the feather.
3. For the child unable to touch finger paints, use a sponge instead of fingers or hands.

Multilevel Instruction:
1. Let the children cut out the turkey feathers before painting. Use a stencil or template and have them trace before cutting.
2. Have the children write the color words on a sheet of paper or on the chalkboard as a reinforcement activity.
3. After the feather paper is completely dried, have the children cut little slits at the edges to simulate feathers.
4. Let children practice snipping the edges of pre-cut feathers with scissors after they take their turns finger painting.

Letter to Parents

Turkey Finger Painting

This week we learned about colors while we made turkey feathers for our class decoration. Each feather was painted using finger paints. We also practiced walking like a turkey and making turkey noises.

Purpose of the Activity

Painting with finger paints has many positive aspects for the young child. This activity helps to increase the child's awareness of his or her fingers and hands. By being more aware of his or her hands the child is able to better coordinate movements of the hand needed for coloring, cutting, buttoning, and cutting. This activity also involves taking turns and group cooperation to complete the project. Working together to achieve a common goal is an important life-long skill. Most of us need to work cooperatively with others in school, with our family, and in the workplace.

Home Activities to Help Your Child Grow

Learning about our hands and fingers is important for later fine-motor skills. One way to increase your child's hand awareness is through tactile or touching activities, especially if he requires discrimination or identification of objects without looking. Set up a feely box at home. Save a shoe box and tape the cover closed. Make an opening in the lid of the box just big enough for your child to get his or her hand in and out of easily. Start by placing two very dissimilar toys inside, e.g., a toy airplane and a small ball. Ask your child to take out one of the objects, e.g., "Get the ball." As your child gets better at the task, make it more complicated by adding more items or making items more alike. For the older child you can use plastic letter magnets to discriminate by touch alone.

November

Educational Goals by Activity

Attention Improvement	Balance Improvement	Bilateral Coordination Development	Body-Scheme and Motor-Planning Improvement	Cognitive Development	Fine-Motor Skills Development	Gross-Motor Skills Development	Group Development	Hand-Dominance Development	Pre-Writing Skills Development	Scissor Skills Development	Self-Help Skills Development	Sensory Processing Improvement	Strength and Endurance Improvement	Visual-Perceptual Development	Activity	Page
									✔			✔			**Cinnamon and Applesauce People**	100
		✔	✔												**Gingerbread Boys and Girls I**	103
			✔			✔									**Gingerbread Boys and Girls II**	106
						✔							✔		**Hat Pass**	108
			✔						✔						**Holiday Wreath Cookies**	110
✔			✔												**Marching**	113
			✔				✔								**Newspaper Ball Snowman**	115
			✔						✔						**Pine Cone Bird Feeders**	117
	✔												✔		**Sleigh Ride**	119
								✔						✔	**Toy Workshop**	121

Cinnamon and Applesauce People

Activity Goals: Sensory Processing Improvement
Pre-Writing Skills Development

Time: 30-to-40 minutes

Objectives: Upon successful completion of this activity, the child will be able to
1. Mix with a spoon
2. Use both hands to roll out the batter
3. Name the members of her family
4. Tolerate sticky materials on her hands without behavioral problems

Materials:
1. Applesauce
2. Cinnamon
3. ½ cup White glue (optional)
4. Large bowl and spoon
5. Rolling pins
6. Gingerbread or bear shape cookie cutters of different sizes.
7. A six-inch piece of ribbon for each figure or cookie shape
8. Wax paper
9. Toothpicks and paper plates
10. Vegetable cooking spray

Procedure:
1. Gather children at the table or circle and talk about what makes up a family. Find out from the children if they have brothers, sisters, mother, father, grandparents, aunts, uncles, etc.
2. Make connection between the holidays and family gatherings.
3. Show the children the cinnamon and let them smell it. Pass around the applesauce and let each child get a taste.
4. Pour the cinnamon into a large bowl and slowly add the applesauce to make a stiff batter. A half cup of white glue can also be added to make the dried ornaments more durable.
5. Have the children each take a turn stirring the batter. Encourage each child to stir with one hand and hold the bowl with the other hand. Sometimes, it's easier for the children stand while stirring.
6. Give each child a small ball of the batter and a rolling pin. Use cooking spray on the children's hands, the waxed paper, or any of the surfaces to prevent sticking, if desired.
7. Have the children first pat the ball flat and then roll it on wax paper with the rolling pin to ¼" thickness.
8. Press cookie cutter into cinnamon and applesauce batter, and while still in place, remove batter outside cookie cutter.
9. Using a toothpick, place a small hole in the top middle of the cookie shape for placing the ribbon.
10. Place figures on racks to dry. This may take several days. Turn them to encourage them to dry flat.

11. After figures are dry, add ribbons and knot at top. It's ready for gift giving, and smells great for a few months.

Adaptations: 1. For the child who cannot grasp the rolling pin with both hands, try a one-liter bottle filled with cold water. Have the child use her palms or fists on the bottle and try to push and roll it over the cinnamon and applesauce batter.

2. For the child with a visual impairment, have her roll the clay inside a cookie sheet.

Multilevel
Instruction: 1. To make the activity using fewer steps, prepare the cinnamon and applesauce clay before the children arrive; however, continue to include the sensory aspect of smelling the cinnamon and tasting the applesauce.

2. Have the children use a clay tool or toothpick to draw a face on the gingerbread person

3. Have the children use a clay tool or toothpick to make the names of family members on the figures such as Jenny, Billy, Mom, Dad, and Aunt Gail.

4. After the shape is dry, have the children attach the ribbons and tie them.

5. Have the children make shapes, letters, or numbers using a cookie cutter; or make them free-form out of the batter (use cooking spray on their hands for easier cleanup).

Letter to Parents
Cinnamon and Applesauce People

This week we talked about our families. We made special sweet-smelling clay with cinnamon and applesauce. We each smelled the cinnamon and tasted the applesauce. Then, we mixed these ingredients into clay that we patted and rolled with a rolling pin. We used a cookie cutter to cut out figures representing our family members. After our people dry for a few days, we will put a pretty ribbon on them and send them home for you to hang in a warm room and enjoy the yummy smell.

Purpose of the Activity

Young children need to use their hands for many different sensory experiences. Some children seem hesitant to touch different materials or textures, while others cannot stop touching everything. The clay used in this activity is a little sticky and grainy. Exploring this texture will help build hand awareness. Using the clay also may help decrease some children's resistance to touching this type of texture. By working on touch and discrimination of materials, children build better hand skills through an increased sense of tactile (touch) discrimination. This type of awareness helps the child control or her hand movements during coloring, cutting, gluing, and play skills.

Home Activities to Help Your Child Grow

Children need lots of encouragement and exposure to all types of tactile activities. Allowing your child to help make holiday cookies, cupcakes, or decorations can be a perfect opportunity for use of sensory discrimination and tactile play. Allow your child to decorate a few cookies by herself Give your child a large baked cookie and let her spread frosting on it with her fingers. Then encourage your child to add a few details to the iced cookie using chocolate chips, colored sugar, candies, or raisins for facial features. If you bake bread, let your child help with kneading the dough. You can also let your child make holiday cards using materials with a variety of different textures such as glitter, glue, paste, ribbon, dried flowers, fake far, lace, velvet, pipe cleaners, rice, and cotton balls

Gingerbread Boys and Girls I

Activity Goals: Body-Scheme and Motor-Planning Improvement
Bilateral Coordination Development

Time: 30-to-40 minutes

Objectives: Upon successful completion of this activity, the child will be able to
1. Follow multi-step directions
2. Walk forward six steps on balance beam
3. Jump a distance of eighteen inches
4. Tolerate deep pressure of a bolster being rolled over her
5. Crawl through tunnel
6. Jump over a balance beam that is 4 inches off ground

Materials:
1. Short version of "The Gingerbread Man"
2. Therapy bolsters
3. Tunnel
4. Therapy mat
5. Masking tape
6. Balance beam
7. Set of portable stairs (optional)

Procedure:
1. Set up obstacle course while children are out of the room - See Step #4.
2. Review the story of "The Gingerbread Man" and explain to the children that they are going to pretend to be gingerbread boys and girls. Adapt your story to the obstacle course.
3. Demonstrate the adventures in the sequence in which they're to be done.
4. Set up the following obstacles/areas:
   a. place where adults can roll bolsters over child
   b. balance beam to walk on
   c. balance beam or other obstacle to jump over
   d. tunnel to crawl through
   e. masking tape in lines approximately 18 inches apart—to represent river
   f. portable steps
5. Children sit on carpet squares in separate area where they can view course.
6. Children proceed through course one at a time starting at the station with bolsters. As adults roll bolsters over children, they explain that they are turning them into gingerbread boys and girls.
7. Children waiting their turn can explain which part the gingerbread boy or girl is going through.
8. Child finishes the course with a short run.
9. As each child finishes course, she can say, "Run, run, as fast as you can. You can't catch me. I'm the Gingerbread Man!"

Adaptations:
1. Child with visual impairments can be paired with an adult or a child without visual impairment.

2. Child in wheelchair can wheel herself through cones or through a pathway defined by masking tape placed on ground. Or, if able, she can go through obstacle course propelling herself on scooter board (lying on stomach).

3. Partially roll bolster over child who is having difficulty tolerating deep pressure from bolster.

Multilevel Instruction:

1. Children can walk backward, heel-toe, or sideways on balance beam.

2. Children can jump over wider or narrower "river," greater or less than eighteen inches.

Learning in Motion

Letter to Parents
Gingerbread Boys and Girls I

This week's activity was loosely based on the story "The Gingerbread Man." We set up an obstacle course and the children went through the course in a sequence similar to the path that the Gingerbread Man took. First, the adults rolled bolsters over the children to turn them into gingerbread cookies, then the children walked on a bridge (balance beam), jumped across a river (exercise mat), crawled through a tunnel, and jumped over a log (balance beam). The last action was to run as the group said, "Run, run, as fast as you can, you can't be caught, you're the Gingerbread Man." The children recalled their actions when they were finished.

Purpose of the Activity

All of the gross-motor activities that were done today helped the children develop strength throughout their bodies, good balance, and bilateral coordination. Going through the obstacle course also helped your child develop better body awareness, and gave her an opportunity to follow single and multi-step directions. When recalling the events of the group, your child needed to use memory, a necessary component of learning.

Home Activities to Help Your Child Grow

You can set up a simple obstacle course in your home using common objects. Your child can walk up and down the stairs, crawl under a card table that has a blanket over it, step or jump over pillows on the ground, and walk along a masking tape line. Use your imagination! Help your child learn to imitate hand movements by using Play-Doh® to make "cookies." Have your child roll a ball between both hands, roll a "snake" using both hands on the table, and roll a ball using one hand on the table. Try varying the amount of dough to build your child's coordination and dexterity. You might find that your child has difficulty rolling dough because he or she doesn't press down hard enough. To enable your child to press down with more force, you can give him or her "hands-on" assistance, place light wrist weights on your child or have him or her stand up to mold the dough. Learning how to "grade force" is important for children, so that they can eventually hold a pencil or crayon with the correct amount of pressure.

Gingerbread Boys and Girls II

Activity Goals: Group Development
Body-Scheme and Motor-Planning Improvement

Time: 20 minutes

Objectives: Upon successful completion of this activity, the child will be able to
1. Lie on stomach or back on command
2. Name four-to-six body parts
3. Tolerate hands on assistance

Materials:
1. Mat or soft surface
2. Rolling pin
3. Gingerbread cookie, picture or toy
4. The book *The Gingerbread Boy*

Procedure:
1. Briefly tell the children the story of the gingerbread boy and show them the gingerbread boy figure. Explain that they are going to be made into a gingerbread boy or girl like in the story.
2. Show the children the rolling pin and explain how they will be cookie dough that needs to be rolled out with the rolling pin.
3. Ask the children to lie on their stomachs. Take the rolling pin and gently, but with even force, roll slowly up and down the child's arms, legs and back.
4. Occasionally stop and roll several times over a particular body part, i.e., elbow, shoulder, foot, hand, etc.
5. Ask the child to name that body part.
6. Then ask the child to lie on his back. Roll the rolling pin over the child's limbs and upper trunk.
7. Stop again over body parts and roll several times with even and firm pressure.
8. See if the child can identify the body part.
9. After everyone has had the deep pressure experience, then take the group together and read the story "The Gingerbread Boy."

Adaptations: For the child who is very sensitive to touch or having a difficult time calming for the activity, try having this child lie on the floor or mat. Place a second mat or large beanbag chair on top of him. With the mat or beanbag chair on top of the child, place your hands or rolling pin on the top mat or beanbag. You can give gentle and sustained pressure to the child, moving over his back, arms, legs and upper trunk.

Multilevel Instruction:
1. Have the children make and bake their own gingerbread cookies and decorate them.
2. Trace the child's body on a large sheet of brown paper and have the children decorate them. They can be sent home or made into a gingerbread mural.
3. Trace a gingerbread pattern on brown paper to cut out and decorate.

Letter to Parents
Gingerbread Boys and Girls II

This week in our group we pretended to be gingerbread cookies. We each lay on the floor and our teacher rolled out the dough. We laid on our stomachs and backs and tried to name our body parts while the teacher rolled the rolling pin over them. When we were done being the cookie, our teacher read us the story of "The Gingerbread Boy."

Purpose of the Activity

This activity has two purposes. The first is to improve the child's ability to name body parts and learn the relationship between them on their bodies. The rolling pin on the child's body provides deep pressure and increases the sensory input to the child's brain through their skin and muscles. The second benefit of this activity is the firm, sustained sensory input applied to the child's back, limbs, and upper trunk that can have a calming and relaxing effect on the child.

Home Activities to Help Your Child Grow

Some activities similar to these can help your child learn his body parts and to provide a calming activity before bed. After his bath take a towel and rub your child firmly. You can take some extra time with your child and have him use the towel to rub a body part. Make this into a game by asking, "Can you rub your shoulder (elbow, ankle, heel, forehead, wrist, etc.)?"

Sustained gentle and firm deep pressure input to a child can have a calming effect. You can try to place your child in his bed and then stack a few pillows, sleeping bag or beanbag chair on top of him for a few minutes. This extra weight sometimes has a calming effect. You can also use the pillow and your hands to provide slow, sustained deep pressure to your child's arms, back and legs. Avoid covering and pressing on his stomach, lower trunk, or face. If you are interested in learning to massage your child, read the book *Infant Massage: a Handbook for Loving Parents* by Vimala Schneider McClure. For more information on massage, contact the International Association for Infant Massage at 1-800-248-5432.

Hat Pass

Activity Goals: Group Development
Strength and Endurance Improvement

Time: 20-to-30 minutes

Objectives: Upon successful completion of this activity, the child will be able to
1. Remove hat from head and place it on feet, while lying on back
2. Pass hat from his feet to another child's outstretched hands, while lying on his back

Materials: Hat for each child

Procedure

Activity I—Hat Pass
1. Children lie on their backs on the floor.
2. Give each child a hat.
3. Child places hat on his head.
4. Using his hands, child removes hat from his head and places it on his feet without sitting up (head, arms and legs should be off floor and child should hold position briefly).
5. Child takes hat off of feet and places it on his head without sitting up.

Activity II—Hat Relay
1. Children lie on floor in two lines, head-to-toe with six-to-twelve inches between them.
2. First child in each line places hat on feet.
3. First child removes hat from feet (with hands), and places it on feet of next person in line.
4. Second person repeats actions above.
5. Actions continue until last person in each line has hat on his head.
6. First line "finished" is the winner!

Adaptations:
1. Child in wheelchair—take hat from lap and place it on his head.
2. Take hat from knees or feet and place on his head.
3. Take hat from another person who is holding it to the side.
4. If child does not have the necessary trunk strength, adult may have to assist child in curling trunk to achieve objective.

Multilevel Instruction:
1. Child uses one hand to place hat on feet.
2. Child repeats activity two to three times before taking a break.
3. Child uses one hand to remove hat and places it on opposite foot.
4. Child places hat on knees rather than feet.

Letter to Parents

Hat Pass

Our group activity this week was "Hat Pass." Each of us had a hat. We lay on our backs on the floor and placed the hats on our heads. The tricky part was putting the hat on our feet and then putting it back on our heads without sitting up. We also played "Hat Pass" in the form of a relay race.

Purpose of the Activity

When passing the hat from his to his feet, your child needs to briefly lift his head, arms, and legs off of the ground. This activity uses flexor muscles, which are the muscles that usually cause body parts to bend. Extensor muscles generally cause body parts to straighten. Flexor and extensor muscles working together allow a child to maintain good posture and balance, which are basic to motor development.

Home Activities to Help Your Child Grow

Taking your child to the playground on a regular basis will help him develop strength and endurance. To help your child further develop his flexor muscles, have him lie on his back with a pillow under his head. Tell your child to remove the pillow, place it between his feet and pass it to you. You can also have your child pass a ball from over his head to his feet and back again. Your child will probably enjoy playing this game with other children and you.

Another fun activity to strengthen your child's flexor muscles is "Knee Sundaes." Have your child lay on his back with knees bent. Place a dab of peanut butter or chocolate syrup on your child's knees. Tell your child to lick the treat off of his knees by bringing his mouth and knees together. This is a yummy way to get those flexor muscles working!

Holiday Wreath Cookies

Activity Goals: Sensory Processing Improvement
Bilateral Coordination Development

Time: 30-to-35 minutes

Objectives: Upon successful completion of this activity, the child will be able to
1. Stir with a spoon for ten revolutions
2. Identify basic ingredients used in cookies
3. Tolerate the texture of the cookie (oral and tactile)
4. Use fingers to mold dough into wreath shape
5. Wait her turn during cooking process

Materials:
1. Ingredients for holiday wreath cookies (see recipe section)
2. Vegetable cooking spray
3. Access to microwave
4. Large microwave-safe bowl
5. Large spoon
6. 8½-by-11 Inch piece of wax paper per child
7. ¼ Cup dry measure

Procedure:
1. Have each child wash her hands.
2. Discuss how some people decorate their homes with wreaths, especially during the holiday season.
3. Show children the ingredients and cooking utensils, and have them identify them.
4. Explain the steps in the cooking process.
5. Have children take turns pouring the marshmallows into the bowl.
6. One child can place the margarine into the bowl.
7. Adult places bowl into microwave and microwaves ingredients on "high" for 2 minutes.
8. Children take turns stirring marshmallow mixture.
9. Adult places bowl in microwave and microwaves for one additional minute.
10. Stir in green food coloring.
11. Have each child add some corn flakes to the mixture.
12. Each child takes a turn stirring mixture until the flakes are coated with marshmallow.
13. Place a piece of wax paper in front of each child.
14. Adult sprays ¼ cup measure with vegetable spray, spoons mixture into cup, and gives ¼ cup measured dough to each child.
15. Lightly spray children's hands with vegetable spray.
16. Have children shape dough into wreaths.
17. Children decorate wreaths with cinnamon candies.
18. Review steps in process of making wreaths.
19. Children wash hands.
20. Let children eat their creations.

Adaptations:

1. For children with decreased ability to grip, build handle of spoon up with a towel or sponge or special foam tubing (see Appendix).
2. Hand-over-hand assistance can be given to children who don't have the necessary strength to stir the mixture.
3. Stirring the mixture when there are fewer flakes is easier for children with decreased arm strength.
4. Place bowl on Dycem® or other rubber material to prevent slipping and add to stability.

Multilevel Instruction:

1. Write out recipe on large paper and have children practice reading simple words like "add," "stir," "mix," and "bowl."
2. Have children count cinnamon candies, number of stirring strokes, etc.

Letter to Parents
Holiday Wreath Cookies

This week we made holiday wreath cookies. The children identified the ingredients, mixed them together, shaped the dough into wreath forms, and decorated the cookies. Of course, the favorite part was when the children ate their creations.

Purpose of the Activity

This activity involved following single and multi-step directions and remembering a sequence of events. The children used their large arm muscles for stirring the ingredients and then used their smaller finger muscles for shaping the dough into wreaths. The children worked with varied textures of different temperatures, which gave them opportunities to discriminate between different touch sensations. These types of experiences will help your child improve his or her hand awareness, which will promote more refined hand skills and the ability to work with a variety of different materials. Skilled use of the hands is necessary for success in almost all classroom activities.

Home Activities to Help Your Child Grow

Helping Mom or Dad cook is a favorite activity for the young child. Your child can assist you in making holiday cookies and breads. Decorating the cookies, kneading the dough, stirring the ingredients, spooning the ingredients onto a cookie sheet and using a cookie press or cookie cutters are activities that will help your child improve his or her hand strength and manipulation skills. Even licking fingers afterwards increases hand and finger awareness!

Marching

Activity Goals: Body-Scheme and Motor-Planning Improvement
Attention Improvement

Time: 15-to-25 minutes

Objectives: Upon successful completion of this activity, the child will be able to
1. March in rhythm to the beat of the music
2. Imitate motions of adult or child leading group
3. Step over objects while listening to music and "playing" drum

Materials:
1. Tape player
2. Music with marching rhythm
3. Newspaper (approximately two Sunday editions)
4. Elastic bands or tape

Procedure:
1. Give each child 4 full sheets of newspaper.
2. Demonstrate how to roll newspaper in order to make drum sticks. Tape the roll so that it does not unravel, or use elastic bands.
3. Children stand up and practice beating drum and/or kneel on rug squares and beat on floor with drumsticks.
4. Turn on music.
5. Following adult leader, children march around room or remain kneeling, beating pretend drum with their drumsticks. Follow rhythm of teacher.

Adaptations:
1. For children with decreased use of their hands, newspaper drumsticks can be made thicker, or eliminated altogether, and the children can beat the pretend drums with their hands.
2. For children with poor grip strength or children who are unable to sustain a grip, the "drum sticks" can be made so that they loop around the child's hands (the opening can be taped shut).

Multilevel Instruction:
1. Children can keep beat to the music.
2. Children can imitate rhythms, shown by the adult, on the drum. For example, 2 beats with left drumstick, 1 beat with right drumstick.
3. Children can take turns leading the marching band.
4. Music can be stopped periodically and all marchers need to stop until music resumes.
5. Obstacles can be placed on the floor of the room. Marchers will have to step over and around them while continuing to play the drum. It's fun to lay down a line of newspaper rolls and march over them.

Letter to Parents
Marching

The children marched while they played on pretend drums, using drumsticks made from rolled up newspaper. They also beat rhythms on carpet squares placed in front of them. They practiced clapping and marching, stopping when the music stopped and marching while stepping over small obstacles.

Purpose of the Activity

Coordinating body movements to music in beginning motor activities such as marching helps develop the child's ability to listen and attend while moving. Starting and stopping on time builds auditory attention. Watching a teacher in order to imitate moving one's hands to "drum" and watching the group to stay in line and step over obstacles helps develop motor planning (body awareness) and visual attention. All of these skills are basic ones that children need when they get older and have to listen, watch, and imitate the teacher, as they learn to read and write.

Home Activities to Help Your Child Grow

Engaging in rhythm activities is a wonderful way to help your child improve his or her auditory attention. Play music and have your child clap to the rhythm. You can make up a pattern of beats and have your child repeat the sequence. Clapping hands, hammering, shaking bells and banging pots with spoons are enjoyable ways to build strength, endurance and coordination in the upper body.

To have more fun using rolled up newspaper, let your child form shapes and letters with the newspaper and then jump over them. He or she can also line up the rolled newspapers and walk on them, pretending that they are a balance beam.

Learning in Motion

Newspaper Ball Snowman

Activity Goals: Bilateral Coordination Development
Gross-Motor Skills Development

Time: 20-to-30 minutes

Objectives: Upon successful completion of this activity, the child will be able to
1. Demonstrate enough hand and finger strength to make paper snowballs
2. Correctly place snowman's body parts
3. Tolerate the feel of crumpled newspaper
4. Accurately throw "snowball" into open bag

Materials: (for each snowman)
1. Newspaper
2. Three white plastic bags—kitchen size
3. Hat, scarf
4. Eyes, carrot nose, mouth, and buttons

Procedure:
1. Child is given large sheet of newspaper, which is ripped in half.
2. Child takes one piece and crumples it into small "snowball" using two hands.
3. Child places ball on floor and repeats steps #1 to #3.
4. When each child has a pile of "snowballs," adult sits in front of group with open bag.
5. Each child takes a turn throwing snowballs into the bag.
6. When first bag is three-quarters full, adult ties off bag.
7. Repeat steps #4 and #5 with a second bag, until it is half-full.
8. Repeat steps #4 and #5 with a third bag, until it is one-third-full.
9. Stack bags on top of one another and attach with masking tape.
10. Children sit in front of snowman and take turns placing scarf, hat, eyes, nose, mouth, and buttons on snowman.
11. Wash hands to remove newsprint.

Adaptations:
1. Children crumple newspaper using only one hand.
2. Children who are unable to crumple newspaper can tear pieces of paper instead.

Multilevel Instruction:
1. Allow children to work in small groups to make snowman.
2. Children draw facial features and buttons on snowman.

Letter to Parents
Newspaper Ball Snowman

We made a snowman this week! The children crumpled newspaper into balls and stuffed three white trash bags with them. Once the bags were stacked on top of one another, the children added facial features, a hat, a scarf, and some buttons to complete the snowman. They even named the snowman.

Purpose of the Activity

Making balls out of crumpled newspaper was a good activity for building hand strength and improving coordination in the hands. Crumpling newspaper also provided a lot of pressure to the palms of the hands, which helps to desensitize them and can prepare the child for less tactilely appealing activities such as painting with pudding or shaving cream.

Eye-hand coordination was needed to throw the newspaper balls into the open white bags. The children also needed an awareness of facial features, hats, scarves, and buttons to place these items correctly on the snowman. Washing the newsprint off of their hands gave them good practice in this important self-help skill.

Home Activities to Help Your Child Grow

Children enjoy ball and target activities. You can place a bucket, trash can, or laundry basket on the floor and encourage your child to throw foam balls or beanbags into it. Fill empty plastic soda bottles with a small amount of rice and have your child throw a ball at the bottle in order to knock it down. Or have your child practice his or her aim by rolling a ball at the soda bottle pins and bowling them over. Place a target (such as a cutout snowman) on the wall and have your child throw foam balls at it. Your child can record his or her "hits" and see the improvement over time.

Pine cone Bird Feeders

Activity Goals: Bilateral Coordination Development
Sensory Processing Improvement

Time: 25-to-30 minutes

Objectives: Upon successful completion of this activity, the child will be able to

1. Use a dominant-assist pattern to spread peanut butter using a knife
2. Touch the textures of pine cone, peanut butter, and birdseed without overreacting

Materials:
1. One pine cone for each child
2. Peanut butter
3. Bird seed
4. Paper plate per child
5. Yarn or pipe cleaners
6. Plastic sandwich bags
7. One plastic knife per child

Procedure:
1. Beforehand, make sample of pine cone bird feeder. Tie yarn or pipe cleaner on pine cones for the class.
2. Discuss what birds eat and why they may need help finding food during the cold months.
3. Children sit at a table.
4. Each child is given a paper plate, a pine cone, and a plastic knife.
5. Place a ¼-cup glob of peanut butter on each child's paper plate.
6. Show children how to spread peanut butter on pine cone.
7. Each child spreads peanut butter on his pine cone.
8. An adult then pours about ¼-cup of birdseed on the plate.
9. Child rolls the pine cone in the birdseed until the seeds cover the peanut butter.
10. Adult places pine cone into sandwich bag and gives to child to take home.

Adaptations:
1. Child with functional use of one arm can perform activity by placing pine cone against edges of tray to stabilize it.
2. Be sure to check for peanut allergies before using peanut butter. Lard or Crisco° can be substituted for peanut butter.
3. If you know that the students may avoid touching the materials because they are sensitive to touch, try preceding the activity with one that provides pressure to the children's hands. For example, the children could squeeze Play-Doh° first.

Multilevel Instruction:
1. Instead of taking pine cones home, children can hang bird feeders in trees or areas around the school. Or, children can make two feeders—one for home and one for school.
2. Take children outside to sprinkle birdseed on ground. This will require good hand and finger control.

Letter to Parents
Pine Cone Bird Feeders

This week, the children made pine cone feeders for our feathered friends, the birds. They spread peanut butter or lard on the pine cones and then coated them with birdseed or oat cereal. The bird feeders can be hung outside from a branch or nail.

Purpose of the Activity

Making pine cone bird feeders requires using your hands in a dominant-assist pattern in order to manipulate the pine cone in the birdseed as well as to spread the peanut butter on the pine cone. Using one hand as dominant while using the other hand to assist is a pattern that is common in classroom activities such as cutting, handwriting, and painting. Making the bird feeders also involves touching and exploring many varied textures, which is always a good experience for the young child!

Home Activities to Help Your Child Grow

It is important for the young child to develop a dominant-assist pattern when performing fine-motor activities that require two hands. You can provide many "two-handed" activities to your child, such as bead stringing, lacing cards, playing with wind-up toys, using scissors to cut out pictures, spreading crackers with jelly, etc. For the child who has not yet established hand dominance, these activities are especially important to help determine which hand is the most skilled. You can make a "feely" bag for your child. For additional touch exploration, place small common items of varied shape, texture, size, etc., inside the bag. Have your child reach into the bag and identify the items by touch alone. If capable, your child can then describe what he or she is feeling. This is good practice for tactile discrimination.

Sleigh Ride

Activity Goals: Strength and Endurance Improvement
Balance Improvement

Time: 20-to-30 minutes

Objectives: Upon successful completion of this activity, the child will be able to
1. Maintain sitting balance on a moving scooter
2. Maintain grip on a Hula Hoop for length of time needed to complete course
3. Successfully navigate through directed course

Materials:
1. Scooter boards for one-half of the children in the class
2. Hula hoops for one-half of the children in the class
3. Small traffic cones or blocks

Procedure:
1. Pair off the children. One child is the rider and the other is the sleigh driver.
2. Sleigh driver holds one end of Hula Hoop.
3. Rider sits on scooter board and holds other end of Hula Hoop.
4. The sleigh driver pulls the rider slowly through the course, which has been marked with traffic cones.
5. Children switch positions and repeat steps 2 through 4.

Adaptations:
1. Children with decreased balance can lie on stomach on scooter board.
2. Children who have weak grasp can go through shorter course.
3. Adult can assist child in maintaining grasp.

Multilevel Instruction:
1. Children can lie on stomach on scooter board. Some of the muscles that allow them to maintain good sitting control will be strengthened in this position.
2. Course can be made more or less difficult depending on the placement of the traffic cones (e.g., large circle vs. serpentine pattern).

Letter to Parents
Sleigh Ride

This week, we pretended to go on a horse-drawn sleigh ride. We formed into pairs with one of the children on his or her stomach on the scooter board (sleigh) and the other partner (horse) pulling the sleigh along by using a Hula Hoop as reins. Everyone had a turn as the passenger on the sleigh, as well as the horse. We also tried to pull the sleigh around and between traffic cones.

Purpose of the Activity

While riding the scooter board on his or her stomach, the child has to lift his or her upper body. This helps to strengthen the muscles of the back and neck, which are very important for developing good posture and balance. Pulling another child on a scooter board is "heavy work" and helps to develop strength, endurance, and awareness of where your body is in space. During seat work in the classroom, it is important that the child has good posture, which requires strength and endurance in the trunk muscles as well as body awareness and balance.

Home Activities to Help Your Child Grow

Activities that involve pulling and pushing heavy objects help develop the large muscles of the arms, legs and trunk. Having stability is necessary for being able to use smaller muscles for refined tasks. In the grocery store, your child can help push the cart, place the items on the checkout conveyor belt and pack the grocery bag. When you get home, he or she can assist you in putting the groceries away.

Your child can load up a wagon or box with stuffed animals and pull them along the floor, pretending to be an engine or horse. As your child's strength and endurance improve, you can add more weight to the wagon or box.

Toy Workshop

Activity Goals: Hand-Dominance Development
Visual-Perceptual Development

Time: 20-to-30 minutes

Objectives: Upon successful completion of this activity, the child will be able to
1. Hit a tee with a hammer
2. Identify shapes and colors
3. Tell about what she constructed

Materials:
1. Styrofoam
2. One wooden or plastic hammer per child
3. Styrofoam pieces e.g., packing material
4. Colorful foam shapes cut from fun foam
5. Colorful golf tees

Procedure:
1. Each child or small group of children gets a large piece of Styrofoam, golf tees, additional pieces of materials to hammer, and a small wooden/plastic hammer.
2. Child hammers small pieces of Styrofoam and Styrofoam shapes into larger pieces by using the golf tees as nails.
3. When completed, children bring their creations to the group circle.
4. Children describe what they have made.

Adaptations:
1. If child is unable to use pincer grasp to stabilize tee while hammering, larger pegs can be used or a helper can hold the tee or start the hammering process.
2. Handle of hammer can be built up by wrapping it with foam or tape so children can grasp it more easily.
3. Visually impaired children can be given tees and foam that have a greater level of contrast.

Multilevel Instruction:
1. Child identifies the shape and color of fun foam pieces that she is hammering.
2. Teacher specifies the category the children are to build (e.g., vehicles, buildings, animals).
3. Children work with partners to build creation.
4. Children describe what they made and the steps involved in the process.

Letter to Parents
Toy Workshop

This week, your child pretended to be a worker in a toy workshop. We used toy hammers, nails (golf tees), wood (Styrofoam), and saws made of cardboard to make wonderful creations. Each child got to tell the group what he had made.

Purpose of the Activity

A great deal of eye-hand coordination is required when using a hammer. Hammering is a wonderful activity to use for children who are still switching hands and have not yet demonstrated a clear hand preference during fine-motor tasks. The children were encouraged to use their assist hand to hold the Styrofoam and their preferred or dominant hand to hold the hammer. This helped them establish a dominant-assist type of hand pattern, which is used in many classroom activities, such as scissors usage, handwriting, and the manipulation of clothing fasteners. Hand and finger strength was also needed to "saw" and pull the "nails" out of the Styrofoam.

Home Activities to Help Your Child Grow

You can make a construction kit for your child. You will need large pieces of Styrofoam (from packaging), colorful golf tees, a toy hammer, smaller pieces of foam (from craft stores or meat trays) and a toy saw or one that you've made out of sturdy cardboard. Place all of these items in a large box and supervise your child as he or she makes wonderful creations. To cut down on some of the mess caused by crumbling Styrofoam pieces, you can cover the large Styrofoam blocks with burlap material.

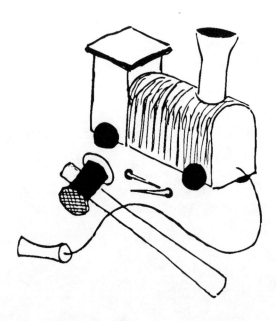

Educational Goals by Activity

Attention Improvement	Balance Improvement	Bilateral Coordination Development	Body-Scheme and Motor-Planning Improvement	Cognitive Development	Fine-Motor Skills Development	Gross-Motor Skills Development	Group Development	Hand-Dominance Development	Pre-Writing Skills Development	Scissor Skills Development	Self-Help Skills Development	Sensory Processing Improvement	Strength and Endurance Improvement	Visual-Perceptual Development	Activity	Page
		✔											✔		Bears	124
				✔										✔	Color Hunt	126
						✔	✔								Color Toss	128
		✔											✔		Fun in the Ice and Snow	130
							✔				✔				Getting Ready for Snow	132
			✔										✔		Peter and the Wolf	134
							✔		✔						Polar Bears	136
		✔	✔												Sliding Seals and Penguins	138
									✔			✔			Snow Painting	140
		✔				✔									The Three Little Kittens	142

Bears

Activity Goals: Strength and Endurance Improvement
Bilateral Coordination Development

Time: 30 minutes

Objectives: Upon successful completion of this activity, the child will be able to

1. Demonstrate enough strength and endurance to perform bear walking
2. Coordinate both sides of the body to imitate bear walking
3. Enjoy touching and wearing "bear fur" or "bear feet"

Materials:
1. Mats, arranged in a line
2. Music* suitable for "bear walking"
3. Real or fake fur coats or a large brown fuzzy bath towel that can be wrapped around the child
4. Animal slippers or commercially made "bear feet" (See Appendix)
5. Light ankle weights

Procedure:
1. Show the children how to bear walk. (Advance the arm and leg on the same side forward, then rock to the weight bearing side as you raise your other arm and leg.)
2. Have the children practice bear walking down the line of mats. Try using music to help them get the rhythm. Give some hands-on help if they seem to need it. Some children may not be able to motor plan to advance the same arm and leg at the same time, but they should all try to "walk" with their legs extended.
3. After the children have some practice, let them try on the bear coats and/or bear feet.
4. Try folding a mat and placing it under another mat to make a "mountain."

Adaptations:
1. If you have a student who cannot "bear walk" due to poor strength or restricted mobility, have the group try crawling, rolling, and using the scooter boards.
2. Some children may not be able to completely straighten their legs when bear walking. This may be because they have reduced flexibility. This activity is a good one for helping children stretch their leg muscles.
3. Since bear walking puts a lot of the body's weight into the hands and arms, check for any restrictions on activities if you have a student who has arthritis.

Multilevel Instruction: Try providing "caves" for the bears using beach towels or cartons on their sides. Close the activity with the "bears" taking naps!

January

* *Songames for Sensory Integration*, a 2-CD collection of children's music that includes "Forest Stump," is available from www.SensoryResources.com

Letter to Parents
Bears

The children learned how to "bear walk" today. They learned to bend over and put their hands down, keeping their knees straight, and walk by rocking from side-to-side, moving the arm and leg on the same side forward at the same time. The children tried on fur jackets as costumes to look like bears, and they tried walking with weights on their feet to see what it might feel like to be a big, heavy bear.

Purpose of the Activity

Bear walking is a very vigorous activity that builds strength and endurance in your child's muscles. Bending over and trying to keep his or her legs straight also helps stretch out many of the muscles that tend to get tight when children grow. We used furry jackets to help motivate the children. They also enjoyed feeling the soft fur! Using the lightly weighted feet helps children feel their legs and feet better and can help children develop better body awareness and motor planning to imitate bear walking, as well as strengthening their legs.

Home Activities to Help Your Child Grow

Let your child try bear walking at home so you can see how easily he or she can assume the position and coordinate moving his or her arms and legs as described above. You might want to try it out, too. Don't be surprised if you have trouble straightening your knees; unless you work out, you probably aren't flexible enough to do it!

One of the good things that come from activities that encourage weight bearing on children's hands is getting their arms, wrists, and fingers stronger. This is very important for young children in order to help them be ready to hold their pencil or crayon for writing and coloring easily and perform the motions without fatigue. Encourage your child to play on the floor with his or her toys at home, knowing that you're helping your child get stronger in a natural way.

Color Hunt

Activity Goals: Visual-Perceptual Development
Cognitive Development

Time: 20 minutes

Objectives: Upon successful completion of this activity, the child will be able to
1. Color a large area with a crayon.
2. Locate and match objects by color.
3. Recall where an object was found and replace it.

Materials:
1. Small white paper bags
2. Crayons in different colors

Procedure:
1. Allow children to choose a crayon and have them each color a bag.
2. Ask them to walk around the classroom and find objects that are the same color as their bags.
3. Warn them that they need to remember where they find each object, they will put them back when the game is over.
4. Have children sit in a circle and show the others the objects that they found.
5. Have the children replace the objects where they found them.

Adaptations:
1. Use various types of crayons, depending on the children's needs, such as large-diameter crayons, anti-roll crayons, chunky crayons, or short pieces.
2. To make coloring easier, allow children to use markers.
3. Arrange some objects ahead of time so they are visible or have children work with a partner if they are having difficulty finding objects to place in their bags.

Multilevel Instruction:
1. To help strengthen more muscles, have the children lie on their stomachs when coloring.
2. After children talk about their objects, put them all together on the floor, have each child take a different color, and sort them out again.
3. Ask children to return each object to its place one at a time, performing a motor skill to get to the location, such as hopping, walking backward, or tiptoeing.

Letter to Parents
Color Hunt

This week the children practiced color identification playing a color-matching game. Each child was given a bag and colored it with the crayon of his choice. Then the children hunted for same-colored objects around the classroom, put them in their bags, and brought them back to the group. When we were all done, the children were asked to put all the objects back, which tested their memory.

Purpose of the Activity

The children worked on strengthening their fingers today when they colored their bags. They had a good time finding the colored objects and talking about them too. Returning objects to their places in the classroom indicated how well the children remembered where everything belonged.

Home Activities to Help Your Child Grow

Helping your child learn to pick up her toys is an important skill to learn. When your child can find the right spot for each toy, he has learned how to be organized with his things. Like putting together a puzzle, it gets easier every time your child practices it. At school, we often find that first grade children are initially disorganized with storing their crayons, pencils, and books in their desks. They need time to decide how they will store them. Providing them with pencil boxes and different-colored folders often helps. The teachers spend time helping the children learn to be organized with their materials because, once learned, the children can be more independent and efficient getting their work done.

You'll be teaching your child an important life skill if you limit the number of toys he has (at least, in one room) and help him learn to put them away in an organized way every day.

January

Color Toss

Activity Goals: Gross-Motor Skills Development
Group Development

Time: 30 minutes

Objectives: Upon successful completion of this activity, the child will be able to

1. Match colors.
2. Accurately toss beanbags into containers.
3. Enjoy crawling through a tunnel without a behavioral overreaction.
4. Cooperate to play a circle game.

Materials:

1. Colored beanbags
2. Matching colored containers
3. Tunnel, either prefabricated or made from a tube of cloth approximately 12-to-15 feet long

Procedure:

1. Line the children up several feet from the colored containers. Give each one a beanbag to throw into the matching container.
2. Give each child a colored beanbag. When his color is called, he crawls through a tunnel and then stands to toss his beanbag into the matching container. (If you use a fabric tunnel, you will need someone to hold either end.)
3. Have the children sit down to make a circle. Show them how to play "Duck, Duck, Goose," using color words instead—such as "Blue, Blue, Red."

Adaptations:

1. Add cues like matching stickers if you have a child who cannot perceive colors.
2. Young children sometimes have difficulty motor planning to let go of something to throw it a distance. Try giving hand-over-hand assistance to swing the arm holding the beanbag and say, "one, two, three" to give him time to get ready to let go of it. Let the child stand very close and encourage him to throw, rather than place, the beanbag.

Multilevel Instruction:

1. Vary the distance the children have to throw the beanbags into targets.
2. Try using suspended targets for the children to practice throwing overhand as well as underhand.

Letter to Parents

Color Toss

The children had fun playing games to learn colors today. They practiced tossing colored beanbags into matching containers and played a game called, "Blue, Blue, Red," which was our version of "Duck, Duck, Goose."

Purpose of the Activity

Our games today had more than one purpose. We wanted to give the children many opportunities to talk about colors in order to make sure that they would have lots of chances to learn them. The children threw beanbags at targets in order to develop a motor skill. Finally, we wanted to help the children develop their ability to work together as a group. A beginning circle game, such as our adapted game, "Blue, Blue, Red" helps each child learn rules and how to cooperate with a group of other children. This is important in school, as most instruction takes place in a group.

Home Activities to Help Your Child Grow

Color identification starts with color matching. Try using things around the house to make color games for your child. For example, you might have a box full of plastic covered paperclips, golf tees, or small blocks. See if your child can find the right color when you name it. Then, see if he or she can name the color when you choose it. If your child already knows the colors well and can name the colors when he or she sees them, try the "I Spy" game. Look around the room for an object that is mostly one color (such as the phone book) and say, "I spy something yellow." Give your child a little time to find the object. If your child needs help, give him a clue, such as, "It is heavy and square."

January

Fun in the Ice and Snow

Activity Goals: Strength and Endurance Improvement
Bilateral Coordination Development

Time: 30 minutes

Objectives: Upon successful completion of this activity, the child will be able to
1. Demonstrate sufficient arm and shoulder strength in order to push own body weight and pull classmates.
2. Demonstrate good coordination between both sides of the body to slide on "skates" and push self over a ball.

Materials:
1. Large gymnastic balls
2. Mats
3. Ice skates made from shoeboxes, half-gallon juice cartons, or pieces of waxed paper
4. Music, such as Strauss waltzes
5. Either several beach towels or plastic sheet sleds with rope handles to pull
6. Scooter boards

Procedure:
1. Set up the mats individually with one therapy ball on each. Have each child take a turn "rolling a big snowball" by lying on top of the therapy ball and rocking over it, pushing with her arms and legs.
2. Next, demonstrate to the children how to put on and take off the "ice skates" by sitting down. Then let them take turns skating around on the floor to the music. Try moving forwards, backwards, and sideways.
3. Using plastic sleds, have the children pull each other along on the mats and/or the floor. The safest position is to have them lie down on their stomachs when they are riding. If you pull the sleds onto a mat and off, the "bump" is fun. To make this even more fun, try putting a folded mat under a line of mats to make a "mountain."
4. Let the children use scooter boards, lying down on their stomachs and pushing themselves along, to pretend they are sledding, too.

Adaptations: Children who are non-ambulatory can often still have fun rocking over a therapy ball and pushing themselves along on a scooter board, but they might need to be held. There are larger scooter boards available that are made to give more support. Some have straps, which help prevent the children from rolling off. Please consult your students occupational or physical therapist for advice on a suitable size and type of equipment.

Multilevel Instruction: The difficulty of this activity is increased by the complexity of the movements you are requiring. A beginning group will be doing well if it can rock over a ball, skate forward using skates, and push themselves and ride on the sleds and scooter boards in a circle. An advanced group will enjoy using the floor and mats in different patterns to skate and sled around.

Letter to Parents
Fun in the Ice and Snow

Today the children had a wonderful time pretending to play wintertime games outdoors. First, they pretended to make giant snowballs. Instead of the usual way of rolling a snowball, they lay on top of the ball and rocked back and forth, pushing with their hands and feet. Next, the children pretended to ice skate, putting boxes on their feet to practice sliding. Last, they pulled each other on "sleds" over the bumpy snow and used scooter boards to practice on their stomachs.

Purpose of the Activity

The activities today helped the children develop their strength and endurance in arms, legs, and trunk muscles. The children also practiced using both sides of their bodies at the same time, which is called "bilateral coordination." For example, when rocking over the therapy balls, the child needed to push with both hands and then with both feet at the same time. If she didn't coordinate pushing evenly very well, she quickly knew it because she would roll off the ball. Sliding along on the "skates" worked on bilateral coordination, too, but the pattern for sliding was reciprocal, in that the children had to move one leg and then the other.

Home Activities to Help Your Child Grow

Your child can practice skating at home with you, too. Try letting her slide on a vinyl floor with waxed paper under her feet. You can also make "skates" using half-gallon juice cartons, cutting off a long side on each, or from two shoeboxes. Learning to glide may help your child have an easier time learning to roller skate.

There are other games you can play to help your child develop good coordination with her legs. Pedaling a bicycle strengthens legs and helps build bilateral coordination. Encourage your child to practice kicking a ball, too. If your child already has good timing for kicking a ball when you roll it to her, try teaching her to stop the ball by placing one foot on top of it. This will help your child develop even better bilateral coordination and better balance, too.

Getting Ready for Snow

Activity Goals: Self-Help Skills Development
Group Development

Time: 30 minutes

Objectives: Upon successful completion of this activity, the child will be able to
1. Put on and take off outerwear over arms, legs, and head.
2. Open and close zippers, buttons and other fasteners.

Materials:
1. Children's outerwear: jackets, boots, mittens, etc.
2. Yarn balls and target

Procedure:
1. Start with the children sitting with you. Go over the various pieces of outerwear and what part of the body they go on. This might be a good time to talk about what is easiest to put on first, second, and last, and how to straighten out the clothing to get it ready.
2. Break the children into two groups or partners, depending on which might work best for their age. Have them arrange their clothing on the floor, helping each other get ready for a "race."
3. At your signal, have the children get their outerwear on as quickly as they can. See which group is ready first!
4. Just so everyone is a winner, make the "prizes" yarn balls to toss at a target, which each child earns as soon as she is ready. Encourage each child to help his or her partner.

Adaptations:
1. For children with limited physical ability to dress themselves, set them up partially dressed to give them a head start.
2. Try pairing a more-able child with a child who has any type of disability that might slow him down.
3. Lay out clothing for each child so that it can be put on easily.

Multilevel Instruction:
1. Increase the challenge for your group by placing clothing in a pile, and asking the children to perform a motor skill each time they go to the pile to pick up another item to put on.
2. Make cards to represent the different pieces of clothing for each child. Have each child arrange the cards in sequence to tell a story of getting dressed.

January

Letter to Parents
Getting Ready for Snow

We practiced getting ready for a snowstorm today. The children talked about how much fun it is to play outside in the snow. Then we played a game with partners. Each pair arranged its outdoor clothing, ready to put it on. At the signal, each child helped his or her partner get dressed! When they were ready, they used pretend "snowballs" to play "outside."

Purpose of the Activity

The children had lots of practice putting on their outerwear by making sure the sleeves were right-side-out, putting it on, zipping, buttoning, and/or snapping. We used hats, gloves, and boots, if your child had them at school. Besides practicing independence with dressing, our activity was designed to encourage helpfulness among the children. We wanted to take advantage of the fact that children often learn better from each other in a structured lesson where they could practice social skills, as well as motor skills.

Home Activities to Help Your Child Grow

Becoming independent with dressing is more than a convenience for parents of young children. As your child learns to ready his or her clothing and put it on, he or she is developing visual perception needed for learning, reading, and writing. You can assist your child with this important step by making sure you provide clothing that is easy to put on. Be sure the shirt or dress buttons are large and slide through the holes easily. When purchasing a jacket, look for a zipper that can be joined easily. Make sure the length of your child's jacket is short enough so that he doesn't have to struggle to join the zipper. If the bottom of the jacket is elasticized, try to make sure it is loose enough that your child doesn't have to stretch it at the same time he is trying to join the zipper. On pants, look for snaps and zippers that are easily manipulated or pants that have elastic waistbands. Rubber boots slide on and off easier if your child puts a plastic bag over his shoe before putting it on. Look for shoes with Velcro® closures to help your child be independent until he is old enough to learn to tie laces.

Peter and the Wolf

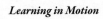

Activity Goal: Body-Scheme and Motor-Planning Improvement
Strength and Endurance Improvement

Time: 20 minutes

Objectives: Upon successful completion of this activity, the child will be able to
1. Imitate animal walks
2. Demonstrate sufficient strength and endurance to perform activity while music is playing
3. Be able to stop and hold a posture when signaled.

Materials:
1. Large cardboard boxes or other materials to make "dens"
2. Music for *Peter and the Wolf*

Procedure

1. Demonstrate to the children how to move like horses by galloping. Let them pretend to be hunters riding their horses, looking for the wolf. Use musical accompaniment and ask the children to stop and hold themselves like "statues" when they hear the music stop.
2. Demonstrate to the children how ducks look when they are flying. Using the music, let them pretend to fly, stopping and freezing when the music stops.
3. Set up "dens" around the room. If you use boxes, place them on their sides, and show the children how to curl up in them.
4. Demonstrate how to move like a wolf. Let the children imitate the movements to music, hiding in their dens when the music stops.

Adaptations:
1. Allow a child who may not be able to walk independently to use his wheelchair or walker when "galloping," "flying," or running like a fox. Provide a "den" he can fit into: a sheet draped over two large chairs, or even a closet.
2. Ensure safety for a child with a visual impairment by marking a large circle on the floor for all the children to follow, laying down carpet squares for a pathway, or grouping the children in pairs.

Multilevel Instruction: Provide puppets or have the children make paper bag puppets, using them to retell the story.

Letter to Parents
Peter and the Wolf

This week the children learned about the story of *Peter and the Wolf*. They practiced being hunters, riding their horses to find the wolf. They practiced being the duck, stopping and freezing when the music stopped. Finally, they practiced running on their hands and feet like a wolf and hiding in a den when they heard the hunters.

Purpose of the Activity

The children practiced animal walks this week using a classic musical piece. One purpose was to work on building their strength and endurance. Not only were the children building their strength performing the movements, they were also building their strength when they had to "freeze" and maintain a position. This activity worked on building the children's balance, too, which is also strengthened by trying to stay still in one position. Starting and stopping to the sound of the music helped the children develop better listening skills, too, so that they improve their attention to their teacher's voice.

Home Activities to Help Your Child Grow

Imitation of gross-motor skills is fun for young children. You can try it out at home with your child, and her siblings, too. Ask your child to imitate an animal she has learned about—a bear, a horse, a rabbit, or a duck. You can tell your child that, when you clap once and say, "Freeze," she must stop moving. Decide ahead of time what position your child will freeze in—on one foot, squatting, etc., and have her practice it. When you clap twice, she can start again. When she plays this game, have your child freeze in a position just a few seconds at first; but work up to ten seconds or longer to build up strength and good balance. Try reversing roles, too; let your child be the leader while you move and freeze. You may find that your child will become more attentive to your directions when you play a game like this. Learning to "freeze" when a parent directs her could also be important for your child in an emergency.

January

Polar Bears

Activity Goals: Pre-Writing Skills Development
Group Development

Time: 30 minutes

Objectives: Upon successful completion of this activity, the child will be able to

1. Squeeze and hold strawberry pickers to pick up cotton balls and put them in a container.
2. Hold container with one hand and pick up cotton balls with the other.
3. Grade force to pull apart cotton balls without tearing them.
4. Glue on cotton balls, staying within the boundaries of the picture.
5. Use glue/paste without avoidance behavior.

Materials:
1. Cotton balls
2. Strawberry pickers, tongs, or tweezers
3. Cups or small bags
4. One large outline or individual outlines of polar bears
5. Glue or glue sticks

Procedure:
1. Give each child a strawberry picker, cotton ball, and container to practice squeezing and picking up the cotton ball.
2. Collect the cotton balls. Scatter them around the room.
3. Tell the children they're going to go on a hunt for a polar bear. The polar bear left "fur" all around the room. They're going to help by finding his fur.
4. Let all the children hunt and pick up the fur. Observe how well they motor plan for this task, how well they are able to walk around the room "hunting" without bumping into the other children, and how well they share.
5. Have the children sit down with their "bear fur." Show them how to pull apart the cotton balls to make them bigger. Let them practice, encouraging them not to pull too hard.
6. Pass out individual pictures of polar bears and glue, and have the children paste on the fur. Or, gather the children around a large picture hung on a wall and let them take turns gluing on the "fur."

Adaptations:
1. Some children might be sensitive to touching soft things, or sticky things like the cotton balls and glue. You can help get them ready by first giving them an activity that puts pressure on their hands, such as bear walking.
2. If you have a child who is having difficulty motor planning to squeeze the strawberry pickers, give him cotton balls clipped with clothespins to practice squeezing to let them drop off.

Multilevel Instruction: For more challenge, have the children cut out outlines of the polar bears before gluing on the cotton.

Letter to Parents
Polar Bears

We went on a polar bear hunt today! The children looked around the room and found cotton balls, which we called "polar bear fur." They practiced picking up the "fur" with special tongs. Then we had some fun playing with the "fur," trying to stretch it out into big clouds. Last, we used the "fur" to make pictures of polar bears.

Purpose of the Activity

Today's activity helped the children develop the muscles in their hands for cutting and writing. We used small tongs to pick up the cotton balls, which required squeezing and holding the cotton ball for a few seconds. Pulling apart the cotton balls worked on learning to grade the amount of force with which the child pulled. If he or she pulled too hard, the cotton ball would tear. Gluing on the cotton helped work on learning to pay attention to staying inside the lines of a figure, which is what your child will do when writing on the lines.

Our activity also worked on developing social skills in a group. The children needed to pay attention to each other while walking around looking for the cotton balls. We tried to encourage them to share them, too.

Home Activities to Help Your Child Grow

Your child would have fun using tongs at home, too, and it's a good way to help him or her develop coordination for cutting with scissors, as well as hand strength. Try giving your child the type of tongs that work by squeezing such as ice tongs or strawberry pickers. Let him or her practice picking up dried cereal or pieces of macaroni and putting them in a cup.

Learning how much force to use, such as when the children pulled the cotton balls, can be a hard task. When children color and write, we find that sometimes they will either press down too lightly or too heavily. You can help your child gain more experience in grading force by playing with Play-Doh® and using cookie cutters and other toys to push into the clay.

Sliding Seals and Penguins

Activity Goals: Body-Scheme and Motor-Planning Improvement
Bilateral Coordination Development

Time: 30 minutes

Objectives: Upon successful completion of this activity, the child will be able to

1. Demonstrate sufficient strength to push body weight in a commando crawl down the inclined mat.
2. Motor plan to learn a new motor skill
3. Coordinate both sides of the body for crawling and rolling.

Materials:

1. Large inclined mat and floor mats
2. Large sheet of plastic, such as a plastic drop cloth sold in hardware and building supply stores
3. Sheets of newspaper
4. Pictures of a penguin and a seal

Procedure:

1. Set up the wedge with a line of mats at the bottom. Spread out and tuck the plastic over the wedge and mats.
2. Talk about how seals move, using your pictures to help the children. Have them lie on their stomachs and practice clapping like seals by raising their upper bodies and clapping their hands together with their arms extended. Let them practice pulling their bodies along by pushing with their forearms, dragging their legs.
3. Have the children take turns sliding down the plastic "ice." Let them tell you what they're pretending to be: a seal or penguin.
4. Give each child a few sheets of newspaper to bunch up into balls ("rocks").
5. Put the "rocks" under the plastic "ice."
6. Have each child roll down the wedge over the "rocks."

Adaptations:

1. For children who are having a hard time coordinating themselves for commando crawling when they are sliding, allow them the time to watch the other children and then practice. If necessary, try wrapping their legs together with a towel to help them learn to slide like a seal.
2. Give a boost to propel the child forward down the wedge as he uses his arms.
3. Allow children to roll if they are unable to commando crawl.

Multilevel Instruction:

1. This is a good activity for giving active children extra turns. You can ask the "seals," who are waiting to do "seal clapping," to keep all the children involved.
2. Follow up this activity with a fine-motor activity such as cutting with scissors. Give the children large round circles of paper with a hole cut in the middle for their faces. They can cut fringe and curl it around their pencils to make fur-trimmed hats.

Letter to Parents

Sliding Seals and Penguins

We had lots of practice sliding this week. We pretended to be seals and penguins sliding down the ice on our bellies into the water! We also had fun imitating seals by lying on our bellies, raising our upper bodies, and clapping our "flippers." We tried walking like penguins, flapping our arms. After our sliding game, we made rocks by crumpling newspaper into balls and placing them under the "ice." The children tried rolling over the bumps created by the "rocks" to see how it felt.

Purpose of the Activity

Our motor skills this week were designed to help the children develop better strength, balance, and body awareness. In order to "slide" down the plastic "ice," the children had to hold up their upper trunks and help push themselves with their arms, like a commando crawl. This helps to strengthen the postural muscles, which helps children sit comfortably during listening and fine-motor activities.

Our activities also gave the children a lot of sensory input. Moving stimulates the vestibular sensory system, and because the children were on their stomachs, they received touch input, too. Using activities that provide a lot of movement and touch input helps the children develop a good sense of their bodies. Children need

this in order to get a good inner picture of how much space they take up and what part of their body is moving, even when they aren't visually guiding it. Good body awareness is a building block for developing motor coordination for higher skills, such as writing, coloring, and cutting with scissors.

Home Activities to Help Your Child Grow

You can incorporate many of the same kinds of sensory and motor challenges for your child that he had today by pulling him on a plastic sheet-type sled outside on the grass or the snow. Let your child try riding it lying on his stomach and sitting up. You could try this indoors using a beach towel if you have a vinyl floor. Make sure you pull your child carefully and have him wear a helmet when sitting up as it can be difficult to balance this way.

Snow Painting

Activity Goals: Sensory Processing Improvement
Pre-Writing Skills Development

Time: 15 minutes

Objectives: Upon successful completion of this activity, the child will be able to

1. Demonstrate good tolerance for touching shaving cream and squeezing newspapers without behavioral overreaction.
2. Copy a snowman and other figures by drawing in the shaving cream.
3. Be able to draw with just the index finger with the other fingers curled under.

Materials:
1. Shaving cream
2. Popsicle sticks
3. Yarn balls
4. Snowman's top hat or other target

Procedure:
1. Stand children either at the chalkboard or around tables. Demonstrate how to make a snowman by spreading out some shaving cream and drawing on it with your index finger. Let the children try, making three circles, features, and arms. Encourage them to "erase" by spreading around the shaving cream so that they can try again.
2. Teach them how to make the snowman's top hat by making a square and drawing a line under it. Let them practice drawing it alone and drawing it on top of their snowmen.
3. When finished, before rinsing off, have the children "shave" the shaving cream off their fingers, scraping gently, to help develop their awareness of their hands and motor-planning skill.
4. After rinsing off, let the children try a target game: throwing yarn balls or newspaper balls ("snowballs") at the snowman's hat.

Adaptations:
1. Some children may be very sensitive to touching soft things, and will either refuse to touch the shaving cream or will become overly excited while playing with it. You can help pre pare the children who may be sensitive by doing activities that put pressure into the hands; for example, making newspaper "snowballs."
2. Add rice to the shaving cream to give more sensation to assist a child who has a visual impairment. Also, play with the white shaving cream on a dark surface.

Multilevel Instruction:
1. Using a vertical surface, such as a chalkboard, for writing activities such as these helps build upper body strength and eye-hand coordination for writing. Use shaving cream for practicing writing letters and numbers, too.
2. Follow up this activity by either providing a square and thin rectangle and three circles or having the children cut them out and assemble a snowman picture to take home. They can also cut a small orange triangle "carrot" for the snowman's nose.

January

Letter to Parents
Snow Painting

We practiced making snowmen this week. We used shaving cream for our "snow" and drew with our fingers. The children practiced making circles for the bodies, the faces, buttons, and arms, and a top hat made with a square that was underlined. To clean off their fingers, the children scraped off the shaving cream with Popsicle sticks, like "shaving."

Purpose of the Activity

This activity helps the children learn to draw basic shapes, circles, and squares. It also helped the children develop better finger awareness and finger control using the shaving cream. Sometimes, children don't have a good sense of their fingers when they are young. When shaving cream covers up their fingers, we find that they need some "hands-on" help to be able to do the activity, because when they are confused when can't see their fingers. Experiences where they use their fingers without being able to see them help these children develop better feeling and position sense. This will increase their ability to do other fine-motor skills, such as cutting with scissors and coloring.

Home Activities to Help Your Child Grow

You can duplicate this activity at home with shaving cream. It's fun to do in the bathtub and a lot easier to clean up! If your child already knows how to make the basic shapes, try teaching him to draw simple figures and his name.

To help your child develop better finger awareness, try making a "feely box" at home. Cut a hole in a large shoe-box that his or her hand can fit through. Place small objects from around the house in the box and see if your child can guess them. To make it easier, put a duplicate collection of the objects in front of your child to match.

January

The Three Little Kittens

Activity Goals: Gross-Motor Skills Development
Bilateral Coordination Development

Time: 20 minutes

Objectives: Upon successful completion of this activity, the child will be able to
1. Push self on scooter board for 2-3 minutes.
2. Assume and hold a snowball (supine flexor) position 10-20 seconds.
3. Roll some yarn into a yarn ball.

Materials:
1. Scooter boards
2. Yarn balls or beanbags
3. Balls or skeins of yarn to wind up into balls

Procedure:
1. Set up obstacle course for scooter boards using large blocks, mats, or chairs.
2. Gather children in circle and tell the nursery rhyme of the "Three Little Kittens." Explain how kittens and cats love to play with yarn and yarn balls.
3. Demonstrate to the children how to move on the scooter boards lying on their stomachs. While moving forward on the scooter board, the children should move or bat the yarn balls with their hands (paws). Have them try to keep the yarn ball moving in front of them through the obstacle course.
4. Next, the children can pretend to sleep like kittens. Show them how to hold a snowball position (supine flexor) by lying on their sides and bending their knees up and their heads forward. Let them hug their knees to hold the position.
5. Ask the kittens to "stretch" and "wake up." Have the children sit up in a circle.
6. Demonstrate to the children how to wind a piece of yarn around a ball. Let the children take turns cutting off a piece of yarn and winding it around the ball. Encourage the children to wind using their dominant hand while their other hand, the assisting hand, holds the yarn ball.

Adaptations:
1. For the child using a wheelchair, encourage him to roll his chair around the obstacles.
2. Have the child with a visual impairment play with a ball that makes a noise when moved. Attach bells to the yarn balls or beanbags, or make an object to push from a paper towel roll with a bell inside.
3. For a child who is unable to hold a yarn ball and wind the string around it, try having him hold a paper towel roll or thick dowel with a yarn end taped on to it and then attempt to wind yarn.
4. For the child with functional use of one hand, have the teacher hold the ball or paper towel roll and let the child wind yarn onto it.

Multilevel Instruction:
1. Have children wind yarn around two donut-shaped pieces of heavy cardboard to create their own yarn balls.
2. With the yarn balls, have the children practice throwing and catching, either as partners or alone.
3. Crawl on hands and knees and push the yarn ball through the obstacle course with their noses.

Letter to Parents

The Three Little Kittens

This week we had fun with the nursery rhyme, "The Three Little Kittens." We went through an obstacle course on scooter boards while pushing a yarn ball, pretending to be kittens playing on the floor. Next, we pretended to be kittens curled up into a ball resting on the floor after our play period. With yarn and yarn balls we practiced winding yarn onto a ball.

Purpose of the Activity

Working on scooter board activities and curling up into a ball helped the children develop strength in their arms, backs, and trunks. These activities help to build strength and endurance needed to sit upright while working on fine-motor activities, such as coloring, writing, and cutting with scissors. Your child will need increased strength and endurance as he or she spends more time sitting in a chair in school. Winding string around a yarn ball is a great two-handed activity to develop fine-motor skills and coordination.

Home Activities to Help Your Child Grow

Your child can develop more strength during playtime if you encourage playing in different positions. Give your child cars or other toys to play with to encourage floor play. Take old shoeboxes and make an opening in them to turn them into garages. Your child can push the cars from one garage to another. Another way to encourage strengthening during play is to give your child a small table that is waist high when he or she is kneeling "tall." Playing in this position helps strengthen leg muscles. When watching television, have your child sit on a stool or small bench instead of a chair for strengthening. If your child likes to color, have him color while lying on his stomach. Try placing a picture to be colored on a wall so that your child is raising his or her arm to shoulder height when working on a picture. Helping your child become strong will develop the strength and endurance that he or she will need for writing and other fine-motor tasks in school.

January

Educational Goals by Activity

February

Candy Clay

Activity Goals: Sensory Processing Improvement
Bilateral Coordination Development

Time: 30 minutes

Objectives: Upon successful completion of this activity, the child will be able to
1. Touch and manipulate the candy clay with enjoyment.
2. Coordinate hands to manipulate the clay into shapes and to use the various tools.

Materials:
1. One or more recipes of candy clay (see recipe on page 147)
2. Waxed paper
3. Cookie cutters, rolling pins, plastic knives, Popsicle sticks, and tongue depressors
4. Ziploc® bags for children to take some candy clay home

Procedure:
1. Have children help you put the softened butter and corn syrup in a bowl and blend it together. Add salt, vanilla extract, and confectioner's sugar and mix well, using hands as necessary.
2. Divide the candy clay among the children and let the children taste it.
3. Let them try to make pancakes, ropes, cut-out shapes, and their own designs.
3. When finished, you can send it home in a plastic bag.

Adaptations:
1. Give a child with a visual impairment a dark surface to work on, as the clay is white.
2. Check your seating for a child who has upper body weakness or who lacks coordination. Using an armchair can make him more secure and will promote better hand coordination. The height of the work surface when the children are seated should be one-to-three inches above the height of their elbows when their arms are bent.
3. If a child appears to have difficulty pressing down on the clay, he may be having difficulty with motor planning. Try giving him a lower surface to work on or ask him to stand so that he or she can use his whole body weight to press down.

Multilevel Instruction: Increase the level of difficulty of this activity by providing samples or giving directions of shapes to imitate. You could use numbers or letters, or ask the children to make "I Love U."

Letter to Parents

Candy Clay

We had fun making candy clay this week. The children helped mix the ingredients and then played with the clay just like Play-Doh. They had a chance to taste it, too.

Purpose of the Activity

This activity helps the children with their coordination by using both hands together, both in manipulating the clay with their hands and also by using tools such as cookie cutters, rolling pins, and play knives. Since the clay is stickier than Play-Doh, it helps the children feel their fingers more, which helps them build a better sense of touch. When your child has a good sense of touch in his or her hands, he or she will find holding and using a crayon or pencil easier. Sometimes children are sensitive in their hands and don't like to touch many things, including sticky things. An activity like this helps the teacher identify the problem and help them. Working with sticky materials in a group encourages a sensitive child to be more willing to participate, as he or she wants to have fun with the other children.

Home Activities to Help Your Child Grow

This is the recipe we used to make candy clay today. It makes four cups of candy.

- ¼ lb. softened butter or margarine
- ½ cup. light corn syrup
- ½ tsp. salt
- 1 tsp. vanilla extract
- 4 cup confectioner's sugar

Directions: Mix the softened butter and corn syrup in a large bowl. Add the salt, vanilla extract, and confectioner's sugar and mix well, using your hands.

Using the candy clay, see if your child can show you how to make ropes, pancakes, and cutout shapes. If you wish, give him a plastic knife or Popsicle stick to practice cutting.

February

Candy Hearts

Activity Goals: Pre-Writing Skills Development
Scissor Skills Development

Time: 20 minutes

Objectives: Upon successful completion of this activity, the child will be able to
1. Rub on paper over poster board candy hearts to show letters and outlines.
2. Pick up candy hearts with strawberry pickers or tweezers, placing them in a cup.

Materials:
1. Conversation heart candy
2. Strawberry pickers or tweezers
3. Small cups or baskets
4. Paper in pastel shades
5. Hearts cut from poster board, on which you have written phrases from the candy hearts, using thick glue and let dry
6. Thick crayons with paper peeled off (Anti-roll crayons work well)

Procedure:
1. Show the children the candy hearts with phrases on them. Set them up with the pastel paper, crayons and poster board hearts that you prepared ahead of time. Let the children make one copy of each candy heart if they wish by placing the paper on top and rubbing with the side of a crayon.
2. While they are working, scatter the conversation heart candy either around the room or on various tabletops. When the children are finished making their pictures, provide them with strawberry pickers and cups to go on a hunt for the conversation hearts.
3. See if the children can match their conversation hearts with those on the table, either by color or by the words, depending upon the group's level.

Adaptations:
1. To make the rubbing activity easier, tack the papers down with tape for the children. Encourage them to use both hands on the crayon for rubbing.
2. To help the children learn to push down harder when rubbing, use a low table and have them stand to do the activity.
3. For the child who has difficulty motor planning to push down on her crayon, try gently pushing down through her shoulders as she rubs; or try having her wear light wrist weights or hand patches.
4. Try using softer waxed crayons: glitter crayons or rub-off style crayons are often a softer wax.

Multilevel Instruction:
1. Let the children who are able to write letters make some of their own conversation heart Valentines by copying the words from the candy.
2. After the children find the candy hearts, play a tabletop game where they each try to pick up as many as they can, one at a time, using just one hand until that hand is full. Who can hold the most without dropping any? Then try laying each heart down, one at a time, trying not to let any drop out of their hands as they do.

February

Letter to Parents
Candy Hearts

The children made Valentines with words on them today. They placed paper on top of cardboard copies of conversation hearts that had the phrases from the traditional candy written on them and raised with glue outlines. The children rubbed on their papers with crayon until they could see the letters and the outlines of the hearts. We also had a hunt for candy hearts hidden around the room. The children filled their candy cups using small tongs to pick up the candy.

Purpose of the Activity

This activity helps the children develop the finger strength and coordination they need to write and cut with scissors. They were encouraged to hold their crayons sideways when rubbing with them so they would pinch the crayon with the ends of their thumb and first two fingers. This helps strengthen the muscles that are used to hold a crayon in a tripod grasp. Using the small tongs to pick up the candy hearts also helped to build the muscles for using crayons. The pincer action helps build strength and coordination for cutting with scissors, too.

Home Activities to Help Your Child Grow

Activities at home that can help your child build strength and coordination for holding a crayon correctly include those that require pinching with some force. Pinching clothes pins or small bag clips, sealing zip lock bags using a pinching motion, and squeezing snaps shut are some examples of ways you could encourage your child to develop strong fingers. Sometimes children also need to be taught how to hold a crayon in a tripod grasp if they aren't using it automatically. To make practicing using a tripod grasp fun, try giving your child short pieces of fat crayons for coloring first. This will help strengthen his or her fingers. Then, try a longer crayon to color with, showing him or her how to hold it. Let your child practice by doing a crayon rubbing activity holding his or her crayon in a tripod grasp. You can make surprise pictures for him or her by tracing simple coloring book illustrations with white glue and letting it harden. Cover them with paper and let your child color over them to reveal the surprise picture.

February

Ferry Boat Rides

Activity Goals: Strength and Endurance Improvement
Bilateral Coordination Development

Time: 20-to-30 minutes

Objectives: Upon successful completion of this activity, the child will be able to
1. Use her arms to pull herself along a rope to cross the room while sitting on a scooter board.
2. Repeat the activity while lying on his or her back.
3. Repeat while lying on her stomach.

Materials:
1. One or more scooter boards
2. Large diameter rope, approximately the length of the room. Knots can be made at one-foot intervals, if desired

Procedure:
1. Children sit at one end of the room to wait their turns.
2. One end of the rope should either be tied to a sturdy table leg (have an adult sit on the table, if necessary) or held by an adult. It is also helpful to have an adult hold the rope at the other end to help keep it straight.
3. Explain what a ferry boat is and demonstrate to the children how they could pull themselves "across the river" sitting, lying on their backs, and lying on their stomachs.
4. Let the children take turns propelling themselves in the various positions. When pulling themselves on their stomachs, let the rope go under the scooter board.
5. When finished, let each child tell which ferryboat ride was the most fun for her.

Adaptations:
1. Let the child in a wheelchair use her wheelchair instead of a scooter board to pull herself or use an adapted scooter board for riding on her stomach.
2. Try to use this activity on a smooth floor, rather than a carpeted one, to make it easier. If you tie the rope to a table leg, be sure to cushion it in case a child goes too quickly.

Multilevel Instruction:
1. Children can count the number of knots as they grab onto them to propel themselves.
2. Children can say which hand they are using as they alternate them: left, right, left, etc.

February

Learning in Motion

Letter to Parents
Ferry Boat Rides

We pretended to be ferryboats crossing the wide, wide river. Our ferryboat was a scooter board, which we propelled by pulling ourselves along using a rope that stretched across the room. We made our ferryboats cross the river while lying on our stomachs, then lying on our backs, and then sitting.

Purpose of the Activity

This activity challenged coordination of two sides of the body by having the children use both arms in a hand-over-hand pattern. It helped the children develop their arm and hand strength by encouraging them to pull their body weight along by their arms. Since the children needed to actively use their trunk muscles to stay steady on the scooter board in a variety of positions, they used their trunk muscles, both for stabilization and for resisting gravity. By developing strength in the trunk muscles and large muscle groups, the children increased their stability. This is needed to provide a stable base for the arms during eye-hand coordination tasks.

Home Activities to Help Your Child Grow

Playground activities, such as climbing, swinging, using a rope glide or monkey bars, work on developing strength in your child's trunk and large muscle groups. At home, you can play "tug of war" with your child or let him or her help you move the chairs when you mop the kitchen floor. You can also help your child wheelbarrow walk: have your child lie face down on the floor, pick him or her up by the knees, have him or her push up with both arms and walk on his or her hands across the room. To make the activity more difficult, you can support your child by the ankles so that he or she is using more arm and trunk strength to support his or her body weight.

February

Gak

Activity Goals: Sensory Processing Improvement
Bilateral Coordination Development

Time: 30 minutes

Objectives: Upon successful completion of this activity, the child will be able to
1. Enjoy touching and manipulating Gak.
2. Coordinate hands together to manipulate Gak into shapes and to use the various tools.

Materials:
1. Elmer's® brand white glue
2. Liquid laundry starch
3. Bowl
4. Large spoon
5. Plastic knives or Popsicle sticks
6. Cookie cutters
7. Ziploc bags to save the Gak or bring some home

Procedure:
1. Mix equal parts of laundry starch and white glue together in a bowl. Use a spoon at first and then let the children try mixing it with their fingers. The Gak will get stiffer as it gets mixed together.
2. Divide the Gak so the children all have some to play with. Encourage them to try cutting and shaping it.
3. When finished, store the Gak in Ziploc bags in the refrigerator. It is fun to use when it is cold.

Note: Some batches may be sticky. If this happens, try adding more liquid starch. It's a good idea to have a sink handy for cleanup if you make this with the children.

Adaptations:
1. If you have a child whom you know will be hesitant to touch the Gak, try having the class do a warm-up activity that involves lots of pressure into the hands. Activities like the crayon rubbing ones may help.
2. Provide a dark surface to work on for a visually impaired child so he or she can see the Gak better.

Multilevel Instruction: For older children, try using alphabet letter cookie cutters or ask them to make the shapes by cutting them out with plastic knives.

Letter to Parents

Gak

We made rubbery clay called "Gak" this week. The children had fun mixing white glue together with liquid laundry starch to make a stiff, rubbery dough. Then they tried kneading it, rolling it, and cutting it with cookie cutters and other tools.

Purpose of the Activity

Our activity helps the children learn to use their hands together and build coordination for bilateral tasks. We used "tools," too, because they help children learn how to use their hands for tasks. The Gak was wet and sticky at first and then became rubbery. This gave the children a touch experience that will help them develop better feeling in their hands. Children need good bilateral coordination and the ability to accurately feel what they are touching when they learn to guide a pencil or crayon for writing or coloring.

Home Activities to Help Your Child Grow

Your child may enjoy making Gak at home, too. To make some at home, simply mix equal parts of liquid laundry starch and Elmer's brand white glue together in a bowl. As the mixture is manipulated, it becomes stiffer. You can try chilling the Gak in the refrigerator to make it feel different.

Your child may resist touching things that are new and unfamiliar. If this is a problem, first try giving her an activity that puts a lot of pressure into her hands. Examples would be to squeeze and wring out a sponge or cloth, rub hard on an object (such as scrubbing a pan or counter) and play exercise games that involve weight bearing such as wheelbarrow walking. If your child seems to be especially sensitive to touching things, including sensitivity to how his clothes feel, what foods she will eat due to texture, or other signs that seem to be related to sensitivity to touch, you might want to consult an occupational therapist for more guidance.

February

I Love You

Activity Goals: Pre-Writing Skills Development
Scissor Skills Development

Time: 30 minutes

Objectives: Upon successful completion of this activity, the child will be able to
1. Stamp with sponge paint within a border.
2. Cut around a curved line to make hearts.
3. Use glue and small decorations to decorate a paper.

Materials:
1. Sets of 3 sponges that spell out "I" "♥" "U"
2. Paper prepared ahead with a large heart drawn on each sheet
3. Poster paint in pastel colors
4. Scissors
5. Smaller paper hearts to cut out
6. Additional decorations to place on the large paper, such as small stars and glitter

Procedure:
1. Demonstrate how to stamp the symbols for "I love you" on a large heart and have each child make one.
2. Pass out scissors and paper hearts to cut out.
3. Glue the paper hearts around the words that were stamped on with paint.
4. Let the children finish decorating their pictures with glitter and stars, if they wish.

Adaptations:
1. Make the lines on the heart thick for beginning cutting. Try folding the hearts in half so that the child only has to cut one side.
2. Try using various styles of scissors, depending on the children's skill level. Generally, scissors with short blades are the easiest to use for beginners. There are also double loop scissors available for hands-on assistance. Consult an occupational therapist if you have a child with special needs.

Multilevel Instruction:
1. To make this a group activity, try hanging a big sheet of paper for a class mural. In addition to the sponge painting and hearts, each child could trace her hand with the third and fourth finger curled under for the symbol "I Love You" in American Sign Language ("ASL")
2. Teach the children how to sign "I Love You" in ASL. Hold up the hand, curl the middle and ring fingers down, and rock the hand at the wrist joint from side to side.
3. Children who have more advanced cutting skills could cut out the hearts using "Crazy Cuts" scissors.

Letter to Parents

I Love You

The children practiced cutting with scissors and getting ready for writing this week by making beautiful Valentine pictures. They sponge painted the words and decorated their Valentines with glitter, hearts, and other adornments.

Purpose of the Activity

Our activity worked on the children's Pre-Writing Skills Development. Using their fingers to stamp and sprinkle helped children develop coordination for using crayons and pencils. Giving them a defined space to work within also helped them learn to cover a whole space and to stay within a border. Sprinkling the glitter this way taught the children to pay attention to these things without the additional challenge of coloring with a crayon.

The cutting skills required for this activity were to be able to cut along a gentle curve. This was adapted if your child was not yet ready for this level of skill.

Home Activities to Help Your Child Grow

You can work on getting your child ready for writing at home, too. Try making cookies and letting your child put colored sugar sprinkles on top. Perhaps you have some other recipes where your child could help you sprinkle on Parmesan cheese, salt, or spices. Try stamping with homemade stamps carved from potatoes, carrots, or apple halves. Try using brown-paper grocery bags. You might end up with some inexpensive wrapping paper this way, and your child will be proud to help you make something you can use!

To help your child practice cutting with scissors, give her the job of cutting coupons from the flyers that come with the newspaper. To make it easier, use a black crayon or marker to darken the lines to be cut.

February

Money

Activity Goals: Sensory Processing Improvement
Visual-Perceptual Development

Time: 20-to-30 minutes

Objectives: Upon successful completion of this activity, the child will be able to
1. Identify a coin by touch alone.
2. Match similar coins.
3. Be able to carry a coin in a spoon to a target.
4. Use a finger to propel a coin toward a target.

Materials:
1. Coins of different sizes
2. Bag or sock
3. Spoons
4. Target, such as a soda bottle

Procedure:
1. Place at least one coin of each denomination into a bag or sock. Place one of each type of coin on a table.
2. Have the children take turns reaching into the bag and grasping a coin. Ask them to either say the name of the coin or point to the coin on the table before they pull the coin out of the bag. Let them match their coin with the one on the table.
3. Have the children form two lines. Let them each carry a coin on a spoon to dump into a target at the other end of the room.
4. Place a large target, such as a soda bottle, down on the floor. Give each child a penny and have him practice flicking a finger at the coin to make it slide to hit the target.

Adaptations:
1. If the children have difficulty flicking a finger to hit the coin, let them try pushing it with the spoon.
2. Try a penny toss into a big bowl of water to make an easier target game.

Multilevel Instruction:
1. Enhance this activity by showing the children how to pick up coins using just one hand. Let each child see how many she can pick up and hold in her hands without dropping any of them.
2. Show the children how to hold several coins in the palm of their hands and lay them down one at a time. Let them practice the technique with several coins.

Letter to Parents
Money

We used money this week to talk about some of our former presidents, including Abraham Lincoln and George Washington. The children played a matching game to feel and identify coins hidden in a sock. Then they played a game carrying coins to a target using a spoon and using their fingers to flick coins towards a target.

Purpose of the Activity

The activities we used this week worked on helping the children develop a better sense of touch in their hands and better eye-hand coordination. Since all the coins were round, feeling the difference in them when they were hidden from view required that the children be able to distinguish a difference in size using just their sense of touch. Although this may have been hard at first, with practice the children learned to be able to tell the difference between large quarters and smaller dimes and pennies.

Being able to carry coins balanced on a spoon required that the children use their eye-hand coordination and sense of their body position in order to walk without dropping the coins. Flicking coins to make them move also worked on eye-hand coordination and helped the children improve their ability to use just one finger, keeping the other fingers still.

Home Activities to Help Your Child Grow

Your child will enjoy playing with play money at home. Perhaps you can allow him or her to have some real coins as well, in order to start becoming familiar with the denominations. If your child needs to bring money to school to pay for a drink or snack on a regular basis, try to let him or her find the correct coins to get the amount ready.

You can play "penny soccer" at home to help your child develop better finger coordination. Try placing a glass on the table and some pennies in a row. See how many coins your child can "flick" and hit the glass. If your child does a good job with his or her index finger, try using his or her middle finger or pair the index, middle, and ring fingers together.

Post Office

Activity Goals: Pre-Writing Skills Development

Gross-Motor Skills Development

Time: 20-to-30 minutes

Objectives: Upon successful completion of this activity, the child will be able to
1. Fold and stamp paper to make cards.
2. Stay within boundaries of design when stamping.
3. Perform various gross-motor skills.
4. Put Valentines through slot, turning to fit.

Materials:
1. Rectangular pieces of paper
2. Rubber stamps with Valentine pictures on them
3. Mailbox with a thin slot
4. Gross-motor equipment for an obstacle course, such as a balance beam

Procedure:
1. Have the children fold their pieces of paper to make Valentine cards and stamp designs on them.
2. When each child has made several Valentines, have the children take turns "going to the post office." They can either negotiate an obstacle course or perform a motor skill, such as hopping, walking backwards, or riding a scooter board. If you use a scooter board, the children will enjoy pretending that it is the "mail truck."

Adaptations:
1. Give pre-folded cards or single sheets to stamp on to eliminate the need for folding.
2. Using a copier, prepare paper with a heart drawn on the front so that the children will know where to stamp after they have folded their Valentines.
3. To make the cards easier to mail, use stiffer paper and/or a larger slot on the mailbox.

Multilevel Instruction:
1. Give the children envelopes with names on them. Provide a mailbox for each child (such as a sandwich bag). Let each child sort the mail by matching the names on the envelopes to the correct mailboxes.
2. To increase the difficulty of the gross-motor component, use heavy cardboard boxes to be mail trucks. Have the children work in pairs, with one child riding in the mail truck, while the other child pushes (she is the "motor"),

Letter to Parents
Post Office

Our class played a mail game this week. They made Valentines by folding rectangular pieces of paper and stamping designs to decorate them. Then, they traveled to the post office to mail them in a variety of ways, such as walking on a balance beam, hopping, and riding on a scooter board "mail truck."

Purpose of the Activity

The children worked on building finger coordination by folding and stamping the papers to make pretend letters. These types of tasks helped ready them for writing. Making the letters also helped the children develop their visual-perceptual skills. They needed to plan where to stamp on their designs, and, when they mailed them, they had to turn the letters to the correct position in order to fit them through the slot in the mailbox.

Home Activities to Help Your Child Grow

Try giving your child other pre-writing activities at home to help him or her get ready for writing. These activities need not involve using a pencil or crayon to help your child. For example, there are many toys available that build up finger coordination and eye-hand coordination, such as playing with doll houses, small "farms," and train sets where your child is arranging the figures and moving them around. Finger-painting with paints, pudding, or shaving cream is another valuable pre-writing activity. There are also toys that your child can write or draw on that are as simple and inexpensive as a "Magic Slate," a waxed board covered with plastic on which you can write and then peel up to erase. Don't forget "writing" with a stick on the wet sand at the beach. It's fun to see how long it will last before the water washes it away.

February

Trains

Activity Goals: Strength and Endurance Improvement

Group Development

Time: 20 minutes

Objectives: Upon successful completion of this activity, the child will be able to

1. Maintain an airplane position on his stomach while being pulled on a scooter board.
2. Maintain sitting balance on a scooter board while being pulled.
3. Cooperate with taking turns with a partner to pull and to ride.

Materials:
1. Scooter boards
2. Lines on the floor to make tracks, such as rope, streamers, or newspaper rolls
3. Hula hoops
4. Mat or chairs for the "station"
5. Stuffed animals
6. Helmets (optional)

Procedure:
1. Set up the train tracks by laying out lines on the floor. You can set this up in a circle (or another shape) with one station; or a straight track with two stations, where first one child takes a turn to ride, and then they switch.
2. Demonstrate to the children how they are to lie down on the scooter boards and be pulled. The children who pull should be shown how to walk—either forwards or backwards. If you wish, the children could wear helmets.
3. After each pair has a turn, direct them to wait at the "station."
4. Try having the children pull each other in a sitting position.
5. The children can give stuffed animals a ride by pushing them on the scooter boards while knee-walking.

Adaptations:
1. If you have a child with poor balance or strength, try using a wagon or a larger scooter board that provides more support.
2. If you have an active group who would benefit by a "heavy work" activity in order to calm and focus themselves for the next task, try using heavy boxes to push or the plastic sleds, which are a heavy sheet of plastic with handles cut into them. You can attach a rope to pull if you use a sled.

Multilevel Instruction:
1. The children can make a longer train by lining up on their scooter boards and holding on to the legs of the child in front.
2. You can add pretend "train tracks" to practice walking over by lining up rolls of newspaper.
3. Follow this activity with one to practice either drawing or cutting. Pretend that the scissors or crayons are the train, and that the child must try "to keep it on the track."
4. Incorporate this activity with the "Post Office" activity. The children could deliver Valentines.

Learning in Motion

Letter to Parents

Trains

We played games pretending to ride on trains this week. The children rode on scooter boards along a "track" pulled by a partner. Our train track started and stopped at a station. We had fun taking turns and using toys that came along as passengers.

Purpose of the Activity

This activity today helped the children build strength and endurance in the large muscles of their bodies, including their trunk muscles. They tried riding on their stomachs, in which they needed to use muscles to hold up their neck, back, and legs. They also rode on the "train" sitting on the scooter boards, in which they were using different arm and trunk muscles. This was a good activity to practice balance and motor planning as each child "steered" the train along the track. We used partners today to pull each other along the train tracks. Each pair took turns pulling and riding, and then changed places with each other when they reached the station. The children practiced pulling carefully so that their partners would have a good ride. This teaches the children beginning rules" for getting along with each other and taking turns.

Home Activities to Help Your Child Grow

Your child would enjoy setting up a train track and station at home. Perhaps you could make this into a helpful activity. A cardboard box or laundry basket could serve as the train. Your child could load up the toys and other objects that need to be put away and steer his or her "train" to the "station," where he or she could unload the cargo by putting them away. Perhaps you could reward your child with a ride back to each spot that has another toy to be picked up and taken back to the "station." You will both get a workout!

February

Trains and Planes

Activity Goals: Body-Scheme and Motor-Planning Improvement
Group Development

Time: 30 minutes

Objectives: Upon successful completion of this activity, the child will be able to
1. Hold his arms and legs up for 15 seconds or more while being held on a gymnastics ball.
2. Steer a tricycle around a marked pathway accurately.
3. Work together with classmates to form a train and walk together.

Materials:
1. Tricycles
2. Large gymnastics balls
3. Traffic cones (or large soda bottles)
4. Lines for train tracks (could be made with streamers from cone to cone or with masking tape on the floor)
5. Small soda bottles filled with some rice or dried beans

Procedure:
1. Have children sit along one side of the room. Discuss the modes of transportation: trains and planes. Talk about the parts of the train: the engine, cars, and caboose. Also, talk about how the train must stay on the track.
2. Discuss and demonstrate how the children will pretend to be an airplane and fly.
3. First, have the children pretend to be trains using the tricycles to ride along the track.
4. Next, arrange the cones in one line. Have the children try guiding the tricycles in a serpentine pattern.
5. Make a people train. The teacher is the engine. He picks up the first passenger by saying, "All aboard," and the child's name. The child stands up, puts his hands on the teacher's waist and follows her around the track. With each pass, the train stops, the teacher says, "All aboard" and another child's name, and picks up another passenger until all the children have joined the train.
6. For the plane activity, have the children return to their places (You could call it the landing pad). Call each child up, hold him on the gymnastics ball, and have him raise his arms and legs to "fly."
7. To keep the children who are waiting occupied, try letting them shake small soda bottles with dried rice or beans in them to make the noise for the engines as each child "flies."

Adaptations:
1. Allow a child in a wheelchair to propel himself along as if on the train.
2. Substitute a push-type riding toy for a tricycle or try Velcro˙ straps to help children keep their feet on the pedals if they are having difficulty with riding a tricycle.

Multilevel Instruction:
1. Add to the difficulty of this activity by increasing the difficulty of the course. This is a good activity for outdoors.
2. Number the cones and ask the children to follow directions, such as: go to the first cone, turn right, then go to the second cone, and stop.
3. Let the children take turns being the engine for the people train.
4. Let the children count to ten/fifteen/twenty while one child is practicing "flying."

Learning in Motion

Letter to Parents

Trains and Planes

Today your child pretended to be a train and a plane. He or she rode a tricycle along a train track on the floor and in and out of traffic cones. With adult assistance, your child climbed on a large therapy ball, tummy down, and held out his arms and legs to fly like an airplane.

Purpose of the Activity

Riding tricycles is a very appropriate and fun activity for this age group. It helps build strength in your child's legs, encourages eye-hand coordination during steering, encourages the use of two sides of the body together, and promotes trunk stability. When flying like an airplane, your child used his back, bottom, and leg muscles to sustain this position.

Home Activities to Help Your Child Grow

Riding toys are such fun for children and, by the age of 3½ years, most children are able to ride a tricycle. Children who are not yet able to master pedaling can use riding toys that they propel with their feet to build up leg strength. To help your child learn to pedal a tricycle, try helping keep his feet on the pedals using some masking tape. Make sure one pedal is at the top of the arc so your child just has to push down. Give a little push at the seat and push down on his knee to get your child to push down on the pedal. Repeat for the other leg, helping him establish a rhythm. Keep the session short if your child seems to be getting frustrated. It probably won't be long before you're trying to figure out how to slow your child down!

It is important to give the young child plenty of opportunities to play actively in a safe environment. Children build their strength and endurance by participating in activities such as climbing, swinging, jumping on a trampoline, jumping rope, playing tag, and swimming. Indoors, children can push stuffed animals around the room in a box, help you vacuum or sweep, use their hands to hit a balloon suspended by a string from the ceiling, or play in a tent made out of a table and sheet, which will encourage crawling. These activities provide force to the large joints and make all the muscles of the body work, building strength and endurance.

February

Valentine's Day Rubbing

Activity Goals: Sensory Processing Improvement
Pre-Writing Skills Development

Time: 20 minutes

Objectives: Upon successful completion of this activity, the child will be able to
1. Demonstrate sufficient grasp strength to hold a crayon and color for 3-5 minutes.
2. Use sense of touch to locate shapes under the paper and color them.
3. Be able to identify colors and shapes when asked.
4. Use cause-and-effect problem solving to color over cardboard and paper figures.

Materials:
1. Mural paper: enough to cover an activity table
2. Masking tape
3. Chunky crayons or wide-diameter crayons
4. Valentine doilies, 4-5 layers thick; or cardboard Valentines
5. Cardboard cupid shapes

Procedure:
1. Place Valentines or cupids on the tabletop and secure them in place from underneath with masking tape to prevent movement when being rubbed. Lay down enough figures for each child to do two or three.
2. Cover the entire table with the mural paper, securing the paper underneath with tape.
3. Have the children feel the tabletop with their hands to see whether they can find the shapes.
4. Offer the children pink or red crayons.
5. Have them color over the shapes, pressing down hard.
6. When the children are finished, either hang up the paper to make a mural or background for other art; or, use the paper to wrap presents.

Adaptations:
1. If the child is having difficulty coloring in one area to reveal the shape underneath, try circling the shape with another color to box it in.
2. This activity can be done individually with small pieces of paper.
3. Use different styles of crayons if grasp strength is a problem, such as the ball type or Chubbi Stumps (see Appendix, page 341).

Multilevel Instruction:
1. To make this a more useful activity for building strength, orient the paper in a vertical plane using a chalkboard, wall, or easel.
2. When finished coloring, the children can cut out the hearts and cupids.
3. Add tracing by having the children trace around the outsides of the figures after coloring them.
4. Use large hearts to make broken heart puzzles. Let the children cut them into three pieces and then take turns trying to assemble them.

Letter to Parents

Valentine's Day Rubbing

This week we made Valentine's Day pictures by rubbing on a big piece of white paper. We took a red or pink crayon and turned it on its side and rubbed on the paper until we saw a picture appear. We also took large hearts and cut them into three pieces to make puzzles. We took turns with each other's puzzles, trying to make them fit together.

Purpose of the Activity

Making crayon rubbings helped to develop strength and endurance in your child's arms and hands. This is important for being able to write and perform other fine-motor skills. Making puzzles helped your child develop visual perception, including visual attention and visual-spatial abilities. Being able to see things that are in parts and put them together to make a whole is a visual-perceptual skill that your child will need when he or she copies letters, words, and numbers.

Home Activities to Help Your Child Grow

The rubbing activity can be done at home with any forms or shapes placed under a piece of paper. You can play "Mystery Picture." Hide a shape or form under the paper without your child watching. You can use old greeting cards for thick paper to make the shapes. Encourage your child to feel the shape first. Once found, have your child use a thick crayon to rub on the shape. See how long it is before he or she can guess what you put underneath. There also are commercially available "mystery" books that use a special highlighter pen that the child rubs with to reveal a picture. This type of activity builds up your child's strength, grasp, and motor planning for coloring and writing.

Have some fun making puzzles at home, too. Take a large picture, paste it on a piece of cardboard (such as from a cereal box), and cut it into three or more pieces. Have your child put it together. Increase the number of pieces to make it harder.

February

Educational Goals by Activity

March

Dr. Seuss Day

Activity Goals: Body-Scheme and Motor-Planning Improvement
Balance Improvement

Time: 30 minutes

Objectives: Upon successful completion of this activity, the child will be able to
1. Jump over objects two-to-four inches high.
2. Walk 6 steps on a low balance beam.
3. Manipulate tongs in order to pick up objects.
4. Balance a short stack of objects in his hands for 5 to 7 seconds.

Materials:
1. Beanbags
2. Balance beam
3. Pink paper
4. Tongs or other "grabbers" (one per child)
5. Cut-out figure of a man (label it "Pop")
6. Masking tape

Procedure: Children should be familiar with Dr. Seuss stories *Hop on Pop, The Cat in the Hat,* and *The Cat in the Hat Comes Back.*

Activity I—*Hop on Pop* Jumping Activity
1. Emphasize the point that you should not actually jump on a person—this is pretend!
2. Place cutout of man on mat.
3. Place beanbag on floor in front of mat.
4. Then, children line up in back of beanbag.
5. First child jumps over beanbag and lands on "Pop."
6. Repeat until each child has at least one opportunity to "Hop on Pop."

Activity II—*Cat in the Hat* Balancing Trick
1. Make available objects to be balanced. Suggestions: small box, beanbag, block, book.
2. Children sit on the floor.
3. One child gets up and chooses 2- to 3- things to balance in his hand.
4. Child then does a "trick," such as standing on one foot, raising his hand, bending over, hopping or walking over balance beam.
5. Other children clap and the next child takes a turn.

Activity III—*The Cat in the Hat Comes Back* Cleaning Up the Pink Mess
1. Have children crumple pink paper of various sizes.
2. Children place crumpled pieces of paper within six-foot circle of masking tape.
3. Children take turns "cleaning up" the *Cat in the Hat's* pink mess by using tongs to pick up paper and placing it into a box or trash can.

Adaptations:
1. Children in wheelchairs can steer over figure of "Pop" (forward and backward).

2. Children with visual impairments can use tongs to pick up larger paper balls that have been made of bright, neon-colored paper.

3. Children who have difficulty balancing objects because of hand tremors can balance a stack of objects that have been stuck together with masking tape.

4. Children with poor balance (or those in wheelchairs) can move forward on masking tape line on floor rather than balance beam.

5. If a child is not able to grasp the tongs, he can pick up paper balls with his fingers.

Multilevel Instruction:

1. Children with adequate balance and body awareness can balance objects in their hands or on their heads while walking across the balance beam.

2. Children can "Hop on Pop" on one foot rather than jumping with two feet.

3. Children can walk backwards on balance beam while balancing objects.

4. Children can use tweezers or "pickle picker uppers" to pick up small pieces of crumpled paper.

March

Letter to Parents
Dr. Seuss Day

In school this week, the children talked about Dr. Seuss and his stories. So, we incorporated some of the antics of his most famous characters. We pretended to be the kids who loved to hop in *Hop on Pop*. Of course, we emphasized that you DON'T hop on your Pop. We practiced jumping over small objects like beanbags. We also tried the *Cat in the Hat's* game of seeing how many things we could hold while successfully performing a trick. We tried holding beanbags and walking over the balance beam, and sitting and bouncing on large balls. Like in *The Cat in the Hat Comes Back*, we made a pink mess with pink paper and used grabbers to pick it up.

Purpose of the Activity

Our activities were designed to work primarily on body awareness and motor planning, balance, and bilateral coordination. It is important that children have good body awareness, which means that they know what part of their body is moving or where it is in space without looking at it. When a child performs a balance activity holding objects, he or she has to rely on awareness of his or her body, as well as automatic balance reactions in order to be successful. This is challenging for many young children.

The children also practiced tearing paper and picking it up with grabber toys in order to work on fine-motor muscle strength and coordination. This helped develop the muscles used for classroom tasks, such as cutting with scissors, squeezing glue bottles, and coloring.

Home Activities to Help Your Child Grow

Try some of the activities at home by having your child jump over a rolled newspaper or other small object placed on the floor. She can carry stuffed animals while walking down a line on the floor. If you have some papers to throw away (and who doesn't get lots of junk mail!) let your child help you tear it up for the trash. In order to help strengthen her hand muscles, your child can also practice picking objects off the floor using kitchen tongs.

March

Fan Folding

Activity Goals: Attention Improvement
Pre-Writing Skills Development

Time: 20-to-30 minutes

Objectives: Upon successful completion of this activity, the child will be able to
1. Follow three-step directions.
2. Hold crayon/marker using functional grasp.
3. Cover 80% of paper surface with coloring strokes.
4. Isolate wrist motions to fan himself.

Materials:
1. Paper for each child (8½-by-11 inches)
2. Model
3. Crayons/markers
4. Paper clip for each fan

Procedure:
1. Show model of fan. Demonstrate fanning yourself and the fact that the breeze that fanning creates makes you cooler. Make connection between March winds and fans.
2. Have children sit at desks or table.
3. Give each child a piece of paper and have him decorate both sides.
4. Have child hold paper lengthwise in front of him (long side toward his belly).
5. Demonstrate how to accordion-pleat paper so that fan is created. Demonstration and oral direction should be given.
6. Place paperclip at base of one end of fan.
7. Have child open fan and fan himself using whole arm motions initially, and then using wrist motion only.

Adaptations:
1. Paper can be clipped to a surface such as a slant board so that child with use of only one arm can fold it into fan.
2. Thick, dark fold lines can be drawn on paper to assist the child with visual impairment to make precise folds.

Multilevel Instruction:
1. To make the activity less challenging, draw "fold lines" on the paper before starting.
2. Use fans to propel feathers or dried leaves around the room.
3. Paper can be pre-folded so that the children can practice creasing it.

Letter to Parents
Fan Folding

This week, we decorated both sides of an 8½-by-11 inch piece of paper. We turned it into a beautiful fan by repeatedly folding the paper. We discussed the windy month of March and created our own wind by using the new fans.

Purpose of the Activity

Your child practiced coloring skills as he or she decorated the fan paper. Coloring helps the young child develop the fine-motor control and visual-perceptual skills that will later be used during handwriting tasks. The children had to visually and auditorily attend to the fan-folding directions and demonstration, remember the sequence of the motor actions, and motor plan to complete the steps necessary to make their own fans. Much of the learning that takes place in the young child's classroom also involves attending to directions, using visual and auditory memory, motor planning, and demonstrating motor control.

Home Activities to Help Your Child Grow

At home, you can have your child write letters, draw pictures, or make cards and then fold them so that they fit into an envelope. Have your child practice folding precisely by lining up the edges of the paper before pressing on the fold with his index finger. Origami, the ancient art of paper folding, can be good practice for the child—large craft stores and libraries usually have books on the art, and these books also show simple figures, such as dogs, that can be made with only a few folds. Your child could make his own book by folding paper in half to make pages. He could illustrate the book, and then you could have fun "reading" it together.

March

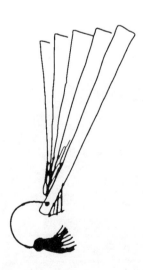

Forsythia Branches

Activity Goals: Pre-Writing Skills Development
Strength and Endurance Improvement

Time: 20-to-30 minutes

Objectives: Upon successful completion of this activity, the child will be able to
1. Pinch tissue paper into small balls.
2. Place tissue paper accurately on tape (on branch).

Materials:
1. Two-inch squares of yellow tissue paper (about 25 per child)
2. One or two small branches for each child
3. Two-sided tape—enough to spiral around each branch

Procedure:
1. Prior to group, gather branches and spiral a piece of two-sided tape down each branch.
2. Show children live forsythia or a sample of the project. Explain what forsythia is and that it is one of the first flowers seen in spring in colder climates.
3. Give each child approximately 25 tissue squares and show him how to roll tissue into small balls (flowers) using 2 hands.
4. Child places "flowers" on two-sided tape.
5. Forsythia branches can be placed in a vase and displayed in classroom.

Adaptations: For the child who lacks the finger coordination or strength to make small tissue balls, the child can use "pre-made" tissue balls or small, yellow pompons available at craft shops.

Multilevel Instruction:
1. Children can make tissue balls in shades of yellow, white, and orange and make a pattern of flowers on their forsythia branch.
2. Children can count the flowers that they've made.
3. Children can use one hand only to make tissue balls.
4. Children can twist 1" x 4" tissue paper, wrap it around a 3" piece of double-sided tape and affix the tape to the branch. Sequence can be repeated until branch is full.

March

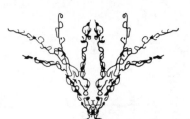

Letter to Parents
Forsythia Branches

Today the children used sticks, two-sided tape, and yellow tissue paper to make forsythia, one of the first flowers of spring. To decorate the room, the group put all of its branches together in a vase, in order to make a beautiful bouquet.

Purpose of the Activity

This activity encouraged the children to use their fingers to form tissue paper into small balls. This helped the children develop strength and coordination in their hands and fingers. Strength and coordination in the small muscles of the hand are needed for success in writing, manipulation of clothing fasteners, cutting with scissors, and other classroom tasks. The children also saw how joining individual parts (their forsythia branch) to their friends' branches helped make a whole group project—the beautiful bouquet in the vase.

Home Activities to Help Your Child Grow

To help your child develop hand and finger strength, have her pop the bubbles in packing bubble sheets using her thumb and index finger or her thumb, index, and middle fingers. If this is too difficult, your child can use a small plastic hammer to pop the bubbles. Tearing paper into small pieces can also develop finger pinch strength. Your child can then make a collage from the pieces of paper that have been torn. Placing stickers in a book, stringing small beads, squeezing clothespins, and pulling very small pop-beads apart are all activities that will help to improve your child's pinch strength.

March

Learning in Motion

Lion with a Linguini Mane

Activity Goals: Visual-Perceptual Development
Sensory Processing Improvement

Time: 20-to-25 minutes

Objectives: Upon successful completion of this activity, the child will be able to
1. Tactilely tolerate the texture of cooked spaghetti for length of time needed to complete this project.
2. Use functional grasp on crayon/marker.
3. Color 80% of lion's face without going outside the lines more than 5 times.

Materials:
1. One pound cooked linguini divided into two parts
2. Copy of lion's face and mane (on the facing page) for each child
3. Crayons/markers
4. Food coloring (paste)

Procedure:
1. Before class, dye ½ pound of cooked linguini orange or yellow and ½ pound linguini brown. To best dye linguini, use food coloring paste and dye it while it is warm, after it has been drained. Rinse the linguini with cold water, and then place it in a plastic bag that contains a little oil.
2. Explain the expression "March comes in like a lion and goes out like a lamb."
3. Give each child the picture of the lion and tell him to color only the face, not the mane. Provide an example.
4. Give each child some orange linguini and some brown linguini.
5. Let child place strands of linguini on lines that have been drawn to represent lion's mane. Children should attempt to match the length of the line (short strands on short lines, long strands on longer lines).
6. Dry lion pictures flat.
7. These are difficult pictures to send home because, as the linguini dries, the paper wrinkles.

Adaptations: If child has difficulty handling the cooked linguini because of tactile sensitivity, pieces of yarn or paper can be used instead. Or, precede this activity with one that provides deep pressure.

Multilevel Instruction: Rather than using linguini to form the lion's mane, the children can practice their scissor skills by cutting along the lines.

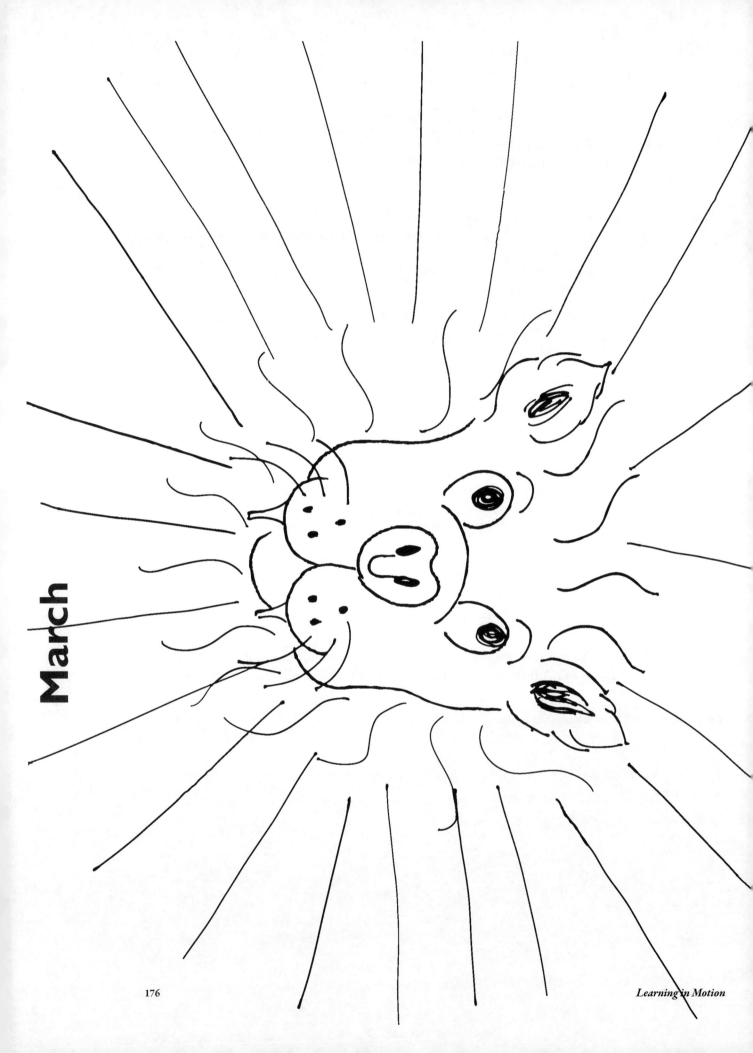

March

Letter to Parents

Lion with a Linguini Mane

This week, we used cold, dyed linguini to complete a project. First, we talked about the meaning of the expression: "March comes in like a lion and goes out like a lamb." Each child then got some linguini to play with and feel. The children were given drawings of a lion's face and crayons to color it in, but something was missing! The mane needed to be made full. The children did this by breaking off pieces of linguini and making sure that the length of linguini was close to, or the same, as the length of the fur in the lion's mane. Then, they pressed the linguini onto the paper, and it stuck!

Purpose of the Activity

Once they were used to it, most of the children enjoyed feeling the cold, slippery linguini. Some of the children were sensitive to this odd texture, and we tried to desensitize their hands by encouraging them to rub their hands with a washcloth or to play with Play-Doh. The lion activity was very engaging for the children and they worked very hard at visually discriminating between "short, medium and long" strands of linguini. The children needed to precisely follow the pattern of the lines on the lion's mane, tear off the proper amount of linguini, and press the pasta down gently using his or her index finger. When coloring the lion's face, it was important to stay within the lines and to cover the majority of space, an important pre-writing skill.

Home Activities to Help Your Child Grow

At home, your child can practice using his or her fine-motor control and visual-perceptual skills in a number of ways. You can purchase coloring books with simple line drawings in them. Have your child color the drawing and then have him or her put glue on the lines and sprinkle glitter on them. When the glue dries, your child can trace the raised lines with his or her index finger. Also, once the glue dries, you can place a blank piece of paper over the line drawing and have your child make a rubbing of the picture.

March

Making Irish Potato Candy

Activity Goals: Sensory Processing Improvement

Group Development

Time: 30-to-40 minutes

Objectives: Upon successful completion of this activity, the child will be able to
1. Stir ingredients in bowl for 10 revolutions.
2. Identify ingredients used in recipe.
3. Break off dough and roll piece in cinnamon.
4. Tolerate tasting and handling food with semi-soft texture.

Materials:
1. Ingredients for Irish Potatoes (see recipe section)
2. Large bowl
3. Large spoon
4. Measuring cups and spoons
5. Paper plate for each child

Procedure:
1. Have each child wash his hands.
2. Explain significance of Irish Potato Candy as it relates to St. Patrick's Day. Show how the candy looks like potatoes, but doesn't have potatoes in it.
3. Show class ingredients and have them identify each one.
4. Follow directions (in recipe section) for making candy.
5. Have each child participate in a part of the cooking process, e.g., adding ingredients, measuring, etc.
6. Allow each child to stir ingredients to blend them.
7. Have each child take turn stirring dough.
8. Place approximately ¼ cup of dough on each child's plate.
9. Sprinkle cinnamon beside dough.
10 Demonstrate how to break off a piece of dough (about one teaspoon) and roll it in cinnamon so that it looks like small potato.
11 Eat and enjoy!
12 Wash hands.
13 Have children recall how they made candy.

Adaptations:
1. For added stability, the bowl and the children's plates can be placed on Dycem or similar non-slide surface.
2. Spoon handle can be built up for children with decreased ability to grip.
3. Knife can be used to cut off small pieces of dough.

Multilevel Instruction:
1. Print recipe and have children read simple words.
2. Before breaking off small pieces of dough, children can shape "snake" into first letter of their name.

Letter to Parents
Making Irish Potato Candy

To help celebrate St. Patrick's Day, we made Irish Potato Candy today. The children placed all of the ingredients into a bowl, mixed them together, rolled the dough into small balls, coated them with cinnamon, and ate the treat!

Purpose of the Activity

While mixing the ingredients together and shaping and rolling the dough, the children were developing strength and awareness in their arms, hands, and fingers. Tactile sense and visual attention to our hands are closely associated and valuable in developing skills, such as coloring, cutting, writing, and tracing. Making and eating the candy allowed your child to experience different tactile and taste sensations.

Home Activities to Help Your Child Grow

At home, given supervision and assistance, your child can help with cooking foods like meatballs, cookies, and bread. Working with a variety of food textures (sticky, warm, cold, chunky, wet) helps to improve tactile awareness and decrease tactile avoidance. If children or adults are not comfortable touching things, it is difficult for them to learn through the important and basic sense of touch. Playing with sand, water, Styrofoam peanuts, and uncooked rice will provide your child with varied tactile experiences. Fill a large wash tub with one of these items, give your child containers, spoons and tongs, and watch what fun he or she has dumping, pouring, and exploring! Place small objects in the tactile materials to make the activity more complex and further develop your child's visual discrimination skills.

Here is the recipe if you want to make Irish Potato Candy at home:

> 2 cups confectioners' 10X sugar
>
> 1 cup coconut
>
> 1-to-4 teaspoons half-and-half
>
> ½ teaspoon vanilla
>
> cinnamon

Mix sugar, coconut, and vanilla with enough half-and-half to make a paste. Knead the dough and then break off a small piece (about one teaspoon). Roll to form a ball or potato shape. Roll the "potatoes" in cinnamon. Eat and enjoy!

March Goes Out Like a Lamb

Activity Goals: Sensory Processing Improvement
Scissor Skills Development

Time: 20-to-30 minutes

Objectives: Upon successful completion of this activity, the child will be able to
1. Use glue from bottle.
2. Draw vertical lines symbolizing grass.
3. Trace his non-dominant hand using a pencil or marker.

Materials:
1. Black and green crayons
2. Cotton balls - 1 large bag per group of 11
3. Pencils or washable markers - 1 per child
4. 1 piece of construction paper 8½-by-11 inches or larger per child
5. Plastic moving eyes

Procedure:
1. Show sample of lamb. Discuss expression "March comes in like a lion and goes out like a lamb." Ask children for ideas about what it means.
2. Give each child a piece of construction paper and a pencil or marker.
3. Show children how to put one hand on paper and trace around it. Hand should be near top edge of paper. Help them stretch their thumbs and fingers wide.
4. Children color the nails of the fingers black.
5. Children turn paper upside-down. Children can practice putting hands right-side-up and upside-down.
6. Ask what picture looks like now (lamb).
7. Children spread/squeeze glue on outline of hand.
8. Give each child approximately six cotton balls. Show him how to pull cotton apart so that it covers greater area.
9. Have children place cotton balls on handprint, being careful not to cover head or hooves.
10. Demonstrate how to draw grass by drawing vertical lines on bottom of paper. Give child green crayon and instruct him to draw lines for grass.
11. Ask children to repeat the phrase about the month of March.

Adaptations:
1. For children who have only one hand (or use of only one hand), allow them to trace someone else's hand.
2. Place paper on non-skid material for the child who has difficulty stabilizing the paper.
3. For child who has difficulty handling cotton balls because of tactile sensitivity, allow him to use tongs to place the cotton balls.

Multilevel Instruction:
1. Give children 2-inch by 11-inch strip of green construction paper. Instruct them to snip paper to make grass.

2. This can be a group project by placing large piece of paper on wall or table and having children trace hands on common piece of paper. Turn paper upside down and repeat steps 4 to 11. Or, have each child cut out his hand and place on mural.

3. Sing "Baa Baa Black Sheep" (but substitute the word "white" for "black").

March

Letter to Parents
March Goes Out Like a Lamb

This week we discussed the phrase "March comes in like a lion and goes out like a lamb." Ask your child what that statement means— you may be surprised at the answer. The children traced their non-dominant hand and used a black crayon to color in the nails of the fingers. When their paper was turned around, they were surprised to see the outline of an animal. After adding a mouth, ears and tail, the children were given cotton balls, which they stretched and used to cover the "body" of the animal. It soon became obvious that the animal with the four hooves and a black muzzle was a sheep! The children completed the activity by snipping green paper or drawing green lines to represent grass.

Purpose of the Activity

This activity gave your child the opportunity to practice using many common tools of the classroom—scissors, glue, crayons, and markers. Completing the picture successfully required following simple, as well as multi-step directions, skills necessary for success in the school environment. By stretching the cotton in order to cover the body of the sheep, your child experienced a different type of texture, as well as increased strength in the small muscles of the hand. Tracing around each finger individually improved your child's awareness of his or her non-dominant hand. Hand awareness is extremely important during handwriting, cutting with scissors, and two-handed tasks.

Home Activities to Help Your Child Grow

Giving your child the opportunity to practice cutting with scissors is important to her fine-motor skill development. By the age of three years, children should hold scissors correctly and be able to snip paper. At five years old, children should be able to accurately cut out a circle and a triangle. Developmentally, children should first learn to snip, then to cut along straight lines, then curved lines, and finally, angled lines. By the age of seven years, children should be able to cut out most shapes and should only be refining their skills with scissors. For practice, your child can cut up junk mail, index cards, or pictures out of a magazine.

March

Learning in Motion

Moving Potatoes

Activity Goals: Attention Improvement
Bilateral Coordination Development

Time: 20-to-30 minutes

Objectives: Upon successful completion of this activity, the child will be able to
1. Roll, in a straight line, the length of a therapy mat (about six feet).
2. Pass a potato in front of, behind, over, and under himself.
3. Cut on a curved line.
4. Place head and arms through correct holes in bag.

Materials:
1. Paper grocery bags—1 per child
2. Music tape
3. Tape player
4. Therapy mat
5. 1 or 2 Potatoes
6. Scissors

Procedure: **Activity #1—Potato Roll**
1. Prior to group, mark paper bags with hole for the child's head, as well as holes for arms.
2. Demonstrate how to cut out holes in paper bag so child's arms and head can fit through the holes.
3. Place paper bag in front of each child.
4. Hand scissors to each child and instruct him or her to cut on the lines in order to cut holes into bag.
5. When child is finished cutting out holes, have child put bag over head and arms through the armholes.
6. Children line up at one end of the mat, and each child takes a turn rolling from beginning to end of mat, pretending to be a potato.

Activity #2—Pass the Potato
1. Have children sit in a circle.
2. Tell the children that they are going to pass the potato to the child beside them. Explain that the children must look at you to see how to pass the potato. Vary the way it is passed, e.g., behind you, in front, over your head, under bent knees.
3. Begin music, and pass the potato. When all or most of the children can imitate the way you have passed it, change your passing style.
4. Have children explain the many ways they passed the potato using prepositions like under, over, etc.

Adaptations:
1. For children who are easily distracted, eliminate the music.
2. Children without adequate scissors control can tear out the circles in the bags, or adults can prepare the bags beforehand.
3. For children who have difficulty rolling, use an inclined wedge with a mat placed over it. Gravity will assist them in rolling.

March

Multilevel
Instruction:

1. Children can stand while in circle and pass potato in more elaborate ways.
2. Children can pass more than one potato at a time.
3. Children can take turns leading the group.
4. Children can roll along mat and knock down bowling pins or cardboard bricks placed at the end of the mat.
5. For an added potato activity, the children could mash cooked potatoes and enjoy eating them for a snack. Or, they could have French fries or potato sticks.
6. Children can pretend they are rolling French fries. Cut bottom of bag out (no arm holes) and slip bag over child.

March

Letter to Parents

Moving Potatoes

We played with, talked about, and pretended to be potatoes this week. We cut holes in paper bags, slipped the bag over our heads, and "Voila!" we became pretend potatoes. We practiced rolling along the length of a therapy mat, being careful to stay on the mat and not roll off. The second game we played involved passing a potato from one person to another while seated in a circle. During this game, we had to pay close attention to the person who was leading us because they were tricky and passed the potato in many different ways.

Purpose of the Activity

The activities that we did this week helped to develop your child's awareness of his or her body and helped your child plan for the coordinated movements that were required. The potato was passed around the circle in many different ways, including over the head, under bent knees and behind the back. The children even tried to pass it using their feet!

During this game, the children had to pay very close attention to the person who was leading them because they were not told how the potato was going to be passed; they needed to observe and imitate the leader's actions. Learning in the classroom often occurs this way, with the teacher demonstrating an activity. You can understand how important it is for your child to be able to attend to an adult in the classroom and to be able to follow directions that are demonstrated, not given orally.

Your child was using motor planning skills and coordinating both sides of his or her body as he or she was rolling along and not going off the sides of the mat. Scissors skills were also needed to cut out the hole for the head in the paper bag potato sack.

Home Activities to Help Your Child Grow

Rolling is such fun for the young child. Weather permitting, take your child outside, and allow him or her to roll along the ground. Rolling up and down a small hill makes this activity even more challenging. An added benefit to the rolling is the fact that vestibular (movement) stimulation is sometimes associated with speech and language development.

March

Paper Airplanes

Activity Goals: Attention Improvement
Pre-Writing Skills Development

Time: 30 minutes

Objectives: Upon successful completion of this activity, the child will be able to
1. Use a functional crayon grasp while coloring.
2. Follow directions to make sample airplane.
3. Use adequate arm motions to fly airplane.

Materials:
1. Crayons
2. Paper clips
3. Paper for each child
4. Direction for making airplanes
5. Sample of airplane

Procedure:
1. Show airplane sample to the group.
2. Have children sit at table or desks, give each child paper and have her decorate both sides.
3. Explain how wind will help the airplanes fly.
4. Explain directions, one step at a time, to children. Demonstrate folds to children as you give them directions orally.
5. When children finish making their airplanes, take them outside or to a large room.
6. Show children how to "launch" airplanes and make them fly.
7. Have each child take a turn flying her airplane.

Adaptations:
1. Since this is a fairly high-level activity, children may have difficulty following the directions to make the airplanes. For these children, the airplanes can be pre-made and the children can decorate and then fly their airplanes.
2. Children can use markers rather than crayons to decorate. Markers offer less resistance and are easier to use than crayons.
3. Fold lines can be drawn on paper to assist children in knowing where to make creases.
4. If children do not have refined grasp patterns, choose adapted crayons or markers for their use.

Multilevel Instruction:
1. Children can "fly" their airplanes through a Hula Hoop target.
2. While walking to a hallway, gym/all-purpose room, or outside, children can pretend they are flying, using their out-stretched arms as airplane wings.
3. Tell children they need to decorate their airplane by drawing a specific shape, pattern, or line on the paper.

Letter to Parents

Paper Airplanes

This week, we talked about the month of March and how things move in the wind. The children made paper airplanes, decorated them, and practiced launching and flying them.

Purpose of the Activity

Folding paper to make an airplane requires fine-motor dexterity as well as the ability to follow multi-step directions. Both of these skills are needed on a daily basis in the classroom. Children need to follow the directions and demonstrations that the teacher gives them in order to complete projects successfully. Launching and flying the airplanes encouraged your child to use his or her eyes to visually track the movement of the airplane. When the airplanes "landed," the children ran and retrieved them, an exercise that required them to make quick adjustments in movement, using good control and balance.

Home Activities to Help Your Child Grow

On a nice windy day this month, send your child outside with some bubbles. To make big bubbles, try putting a fairly strong solution of "No More Tears" shampoo or dish detergent with water in a bucket. Give your child a disposable plastic cup with the bottom cut out. Show him or her how to dip it in, hold it up, and let the wind blow through it to make big bubbles. Your child can also have fun blowing through the cup.

This activity will help your child get a lot of running practice, too. Playing with bubbles encourages the children to use their eyes for visual tracking, which is a very important type of exercise we usually don't think about young children needing. However, children need to be able to use their visual tracking skills in order to follow the teacher's demonstrations and other children's movements, for many of the activities in school.

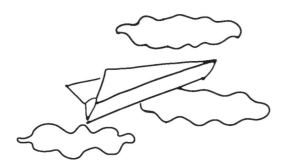

Paper Plate Puppet Faces

Activity Goals: Body-Scheme and Motor-Planning Improvement
Pre-Writing Skills Development

Time: 30 minutes

Objectives: Upon successful completion of this activity, the child will be able to

1. Use her index finger to draw a circle in shaving cream.
2. Correctly orient eyes, nose, and mouth on face.
3. Tolerate texture of shaving cream.

Materials:
1. Paper plates —1 per child
2. Yarn—brown, black, and yellow
3. Craft sticks —1 per child
4. Magazine pictures of facial features (eyes, noses, mouths, ears)
5. Shaving cream
6. Mirrors
7. Paper towel
8. Tacky glue

Procedure:

Activity I
1. Children are seated around table.
2. Each child takes a turn looking into a mirror. If available, each child has her own mirror to look into.
3. Discuss facial features, differences, and similarities.
4. Collect mirrors.
5. Squirt 3-inch-diameter dollop of shaving cream in front of each child.
6. Child uses hands to spread shaving cream on tabletop.
7. Give instructions to draw a face in the shaving cream. Ask the children to include as many features as they can.
8. Each child wipes her area of the table clean with wet paper towels.
9. Each child washes her hands.

Activity II
1. Show children sample of paper plate puppet face that has already been made.
2. Each child gets a paper plate, some yarn (that resembles her hair color) and facial features.
3. Children glue facial features and hair onto paper plates.
4. Children are given craft sticks to glue or tape on to back of paper plate.
5. Children sit at table and learn song. "My face—it has two eyes; My face—it has two ears; My face—it has a mouth and nose; and lots of hair!" Sing to the tune of "The Farmer in the Dell." They can point to the facial parts as they sing the song.
6. Children march around table waving their paper plate puppets in the air.

Adaptations: 1. Allow child with visual impairment to feel her face as well as the face of someone else before attempting to draw face or make puppet face.
2. Child with visual impairment could use Wikki Stix® to "draw" facial features (see Adaptations).
3. Use three-dimensional items, such as buttons or foam cutouts, for facial features if the child has visual impairment.

Multilevel Instruction: 1. Children can be instructed to draw faces in shaving cream that show different emotions (e.g., happy, sad, surprised, scared).
2. Instead of giving each child the correct number and type of facial features, each child can choose features from a common pile.

March

Letter to Parents

Paper Plate Puppet Faces

This week, the children looked into a mirror and at each other and discussed the facial features that they saw. They drew faces in shaving cream and then made faces on paper plates by gluing facial features, cut out of magazines and yarn, onto the plates. They completed the activity by adding a craft stick and making puppets out of the plates. Then they sang the following song: "My face it has two eyes; My face it has two ears; My face it has a nose and mouth; and lots of hair" (sung to the tune of "The Farmer in the Dell.")

Purpose of the Activity

It is important for children to have an accurate internal concept of their faces and bodies because good body awareness allows a child to develop motor skills easily. While drawing a face in the shaving cream, the children were demonstrating whether or not the image of their face was internalized. By making paper plate puppets, the concept of what a face should generally look like was reinforced. The children also experienced varied tactile sensations from the yarn, glue, and shaving cream used in the projects.

Home Activities to Help Your Child Grow

You can make simple puzzles for your child by cutting out pictures from a magazine, gluing them on to cardboard and cutting the picture into pieces. Your child will have fun putting the puzzle together. You can make them more durable by covering the picture, mounted on cardboard, with clear contact paper. The "busier" the picture and the greater the number of pieces and straight line cuts, the more difficult the puzzle will be to put together. To reinforce body awareness, make puzzles out of pictures featuring faces or whole bodies and have your child assemble them.

March

Learning in Motion

Potato Play

Activity Goals: Group Development

Visual-Perceptual Development

Time: 20-to-30 minutes

Objectives: Upon successful completion of this activity, the child will be able to
1. Play simple group games.
2. Catch a thrown potato 3 out of 5 times.
3. Throw a potato accurately 3 out of 5 times.
4. Follow directions.

Materials:
1. 6 to 10 potatoes
2. Tape recorder
3. Musical tape

Procedure:

Game 1—Hot Potato
1. Children sit in circle and adult starts music.
2. Children begin passing potato in one direction. (Reverse the direction in later rounds).
3. Adult stops music and child holding potato when music stops is the "Hot Potato" for that round.

Game 2—Toss/Catch the Potato
1. Children get into pairs and stand 4 to 6 feet apart.
2. One child is given potato, and he tosses potato to a partner who catches it.

Game 3—Potato Relay
1. Children get into 2 equal lines with approximately 3 feet between each child.
2. Children get down on hands and knees holding spoon in one hand.
3. First child gets a potato and uses spoon to push potato to next child in line.
4. Repeat sequence until last child gets potato.
5. When last child receives potato, the line stands up.
6. The order of the children in line can be reversed or changed so each child gets to push the potato.

Adaptations:
1. For children with visual impairment, the potato can be wrapped in aluminum foil or brightly colored paper.
2. The larger the potato, the easier it will be to grasp.
3. The relay race can be done without using spoons to push the potato if children are having difficulty coordinating their arm movements.

Multilevel Instruction:
1. For a higher-level Hot Potato game, pass 2 potatoes at the same time.
2. Children can stand closer or further apart, depending on their ability, during the Toss/ Catch the Potato game.
3. For a higher-level relay race the children can stand, balance the potato on a spoon, and walk it to the next person without dropping it.

Letter to Parents
Potato Play

This week, we played three games using potatoes. First, we played "Hot Potato," passing the potato quickly from one person to another. Next, we formed pairs and tossed potatoes back and forth to each other. The last game we played was a potato relay, in which the children used a spoon to push potatoes to one another.

Purpose of the Activities

The activities we participated in today were group activities. Your child had to attend and perform within a group setting, which is generally how learning occurs in the classroom. While passing, catching, throwing, and pushing a potato, children must coordinate their eye and hand movements. Accurate eye-hand coordination is required for many classroom activities, such as handwriting, coloring and cutting.

Home Activities to Help Your Child Grow

Playing catch at home with you and/or siblings can be engaging for the pre-school child. Beginning catch and throw activities should use slower moving objects to allow the child time to respond, therefore increasing success. Try balloons, Koosh balls, scarves, or Wiffle® balls at first. As skill improves, you can increase the speed or direction that you throw the object. You can work on a rolling type activity at home by taking a large cylinder such as an oatmeal container or an empty soda can and, with a wooden spoon, having the child push it from one end of the room to the other.

For added fun and challenge, you can make a small obstacle course using toys, chairs, or pillows. Have your child use a spoon to push the can around or over the obstacles.

Learning in Motion

Rainbow Day

Activity Goals: Strength and Endurance Improvement
Body-Scheme and Motor-Planning Improvement

Time: 20-to-30 minutes

Objectives: Upon successful completion of this activity, the child will be able to
1. Crawl through the tunnel.
2. Propel herself on scooter board.
3. Jump over objects on ground.
4. Wait her turn to go over, under, through the rainbows.

Materials:
1. Streamers in a variety of rainbow colors
2. Traffic cones
3. Tunnel (preferably multi-colored fabric)
4. 1 or 2 Scooter boards

Procedure: Set up room with 3 different stations: Over the Rainbow, Under the Rainbow, and Through the Rainbow.

Activity I—Over the Rainbow
Children line up and take turns jumping over the rainbow.

Activity II—Under the Rainbow
1. Suspend streamers from tops of cones placed approximately 4 feet apart. Rainbow bridge should be about 6 to 8 feet in length.
2. Children line up in front of the bridge.
3. First child lies on stomach on scooter board.
4. First child propels herself under rainbow bridge and around the cones to next person in line.
5. Repeat steps 3 and 4 until all of the children have gone under the rainbow.

Activity III—Through the Rainbow
1. Open tunnel and place it on ground.
2. Children take turns crawling through the tunnel (through the rainbow).

Adaptations:
1. Rainbow can be made narrow or wide, depending on placement of streamers on ground in "Over the Rainbow."
2. Child in wheelchair can wave different-colored streamers and class can take turns running through or past them.
3. Child in wheelchair can propel herself through a pathway of different-colored streamers.

Multilevel Instruction: Children can tape streamers to cardboard tubes (rainbow wands) and wave them following a different direction (e.g., up, down, to the side, behind). Or children can wave "rainbow wands" in rhythm to music being played.

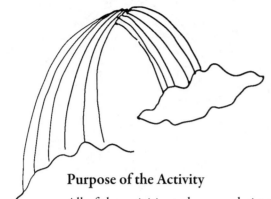

Letter to Parents
Rainbow Day

This week, the children had fun going under, going over and going through the rainbow. They pushed themselves on scooter boards under streamers that had been attached to cones to raise them. We called that going "under the rainbow." Then, we went "over the rainbow" by jumping over the streamers. Then the children crawled through a fabric tunnel, pretending they were going "through the rainbow."

Purpose of the Activity

All of the activities today were designed to help your child develop body scheme and motor planning skills, build up strength and coordination, and also to provide a lot of "heavy work." "Heavy work" means that the activity is encouraging the child to either weight-bear on his arms and legs, as when jumping, or to use his muscles vigorously as when pushing himself on a scooter board. For children who need it, "heavy work" activities help the child become more focused and alert. They also help the child who is sensitive to touch and/or movement become less sensitive, especially if the child does them every day. "Heavy work" activities also have a positive effect on stimulating spontaneous language.

Home Activities to Help Your Child Grow

Taking your child to a playground and encouraging exploration of all of the types of equipment will help your child develop a good sense of how to move his or her body through space. While having fun, your child will be building strength and endurance as well as learning how to plan movements so that he or she can be successful in an activity.

You might want to get your child some bingo markers, which can be purchased at dollar stores, to help him or her with fine-motor development and to provide opportunities for "heavy work" for the arms and hands. Use either coloring book pages or plain paper—even newspaper—hang it on a wall and let him or her make a picture. The markers can be used to either make dots or to paint. Your child will be strengthening his hands while using visual-perceptual skills and fine-motor control to practice staying within the lines. This is a good activity for children who are not enjoying coloring because they have not yet developed good control while using crayons.

March

Rainbow Mural

Activity Goals: Visual-Perceptual Development

Group Development

Time: 20-to-30 minutes

Objectives: Upon successful completion of this activity, the child will be able to

1. Use paint or bingo marker to color for a period of 5 minutes on a vertical surface.
2. Work on an individual task with a group.
3. Realize that their part of the group contributed to the end product or goal of the group.
4. Consistently use one hand for manipulation of brush or bingo marker.

Materials:
1. Large piece of bulletin board paper (approximately 10 feet long)
2. Bingo markers (can be found in dollar stores) or paint brushes for each child
3. Smock for each child
4. Black marker
5. Newspaper (2-3 sections)
6. Q-Tips® for each child
7. 8½" by 11" piece of drawing paper with rainbow drawn on it
8. Paint and paint dishes/plates

Procedure:
1. Before group, draw large outline of rainbow on mural paper. Make lines to separate colors.
2. Hang paper on a flat wall at children's height. Place newspaper underneath against wall to catch any paint drips.
3. Discuss rainbows with children and explain the many colors that make up a rainbow.
4. Children are divided into two groups.
5. Have children put on smocks.
6. Call half of the children up at a time to begin painting.
7. Give children a different color bingo marker or a brush with different color paint on it.
8. Instruct children to paint within their lines of the rainbow.
9. The other half of the group sits at a table.
10. Each child receives an 8½" by 11" piece of paper with a rainbow drawn on it.
11. Instruct children to use one color per stripe.
12. Give children Q-tips that they can dab into individual small paint dishes/plates.
13. Tell them to try and make colored dots within the lines of the drawing without mixing colors. Be aware of children switching hands and encourage them to use a good grasp with their preferred hand.
14. Have groups switch activities after approximately 10 minutes.
15. Hang small pictures next to large mural and discuss what the children see. Ask them to identify the colors of the rainbow.

Adaptations:
1. Built-up handles, using foam or a cloth wrapped around the handle, or brushes with an adapted grasp, will afford the child with less-refined grasp patterns more control and greater success.
2. Children with decreased balance or strength can paint on the mural while sitting in a chair.

3. Children with impaired vision can have outlines of rainbow stripes that are raised using Elmer's glue (allow to dry 4 to 6 hours).

Multilevel Instruction:

1. Children can name colors.
2. Children can read names of colors.
3. Children can color rainbow according to actual color of rainbows: red, orange, yellow, green, blue, indigo, and violet.

March

Letter to Parents

Rainbow Mural

Your child made two beautiful rainbows this week. The children made a large rainbow as a group project using mural paper and bingo markers. Another rainbow was smaller and was made individually by applying paint to paper using Q-Tips.

Purpose of the Activity

Making the rainbow mural provided a great deal of "heavy work" for the children. "Heavy work" means that the activity involves bearing weight through the arms or legs, as in jumping and crawling, or moving the muscles vigorously, as in propelling a scooter board. For children who need them, "heavy work" activities help the child become more focused and alert when used on a consistent basis. They also help the child who is overly sensitive to touch and/or movement become more tolerant of these sensations.

After the children used the markers to make a rainbow, the paper was hung on the wall. The markers, which are like bingo markers, are heavy, and when the children hold them to press against a wall, they are helping to strengthen the muscles in their wrists and hands. These are the same muscles that they need for using crayons and scissors in the classroom. A high degree of eye-hand coordination and control was needed to complete the small rainbow picture. The children were encouraged to hold the Q-Tip as they would hold a pencil (tripod grasp) which gave them a lot of practice for pre-writing and writing activities in the classroom.

Home Activities to Help Your Child Grow

By writing and drawing on vertical surfaces, such as a wall-mounted chalkboard, your child will further develop his or her arm strength and endurance. You can send them outside with a brush and bucket of water and encourage them to "paint" the outside of the house or the sidewalk. Bingo markers can generally be found at dollar stores, and it is very exciting for young children to use them to create masterpieces. The markers are heavier than regular paintbrushes, and because of this, they provide a lot of feedback to the user about how his or her arm and hand are being used. Many children who do not yet have the control to color with a crayon or paintbrush enjoy these markers.

March

Windsocks

Activity Goals: Pre-Writing Skills Development
Body-Scheme and Motor-Planning Improvement

Time: 20-to-30 minutes

Objectives: Upon successful completion of this activity, the child will be able to
1. Color within oak tag strip.
2. Use stapler to attach streamers to oak tag strip.
3. Use hole-punch to punch holes in oak tag.
4. String yarn through holes in oak tag.
5. Imitate movements of leader.

Materials: For each windsock:
1. Oak tag paper; 3-by-24-inch strip
2. 20 inch length of yarn
3. Four 24 inch streamers
4. Crayons
5. Hole punch (to be used by group)
6. Stapler (to be used by group)
7. Music

Procedure:
1. Cut oak tag, streamers, and yarn into correct lengths prior to group.
2. Each child colors/decorates her oak tag strip. They can decorate both sides.
3. Child can staple 4 streamers to each oak tag strip.
4. Child can help staple oak tag strip together so that it forms a circle.
5. Child can help punch 2 holes in top of oak tag (opposite side of streamers). Holes should be placed opposite one another.
6. Child can string yarn through both holes in oak tag. Adult ties ends of string together.
7. Children stand up and get in line. Adult begins playing music.
8. Adult, who is leading the line, performs movements that children follow (e.g., holding windsock above head and marching, holding windsock out to the sides and jumping).
9. Children sit down and recall steps involved in making windsock.

Adaptations:
1. For child who has difficulty using crayons, markers can be used as they offer less resistance.
2. Children can stand while using stapler. They can use more body power in this position.
3. Place tape on the end of yarn to make it easier to string through the holes.

Multilevel Instruction:
1. Children can cut out their own oak tag strips
2. Children can draw a specific scene on the oak tag (e.g., flowers, clouds, or pattern).
3. Children can write their names on the oak tag.

Letter to Parents
Windsocks

This week we talked about the wind. Then, the children made windsocks out of oak tag paper and crepe paper streamers. They decorated the windsocks, helped assemble them, and ran and walked with the windsocks trailing behind them.

Purpose of the Activity

The children used crayons to decorate their windsocks. They were encouraged to use a tripod or mature grasp on the crayon and to stay within the boundaries of the paper. Using a mature grasp during crayon use is good practice for later handwriting skills. The children practiced using a stapler and hole punch while assembling the windsock. The deep pressure required to use these tools gave the children good input on where their hands were in space and required them to use hand and arm strength. Waving the windsocks to music encouraged the children to use large arm movements, another activity that builds strength and endurance, and to move in rhythm to the beat of the music.

Activities to Help Your Child Grow

Your child can practice many pre-Writing activities at home. Generally, by the age of 4-½ years, children usually demonstrate a hand preference during fine-motor tasks and should be encouraged to use a preferred hand during pre-Writing tasks, such as coloring. At home, your child can have fun developing pre-Writing skills by using sidewalk chalk, painting on the driveway with water or using his index finger to "write" in dirt or sand.

March

Educational Goals by Activity

Attention Improvement	Balance Improvement	Bilateral Coordination Development	Body-Scheme and Motor-Planning Improvement	Cognitive Development	Fine-Motor Skills Development	Gross-Motor Skills Development	Group Development	Hand-Dominance Development	Pre-Writing Skills Development	Scissor Skills Development	Self-Help Skills Development	Sensory Processing Improvement	Strength and Endurance Improvement	Visual-Perceptual Development	Activity	Page
			✔			✔									Baseball and Softball Practice	202
✔													✔		Boats. Bridges, and Kites	205
									✔				✔		Butterflies	207
		✔											✔		Egg and Log Rolling	210
			✔			✔									Jump Rope and Baseball	212
						✔							✔		The Nimble Cow	214
			✔				✔								Silly Spring Eggs	216
			✔										✔		Stars and Rolling	218
			✔										✔		"This Old Man" at "London Bridge"	220
						✔	✔								"A Tisket, a Tasket and "In and Out the Windows"	222

April

Baseball and Softball Practice

Activity Goals: Body-Scheme and Motor-Planning Improvement
Gross-Motor Skills Development

Time: 20-to-30 minutes

Objectives: Upon successful completion of this activity, the child will be able to
1. Throw an adapted ball to a partner.
2. Catch an adapted ball from a partner.
3. Imitate a series of motor schemes with verbal and visual prompts.

Materials:
1. Tennis or Wiffle balls—enough for half the class
2. Long tube socks—enough for half the class
3. Picture of a baseball or softball player
4. Rug squares or masking tape to make squares on the floor

Procedure:
1. Gather children in a circle and describe the game of baseball or softball with emphasis on the practice and the conditioning part of spring workouts. Show the children a picture of a softball or baseball player.
2. Using rug squares, space children to allow for enough room between them to stretch out while exercising.
3. Start with this stretching routine:
   a. Standing upright, have children stretch arms over head, out to sides, then attempt to reach toward toes.
   b. Spread 10-to-12 inches. Have the children take their right hand and rotate to stretch toward their left foot and then perform the opposite stretch.
   c. Sitting on the rug square with feet together, have the students stretch up in the air then stretch toward their feet.
   d. Sitting on the rug square, have the children spread their feet approximately 10" apart then reach with both hands toward the right foot. Go back to neutral position; then stretch to the left foot with both hands together.

Note: Repeat all these stretches 5-10 times and do so slowly—you can play music during the stretches that would promote rhythmic movement and slow stretching.
4. Once the stretching is completed, set up students with partners standing 5-7 feet apart and facing each other.
5. Place tennis or Wiffle balls all the way inside the tube socks.
6. Show children how to throw the ball inside the sock. Have them practice by placing their hand over the ball inside the sock not on the tail. This permits better control and encourages proper throwing skills.
7. Have the student practice catching the ball. The tube sock adds extra length to catching time and slows the ball slightly.
8. Set up partner and have the children attempt to throw and catch ball with their partners.

Adaptations:
1. Try using a beach ball or a Gertie Ball˚, which are slower moving balls, to slow the speed of the ball for the child with poor hand skills.

Learning in Motion

2. For students using wheelchairs, have them perform the stretches in the chair.

3. For the visually impaired student, teach exercises hand over hand.

Multilevel Instruction:

1. Have the children roll a large ball to each other.

2. Make the game more challenging by removing the tube sock or increasing the distance between the partners.

April

Letter to Parents
Baseball and Softball Practice

This week we talked about rites of spring. They included flowers, trees blooming, birds singing and baseball season. Today we did conditioning and stretching exercises as our warm up. Then we practiced throwing and catching a special ball.

Purpose of the Activity

Working on these exercises involved visually attending to the demonstration and listening to the verbal directions while in a group. Many learning situations in school involve processing information that is presented both visually and auditorily while in a large group. Often, there is a motor component involved with the teacher's directions such as, "Go over to the board and write that word." This is how art projects, gym classes, and learning to make letters and numbers are taught. The teacher demonstrates the movements necessary to complete certain activities and the children are required to reproduce them.

Home Activities to Help Your Child Grow

We worked on ball throwing and catching this week. Children need these skills when they begin to learn group games and activities. In many communities, sports activities are a means of socialization for children. The child who can throw and catch a ball will feel more confident in community sports, at the playground, and during gym class. To work best on ball skills, start with your young child rolling a ball and catching it by trapping it with his or her body. Throwing skills come before catching.

Have your child practice throwing balls at targets. Start with a playground ball and encourage your child to throw it with both hands. Change the position and increase the distance of the target as your child improves in this skill. Begin catching with a safe, slow moving ball such as a beach ball, balloon, or a Nerf ball. Encourage your child to try to catch the ball with both hands and cue your child to "Keep your eyes on the ball." Throw the ball slowly and make sure your child is attending. Later, when your child's skills improve, you can change to a smaller ball. You can place a small ball in the toe of a tube sock. This will increase your child's catching success rate.

April

Boats, Bridges, and Kites

Activity Goals: Attention Improvement

Strength and Endurance Improvement

Time: 20-to-30 minutes

Objectives: Upon successful completion of this activity, the child will be able to

1. Hold a static crab position for 1-to-2 minutes
2. Use musical cues to start and stop movement
3. Commando crawl forward 3-to-5 feet

Materials:
1. Children's music
2. Streamers
3. Picture of a kite

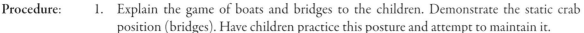

Procedure:
1. Explain the game of boats and bridges to the children. Demonstrate the static crab position (bridges). Have children practice this posture and attempt to maintain it.
2. Break the class into small groups and form "bridges" around the open area of the room.
3. Have the first group get into the static crab position (bridge) and hold it while the other children take turns commando crawling (arm crawl) under the bridges.
4. Reverse roles and change the bridges as frequently as needed.
5. Then gather the children back into the circle to talk about kites and show them a picture of a kite. Explain how the kite flies in the air driven by the wind. Tell the children that they are going to pretend that the music is the wind, and when the music stops, the wind and the kites stop.
6. Demonstrate how the kite will float around the room by having your arms outstretched, holding a streamer or streamers in one or both hands.
7. Have children practice being a kite while holding the streamer (kite tail).
8. Introduce the music and demonstrate to the group how to start and stop the floating kite movement with the music.

Adaptations:
1. For the children unable to hold the streamer, tape the streamer around the child's wrist and encourage arm movement to make the kite tail move.
2. For the child unable to hold a static crab position, try having him or her assume and hold a bear walk posture (bend over at the waist and place hands and feet on the floor).
3. For the child unable to commando crawl, try pushing the child under the bridges while lying on his or her stomach on a scooter board.
4. For the child using a wheelchair, have him or her go through a drawbridge (children stand up facing each other and hold hands) while standing approximately 24-30 inches apart.

Multilevel Instruction:
1. Make the activity of getting through the bridges a sequential memory task by establishing patterns such as: "Go under Tom, to Katie, to Jennifer, to Eric," etc.
2. Just have one bridge and have each child take a turn climbing through.
3. Make up a pattern with streamer movement to music and have the children imitate the pattern.

April

Letter to Parents
Boats, Bridges, and Kites

This week we pretended to sail our boats on the lake and fly kites in the wind. We each had a turn to make our bodies into bridges and hold still while our friends commando crawled under us, pretending to be the boats. While holding on to streamers and listening to music, we pretended to fly on the wind; but when the music stopped, we stopped.

Purpose of the Activity

All the activities we did this week involved holding our bodies in different patterns or imitating the teacher's movement patterns. We also had to attend to music (auditory attention) to stop and start our kite flying. The activities worked on building our body strength, balance, and imitation skills. The child needs to be able to hold a static position often in school, e.g., when sitting in his or her desk, standing in line, working at the chalkboard, etc. These activities will help your child build strength and endurance necessary for these school postures. This activity also builds cooperation and turn-taking skills for the children in the group. In school, it is important for your child to be able to wait for his or her turn to answer questions, use the water fountain, swing on the swing, play with the blocks, etc.

Home Activities to Help Your Child Grow

Staying in one a position and using large muscles of the body can be made into a game at home. Most children love the "Freeze Game." Children start the game by dancing to music. When you periodically stop the music, the children must freeze in their positions. Increase the challenge by moving from simple dance to more difficult movement patterns, such as jumping on one foot, walking heel and toe, skipping to music, etc. Stop the music and see if they can hold these positions for five-to-ten seconds before starting the music again. Maintaining a "frozen" posture will require your child to attend and use balance, strength, and muscle control.

April

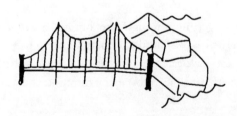

Butterflies

Activity Goals:	Pre-Writing Skills Development
	Visual-Perceptual Development
Time:	20-to-30 minutes

Objectives: Upon successful completion of this activity, the child will be able to
1. Refine control of his pincer grasp
2. Squeeze a clip clothespin to open it
3. Follow two-step verbal command with visual cues
4. Visually attend to a fine-motor task for 2 minutes

Materials:
1. Food coloring
2. Vinegar
3. Automatic coffee filters
4. Eye droppers
5. Clip clothespins
6. Black crayon
7. Pipe cleaner
8. Picture and completed model of a butterfly

Procedure:
1. Pre-mix the food color and water with a tablespoon of vinegar in small shallow bowls or cups. You only need to make up 2-3 ounces of colored water for a group of 10 children.
2. Gather children at the table and show them the finished butterfly and butterfly picture.
3. Give each child a coffee filter.
4. Place one eyedropper in each colored water cup and pass it around. Let each child squeeze one dropper of each color on his or her coffee filter. Use all colors; then start a second pass with the colors if the children have not yet colored most of the coffee filter.
5. While the coffee filter is drying either on a line by the window or over the heater, give each child a clip clothespin.
6. Demonstrate how to color the entire clothespin (butterfly's body) with the black crayon.
7. When the coffee filter is dry, demonstrate how to gather up the coffee filter in the middle and clip on the clothespin.
8. Gently spread the coffee filter (butterfly wings) on either side of the clothespin.
9. Take a black pipe cleaner and wrap it around the top end of the clothespin to make the antennae.
10. Add a string or self-adhesive magnet strip to the back of the butterfly.

Adaptations:
1. For the child with poor finger pinch or hand use, try using a large-handled paintbrush to apply the dye water—or bingo markers can be used to make the design on the butterfly.
2. For the child with a visual impairment, place the coffee filter in a pie tin to provide a boundary.

April

Multilevel
Instruction:

1. Instead of an eyedropper, try the same procedure using straws to apply the color to the coffee filter. Place straws in the colored water and have the child place his thumb over the top opening until ready to dispense on the coffee filter. The colored water will run out of the straw when the child moves his thumb off the top of the straw.

2. Have the children paint the clothespin with black paint.

Letter to Parents

Butterflies

This week, we used coffee filters, food coloring, eyedroppers, and clip clothespins to make butterflies.

Purpose of the Activity

In this activity, we used eyedroppers to drop the colored water on our coffee filters. Controlling the fluid in the eyedropper and squeezing the proper amount in the area needed requires refined pinch. This type of control is needed for fine-motor activities such as drawing, writing and tracing. While

waiting for the wings of the butterfly to dry, we colored the clip clothespin black. While coloring this small object, we used both hands together in a dominant-assist pattern; that is, one hand stabilized the clothespin while the other colored it. When children are coloring, writing, or cutting with scissors, they must use both hands together: one to stabilize or manipulate the paper and the other to use the pencil, crayon, or scissors.

Home Activities to Help Your Child Grow

Developing grip and pinch strength is necessary for children to be able to perform self-care skills, such as buttoning, zippering, and opening food packages. There are many common objects around the house that you can use to help your child develop hand and finger strength. For the young child, have him or her pick up soft and small objects with toaster or salad tongs. Picking up sponge pieces, cotton balls, beanbags, paper balls, or small stuffed animals can help to develop grip strength. Let your child pick up small objects with tweezers.

Allowing your child to help you clean the table by spraying it with a small spray bottle filled with water, or painting the concrete with a spray bottle or paint brush, will also build arm and hand strength. For the older or more physically mature child, have him or her use clip clothespins to place around the edge of a plastic container. Set up art activities that can be painted using an eyedropper filled with paint or small pieces of sponge dipped in paint. Try these and other activities to help your child build finger and pinch strength needed for independence in self-care and school activities.

April

Egg and Log Rolling

Activity Goals: Strength and Endurance Improvement
Bilateral Coordination Development

Time: 20 minutes

Objectives: Upon successful completion of this activity, the child will be able to
1. Hold a tucked position with head and knees to roll a distance of 6 feet
2. Roll with straight body, arms above head for a distance of 6 feet

Materials:
1. Large mat or carpeted floor

Procedure:
1. Gather children around mat or rolling area. Have a child demonstrate egg rolling. The child brings knees to chest, holding his knees with both hands and tucking his chin to his chest. In this position, the child rolls from one side of the mat to the other.
2. Each child takes a turn or several turns performing this pattern of egg rolling.
3. Gather the children together again and demonstrate log rolling. The child straightens out his body with arms straight overhead. The child rolls from one side of the mat to the other.
4. Have the children each take several turns.

Adaptations:
1. For the child unable to roll in either position, provide hands on assistance and practice in this posture.
2. For the child who has a visual impairment, provide hands on assistance and/or verbal cues to learn this new motor pattern.

Multilevel Instruction:
1. First practice holding an egg-roll position with knees to chest using arms around knees and chin tucked to chest. Then practice rocking side to side in this position before practicing rolling.
2. Use an incline mat to facilitate downward rolling in these postures.
3. To increase the challenge, provide incline mats and have the children roll up the mats in the log-roll or egg-roll posture.
4. While rolling in an egg-roll posture, have the child hold a bean bag under his chin.
5. While rolling in a log-roll posture, have the children hold a softball or stuffed animal above their heads.

April

Learning in Motion

Letter to Parents
Egg and Log Rolling

This week we practiced egg and log rolling. To roll like an egg, we hugged our knees to our chests with our arms as we tucked our chin to our chest. To do a log roll, we stretched our bodies straight and put our hands above our heads and rolled, trying to roll straight across the floor.

Purpose of the Activity

Rolling and holding these body postures provides the child with sensory input and strengthens the entire body. For the child to be able to hold these postures demands strength and endurance. The child then works to move his or her body across the floor in one direction, adding coordination of the two sides of the body to achieve this feat. Vestibular or movement sense is stimulated by this rolling activity. This type of input can have a positive effect on the child's ability to attend and visually focus on activities. Strength, endurance, and the ability to visually focus on tasks are important in the school environment especially when the child is trying to learn new visually presented information such as spelling words or following the teacher's directions.

Home Activities to Help Your Child Grow

Rolling activities such as these can be done inside or outside. With the nice weather, go outside and try rolling on different surfaces and terrains. You can try rolling down or up a hill, over a bumpy area, on grass or sand, etc. Indoors, you can set up pillows or sofa cushions to roll over. Have your child pretend to be a giant steamroller as he or she rolls over the different surfaces, terrains, and materials.

April

Jump Rope and Baseball

Activity Goals: Body-Scheme and Motor-Planning Improvement

Gross-Motor Skills Development

Time: 30-to-40 minutes

Objectives: Upon successful completion of this activity, the child will be able to

1. Jump and clear the ground
2. Hit a suspended ball with a bat
3. Catch a yarn ball with both hands
4. Visually attend to an activity for 2-to-3 minutes

Materials:
1. 8-to-10 foot rope
2. Yarn balls, pompoms or Wiffle balls
3. String
4. Streamers
5. Masking tape
6. Empty paper towel roll

Procedure:
1. Set up by placing two six-foot-long streamers five feet apart.
2. Demonstrate for the group the following jumping patterns: jump across the streamers, jump sideways over the streamers and jump backward over the streamers.
3. The children practice these jumping patterns.
4. Set up the jumping rope by attaching one end to a stable base.
5. Hold the rope two-to-four inches above the ground and demonstrate the same jumping patterns as above.
6. Have the children practice jumping over the rope.
7. Tie string to yarn ball and suspend from the ceiling or other surface to reach the child at approximately 3" below shoulder height.
8. Demonstrate hitting pattern with empty paper towel roll.
9. Give each child one or several opportunities to try to hit the ball with the paper towel roll.

Adaptations:
1. For the child with a visual impairment use a high-contrast ball or place a bell on the ball to reinforce and encourage the child to hit it. Give verbal cues as needed and provide a small rug square as a means to position the child near the ball.
2. For the child with decreased motor ability or a wheelchair user, set up an obstacle course instead of asking for a jumping pattern.
3. For the child unable to bat the ball due to decreased strength, place the ball on a tabletop or lap tray and allow the child to hit it with the paper towel roll or his hands.

Multilevel Instruction:
1. Start this activity by jumping on a trampoline or foam pad to reinforce the idea of jumping. Encourage the children to bend their knees and clear the ground as they jump.
2. Raise the height of the rope as the children easily clear it.
3. Use a batting tee or throw the ball to the batter.
4. Move the rope up and down in a wave motion when the children try and jump over the rope (High-Low Waters).

April

Learning in Motion

Letter to Parents
Jump Rope and Baseball

This week we played jump rope and baseball. We practiced jumping forward, sideways, and backwards. Our teacher made this more challenging by taking a jump rope and raising it off the ground while we practiced jumping again. We practiced our batting swing by taking a paper towel roll and hitting a suspended ball. Then we practiced throwing and catching with yarn balls.

Purpose of the Activity

The activities we practiced today are helpful for developing skills needed later for real jump rope and baseball. Some areas that are developed in these activities are visual attention, eye-hand coordination, hip and leg strength, and the motor planning skills needed to execute these demanding activities. The ability to attend to visual information and motor planning skills is also important in academic situations, such as reading, handwriting, and cutting with scissors.

Home Activities to Help Your Child Grow

At home, you can help your child develop visual attention using batting and ball skills. Take a softball size Wiffle® ball and suspend it from an inside doorway. Place the Wiffle ball at the child's eye level. Instruct your child to hold the paper towel roll with one hand on either end (like a rolling pin, not a baseball bat). Make a game out of trying to hit the ball and keep it moving. This involves sustained visual attention, eye-hand coordination, visual tracking, and upper-body strength. You can add stickers to the ball to make it more appealing. For a younger or less-experienced child, try the same activity by suspending a balloon and use the same hitting pattern of both hands on the empty paper towel roll, dowel, or rolling pin.

April

The Nimble Cow

Activity Goals: Gross-Motor Skills Development
Visual-Perceptual Development

Time: 20 minutes

Objectives: Upon successful completion of this activity, the child will be able to
1. Jump over a four-inch-high object without falling
2. Plan a running jump to clear a four inch high wall of blocks
3. Perform a standing jump
4. Listen for a cue word to start a jump

Materials:
1. Large plastic or cardboard blocks and/or a wide-based candle
2. Several blocks set up in a row with a paper moon crescent attached to the front of the blocks

Procedure:
1. Have the teacher set up a 4" candle or block in a vertical position. Also set up 4 or 5 large blocks horizontally to create a low wall. Tape on the cardboard or oak tag crescent moon-shape in the front and middle of the low wall.
2. Gather children in the circle to explain and repeat the two nursery rhymes "Jack Be Nimble" and "The Cow Jumped Over the Moon."
3. Demonstrate to the children how to perform a standing jump over the candle and a running jump over the moon. Explain to the children that they will all have a turn to try jumping over the candle and the moon.
4. As each child takes his turn, the teacher and children repeat the appropriate nursery rhyme. When jumping over the moon, the teacher and children repeat the rhyme. The jumping child must listen for the cue phrase "The Cow Jumped Over the Moon" and start his running jump then.
5. The teacher and children repeat the "Jack Be Nimble" rhyme while the jumping child practices a standing jump over the candle.

Adaptations:
1. For the child unable to jump over the candle or the moon, try walking over the candle.
2. For the child using a wheelchair, have them push their chair either over or around the obstacle.
3. For the child with a hearing impairment, you can sign the nursery rhyme.

Multilevel Instruction:
1. Set up several candles/blocks in a row about 2-3 feet apart and have the children jump over them in a series.
2. Beginning jumpers could jump from one rug square to another, or over a paper moon or candle taped to the floor. Encourage the children to jump with both feet together.
3. Pre-jumping groups could bunny hop (jump with both feet together) to the candle or moon.
4. If available, try using a trapeze and teaching the children to swing over the candle.

Letter to Parents

The Nimble Cow

This week, we did jumping activities related to two nursery rhymes. During one rhyme, "Jack Be Nimble," we pretended to jump over the candle; and during the other, "The Cow Jumped Over the Moon," we pretended to run and jump over our paper moon.

Purpose of the Activity

Jumping over stationery objects, either from a standing position or while running, involves planning our body's movement with appropriate speed, direction, force, and timing. This requires a complex coordination of a number of factors including: visual perception, attention to the task, prior movement experiences, and memory. All of these factors help your child move with confidence in a new or unfamiliar setting. Attention to task and ability to coordinate movements help your child to refine fine-motor skills as well as to reinforce spatial concepts such as over, next to, and on top.

Home Activities to Help Your Child Grow

Any task that involves jumping over, in, on top of, next to, etc., will help your child develop motor planning skills. I am sure many of us remember childhood games such as "Don't Step on the Crack," "High, Low Waters," and "Snake or Waves" (moving a rope along the ground and trying to jump over it). These activities were games that helped us learn to visually attend better and refine our timing and motor planning skills. Try to introduce these games to your children or play similar types of games during daily tasks. For example, have your child jump on the dark colored tile squares at the supermarket or at home, place a rug square and other non-slip mats on the floor and have your child pretend to be a goat hopping from rock to rock. Jumping over puddles or leaves on the ground will help your child further develop visual perception and gross-motor skills.

April

Silly Spring Eggs

Activity Goals: Body-Scheme and Motor-Planning Improvement
Group Development

Time: 20-to-30 minutes

Objectives: Upon successful completion of this activity, the child will be able to
1. Follow two-step verbal directions.
2. Work together with another classmate.
3. Match 6 body parts with verbal commands.

Materials:
1. Egg-shaped foam cut from about 1"-2" thick foam rubber. Cut one for each child and make the eggs approximately 6 inches in size
2. Spinner from a game, adapted to include body parts such as, hand, wrist, elbow, knee, shoulder, head, hip, etc.
3. Rug square or other target area

Procedure:
1. This game is a cross between Twister and a three-legged race. Use two children to demonstrate how the game is played. One child gets the foam egg. The spinner from the Twister® game is spun to tell him which body part to hold it with; and then his partner is directed to use another body part, based on a spin. For example, the child with the foam egg might get "wrist" and his partner may get "elbow." They try to hold the egg between one child's wrist and the other's elbow.
2. Then the partners attempt to walk to a rug square or other target, approximately 6 feet away, and walk back to the starting position.
3. Those partners return to their seats or rugs squares and the next pair begins.
4. Repeat the activity several times and allow each pair to have one or more turns.
5. Use the game to review body parts such as shoulder, neck, forehead, chin, shoulder, hip, ankle, heel, calf, forearm, wrist, thumb and palm.

Adaptations:
1. For the child who is restricted in movement, pick body parts on the upper body or areas that you know the children can reach. For example, the child using a wheelchair may get "palm" and his partner may get "thumb."
2. For the child with a visual impairment, first give the instructions, and then allow the children to cooperate together and find the body parts. To help this pair walk together, the visually able child might need to let the child with a visual impairment hold his elbow.

Multilevel Instruction:
1. Vary the way the children walk to the target and back to the starting position. For example, have them walk sideways, backwards, etc.
2. Use flashcards with body part names on them. Each partner picks a card from the pile and the pair performs the activity.
3. Use just one body part per pair. The partners try to carry the foam egg with their shoulders, hips, thumbs, etc.
4. Do this activity as a relay race. Have one pair start the race and the next pair pick up the egg and move toward the target in the same manner until all pairs have competed.

April

Learning in Motion

Letter to Parents

Silly Spring Eggs

This week we played a funny game called "Silly Spring Eggs." Using a spinner, each child was given a body part to help hold an "egg." We tried to carry our eggs (foam rubber shapes) with a partner using different parts of our bodies and not drop them until we reached our teacher. This game was a combination of a three-legged race and the game Twister˸.

Purpose of the Activity

This activity helped to develop the children's ability to motor-plan novel activities and learn body parts at the same time. The internal knowledge gained by these types of motor and sensory experiences helps your child become more efficient when learning new motor activities. It also helps your child develop balance, strength, awareness of others, and the ability to cooperate with a partner. The ability to work cooperatively with others is an important school and life skill.

Home Activities to Help Your Child Grow

Children really enjoy doing activities in novel or "silly" ways. This novelty is what enhances motor planning and makes motor learning in the future easier. Try to make games out of everyday activities. When your child needs to put her coat away, have her carry the coat to the closet on her elbow. Or, have your child carry a beanbag to the toy chest on his or her knee, wrist, hip, or back. You can think up many more inventive motor-planning games to play during everyday activities.

April

Stars and Rolling

Activity Goals: Body-Scheme and Motor-Planning Improvement

Visual-Perceptual Development

Time: 20-to-30 minutes

Objectives: Upon successful completion of this activity, the child will be able to

1. Roll down an incline
2. Roll up an incline
3. Roll toward a target
4. Throw a beanbag 3-to-5 feet at a 36-inch target

Materials:
1. Large incline mat or an inclined surface, such as a ramp
2. Large mat
3. Plastic sand bucket
4. Flashlight
5. Three Hula Hoops®
6. 4-5 beanbags or pompoms

Procedure:
1. Gather children together and explain the movements for the nursery rhyme, "Jack and Jill."
2. Have children practice repeating the rhyme as they do the activities.
3. Have a child demonstrate rolling down the incline.
4. Let each child take a turn rolling down the incline.
5. Have one child demonstrate rolling up the incline.
6. Let each child take a turn rolling up the incline.
7. On a large mat or rug, set a bucket up at one end or one corner. Have the children try to knock over the bucket as they roll to it. This is like body bowling.
8. Gather the children and read them the nursery rhyme "Twinkle, Twinkle, Little Star."
9. Set up three Hula Hoops in a line approximately three feet away from the children. Conduct the game in a darkened room. Have a child stand three feet away but in the middle of the line of hoops. Shine a flashlight inside one hoop and that is the hoop the child is aiming for with her beanbag. Cue the child with "See if you can throw your beanbag inside the twinkling star's hoop."
10. Give each child a chance to throw four or five beanbags and change the hoop lighted by the flashlight for each try.

Adaptations:
1. For the child unable to roll independently, assist the child to roll down the ramp or incline.
2. For the child with a visual impairment, give verbal cues about the location of the light such as "It's in the hoop right in front of you or off to your right," etc.

Multilevel Instruction:
1. Have the children hold a large softball or toy above their heads as they roll.
2. Have the children roll with their eyes closed.
3. Try to set up several things on the mat and let the children choose which one they will roll into and knock over with their bodies. The teacher can set up a bowling set on the mat and have the children attempt to knock down as many pins as they can by rolling into them.

April

Learning in Motion

Letter to Parents

Stars and Rolling

This week we pretended to be "Jack and Jill." We had an opportunity to roll down and then roll up a hill. We also had a turn rolling toward a toy and knocking it over. Our teacher told us the nursery rhyme, "Twinkle, Twinkle, Little Star." Then we played a game where we had to throw our beanbags inside the hoop where the twinkle star (a flashlight beam) landed.

Purpose of the Activity

This activity incorporates movement of the body with visual input. In order to roll down the hill, both sides of the body have to work in opposite patterns, while visually the child must locate the end of the mat. Rolling activities help to develop motor planning skills, visual tracking skills, eye-hand coordination, and overall body strength. These areas of motor and visual-perceptual development are important for the young child when he or she needs to copy from the chalkboard and form letters and numbers on paper.

Home Activities to Help Your Child Grow

Children love flashlight play and it can be fun to incorporate into a bedtime activity. While your child is lying in bed in a darkened room, have him or her hold a flashlight with both hands and attempt to follow your slowly moving flashlight beam around the room. Or, try turning on your flashlight and have your child find your beam with his or her flashlight as quickly as he or she can. You can also turn your light on an object in the room quickly and have your child tell you where the light is shining. This is a great way to increase your child's ability to visually track movement, visually attend, and quickly locate an object while increasing his or her vocabulary.

April

"This Old Man" at "London Bridge"

Activity Goals: Body-Scheme and Motor-Planning Improvement
Visual-Perceptual Development

Time: 20-to-30 minutes

Objectives: Upon successful completion of this activity, the child will be able to

1. Follow a series of five motor patterns in imitation
2. Isolate finger motion needed to demonstrate finger counting to ten
3. Climb over and under obstacles without falling
4. Demonstrate concept of over and under while performing a motor skill

Materials:
1. Words and music from the nursery rhymes, "This Old Man" and "London Bridge"

Procedure:
1. Explain the nursery rhyme "This Old Man." Have the children practice the routine with you to learn the motor sequence to the rhyme. Remember that children will need multiple practices over several days and weeks to learn the complete sequence.
2. Slowly practice together the motor sequence of the rhyme.
3. Next, demonstrate the "London Bridge" rhyme.
4. Have the children practice being the bridge: practice the motor sequence of raising both arms overhead for "all built up," arms at waist height for "½ built up," and children squatting with hands near the floor for "all fall down."
5. Choose two children to be the bridge. Have the others take turns going under (or over) the bridge, with the teacher and children repeating the nursery rhyme. Have the children decide which way to perform the motor skill: standing, crouching, or crawling under the bridge or stepping over the bridge.
6. Exchange roles and allow the children who were the bridge to join in and pick two new children to create the bridge.

Adaptations:
1. For children with visual impairments or motor planning problems, teach the motor sequence for the rhymes with hand-over-hand assistance to provide physical modeling.
2. To help the child with a communication or hearing impairment, the rhymes for "This Old Man" and others are fun for all the children to learn in American Sign Language.
3. To help the child with limited expressive language, have him use a switch, cards, or an augmentative communication device to say the numbers during the "This Old Man" rhyme.
4. Children who use a wheelchair can easily be half of the bridge while playing "London Bridges."

Multilevel Instruction:
1. Have each child perform a sequence for "This Old Man." For example, one child would be doing all of "one," next child would do all of "two," etc.
2. Have the group try to say and perform the "This Old Man" rhyme slowly, then quickly.

April

Letter to Parents
"This Old Man" at "London Bridge"

This week we listened to two nursery rhymes. The first one was "This Old Man." We learned a motor play to go with the rhyme. Then we played "London Bridge" and tried to get either over or under the bridge.

Purpose of the Activity

While playing "This Old Man" we worked on learning to imitate and remember a sequence of motor actions. This requires a good sense of our body, visual attention, and memory of the movements. This ability to remember a sequence for motor movements is important later in school, because to form letters correctly, we need to remember what direction to move our hand. Also, much information in school is presented visually by the teacher, so your child will need to attend to this information to be able to perform the tasks.

The second activity involved climbing over and under "London Bridge." Your child needs to have good awareness of his body scheme or image and the ability to use visual information to judge size and position to perform this activity. These skills of spatial awareness and visual perception will help the child with learning concepts like size, shape, distance, and figure-ground perception.

Home Activities to Help Your Child Grow

Learning finger plays and motor imitation to music or rhymes can be another way to help your child learn new information. We all know that the child often learns to sing the alphabet before saying it. Using songs and rhymes as ways to remember information can help a child learn rote skills such as letters, numbers and counting, colors, months of the year, and days of the week. Using this method as a way to help your child learn also develops memory and auditory attention. Often, along with the rhymes, we practice motor sequences such as "This Little Piggy" or 'The Noble Duke of York." By adding motor sequences, we tap into another area of the brain that helps reinforce the learned information and aids in recalling it. Ask your child to show you how to perform "This Old Man."

April

"A Tisket, a Tasket" and "In and Out the Windows"

Activity Goals: Group Development

Gross-Motor Skills Development

Time: 20-to-30 minutes

Objectives: Upon successful completion of this activity, the child will be able to

1. Step over an obstacle 6-to-12 inches off the floor without falling
2. Carry a one-pound to two-pound weight
3. Play a game cooperatively with simple rules

Materials:
1. Bucket or a basket with a handle
2. A one-pound to two-pound weight or a cup of sand to use as weight

Procedure:
1. Gather children in a circle and talk about the nursery rhymes "In and Out the Windows" and "A Tisket, a Tasket, a Green and Yellow Basket."
2. Have the children form a circle holding hands with each other. Demonstrate the rhyme and the motor actions with it. When the rhyme says "In and out the windows," the children need to be standing and holding their hands up high. For "Up and down the door steps," the children need to crouch down and place their hands together near the floor. Have the children take turns weaving in and out of the circle. Physically direct the children initially or cue with masking tape or verbal cues.
3. Allow all the children to take a turn going through the windows and doors as the other children sing the nursery rhyme.
4. Make another circle and demonstrate the game that goes with the nursery rhyme "A Tisket, a Tasket, a Green and Yellow Basket." One child is given the basket or bucket with the weight inside. He either walks or skips around the circle while the children sing the rhyme. At the end of the rhyme, while the children are singing "He lost it, he lost it," he leaves the basket/bucket behind one child. That child then chases him and tries to get back in his space before the child who dropped the basket gets there. It is the same idea as "Duck, Duck, Goose" with visual, not verbal cues.
5. Give each child an opportunity to try to be the basket carrier.

Adaptations:
1. For the child using a wheelchair, when performing "In and Out the Windows," instead of going all the way to the floor for doorsteps have the children lower their hands to just above the child's head. For "A Tisket, a Tasket," have the child place the basket in his lap and have a physically capable child or adult push the child if he is unable to do this independently.
2. If the child is unable to bend or reach down to drop the basket to the floor, try placing a small rope on the basket handle and allow them to lower the basket to the floor.
3. For the child with visual impairment, performing these motor activities will involve physical assistance and verbal cues such as "Lift your foot and walk over the children's hands."
4. For the child with weak hands or decreased grip, you can enlarge the handle of the basket and/or decrease the weight in the basket.

Multilevel Instruction: If moving around a circle or in and out of the circle is too confusing for the group, try the same circle type games, but have the children holding hands standing in a straight line. Gradually increase the curve of the line until it becomes a circle.

Letter to Parents
"A Tisket, a Tasket" and "In and Out the Windows"

This week, we learned nursery rhymes and games to accompany them. We played "In and Out the Windows" in a big circle with our classmates. We each had a turn to go in and out of the circle while we sang the rhyme. Then, as we sang "A Tisket, a Tasket, a Green and Yellow Basket," we had a chance to drop the basket behind a friend.

Purpose of the Activity

"In and Out the Windows" involves using balance and planning movements as related to height, distance, and the correct perception of the child's body size and position. "A Tisket a Tasket" involves timing of the movements, listening skills, the ability to take turns and following multi-step directions. If your child has a good sense of his or her body (body scheme) and is confident and efficient when performing coordinated or novel activities, he or she will be better able to participate in school-related activities. Many refined motor activities such as cutting, coloring, writing, drawing, tracing, etc., are part of the educational program.

Home Activities to Help Your Child Grow

Planning activities that work on balance as well as size and height perception can be done easily at home. When you come home from shopping, have your child step in and out of shopping bags or large boxes. Also, help your child set up an obstacle course inside or outside. Use empty shoeboxes or large boxes to walk around or over, depending on the size of the box or the verbal directions you give. Try to save a large appliance box (from an oven, refrigerator, or computer) and make varied-size doors in it by using scissors or a knife to cut them on different sides of the box. Give your child a direction and see if he can go through all of the doors a certain way: standing up, crawling, kneeling, or on his stomach. This helps the child experiment with movement and body size. Leave this large box around as a playhouse or a quiet spot.

April

Educational Goals by Activity

May

Attention Improvement	Balance Improvement	Bilateral Coordination Development	Body-Scheme and Motor-Planning Improvement	Cognitive Development	Fine-Motor Skills Development	Gross-Motor Skills Development	Group Development	Hand-Dominance Development	Pre-Writing Skills Development	Scissor Skills Development	Self-Help Skills Development	Sensory Processing Improvement	Strength and Endurance Improvement	Visual-Perceptual Development	Activity	Page
			✔											✔	Balloon Tennis	226
		✔												✔	Balloon and Tennis Ball Games	228
		✔											✔		Big Ball Kick-Off I	232
	✔	✔													Big Ball Kick-Off II	234
											✔	✔			Edible Dirt	236
									✔	✔					Festive Boleros	238
		✔	✔												King Humpty Dumpty's Horses	240
						✔	✔								Large Ball Pass	242
											✔	✔			Moving Bugs	244
										✔		✔			Piñata	246
									✔					✔	Special Flowers	249
											✔			✔	Wash Day	251

Balloon Tennis

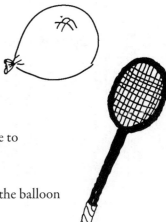

Activity Goals: Body-Scheme and Motor-Planning Improvement
Visual-Perceptual Development

Time: 20-to-30 minutes

Objectives: Upon successful completion of this activity, the child will be able to
1. Visually attend to an activity for two-to-three minutes
2. Hit a balloon with a racket
3. Isolate arm movement from body movement when striking the balloon

Materials:
1. Balloon
2. String
3. Metal clothes hangers (see appendix for instructions in making rackets)
4. Rug squares or other space-defining materials

Procedure:
1. Set up balloons suspended by a string at approximately the child's chest height.
2. Demonstrate batting the balloon with the racket. Encourage the child to watch the balloon and try to hit it consecutively while standing on a rug square. Tell the child that the rug square acts like the batter's box.
3. Let each child have a turn or several turns.
4. After practice with the racket and the suspended balloon, take the balloon off the string. Have the child practice hitting the balloon in the air with the racket. As each child takes a turn, the other children or teacher can count the times he or she hit the balloon in the air.

Adaptations:
1. For the child with visual impairments, place rice, beans, or bells inside the balloon. Also, place shiny or reflective ribbons on the ball to attract the child with low vision. In a darkened room, use a flashlight on the balloon with reflective ribbons to help the child focus on the object.
2. For the child unable to grasp the racket, try using Velcro catching mitts or disks on the child's hand to enlarge the surface of his or her hand.
3. Allow the child with poor balance, or in a wheelchair, to sit during this activity.

Multilevel Instruction:
1. Set up a rope with streamers hanging from it or a badminton or tennis net across half the area. Set the children up in pairs and have them try to hit the balloon with the racket across the net to their partners.
2. Play this game like balloon baseball. Set up bases and have the pitcher toss the balloon to the racket holder. If he or she hits the balloon, the batter runs the bases.
3. Instead of using a racket, try having the children hit the balloon with their hands.

Learning in Motion

Letter to Parents
Balloon Tennis

This week we played a special tennis game with a balloon and a homemade racket. We practiced hitting the balloon attached to a string suspended from the ceiling. After our practice, the teacher took our balloon off the string. Then we tried to hit the balloon with our racket and keep it in the air as long as we could.

Purpose of the Activity

Attempting to follow a slow moving target with our eyes and hands is a great way to increase visual attention and eye-hand coordination. Placing the balloon on the string and hitting it without moving helps the child build attention and motor planning skills.

Eye-hand coordination is important for ball skills and fine-motor activities. When reaching for an object, it is the coordination between the hands and eyes that helps us judge the distance, direction, height, and size of the object to be retrieved. Visual tracking, the ability to move the eyes to follow a target, is also reinforced in this activity. Visual tracking is an important school skill for reading, copying information from the board, watching the teacher at the front of the class, and finding information in books.

Home Activities to Help Your Child Grow

You can play some of the same games at home. Get a balloon or beach ball and make a racket from a metal clothes hanger stretched into an oval. The metal oval is then covered with a knee-high stocking. The hook part of the hanger is bent and folded in half. Tape up the handle or bent hook to eliminate sharp metal ends. You can play this game with your child inside or outside.

Start the game inside with the balloon attached to a string. Hang the balloon from the ceiling or a doorway. Have your child practice standing still and hitting the balloon. Later, as his or her skill improves, take the balloon off the string and see if your child can hit the balloon several times. Work on increasing repetition without missing or without the balloon falling to the ground. You can also play this game across a net with a partner (like tennis).

Balloon and Tennis Ball Games

Activity Goals: Bilateral Coordination Development
Visual-Perceptual Development

Time: 30 minutes

Objectives: Upon successful completion of this activity, the child will be able to

1. Balance himself using his trunk and legs to maintain posture while in prone, sitting, kneeling, standing, and half kneeling
2. Hit a balloon with a rolling pin using two hands
3. Sustain visual attention to a moving target for two-to-five minutes

Materials:
1. Scooter boards
2. Balloons
3. String
4. Rolling pins or foam pipe insulation cut into 2-foot lengths
5. Clip clothespins
6. Tennis ball or Nerf ball

Procedure:
1. Hang balloons from strings and use clip clothespins to vary distance of balloon from the floor. Balloon should be at chest height for the child sitting and kneeling and at eye level for the child lying on his stomach.
2. Demonstrate how to hit the balloon and keep it moving with one hand on each end of the rolling pins or on the rolling pin handles.
3. Have the children assume these different positions and hit the balloons with the rolling pins.
4. Hit the balloon while tall-kneeling, half-kneeling, sitting on the floor, and lying on his or her stomach.
5. Demonstrate to the children how to lie on their stomachs on scooter boards. Once on their stomachs, pair two children and have them face each other on the scooter boards 7-feet apart using the rolling pins as bats with one hand on each end. Goal of the game is to hit the tennis ball or Nerf ball back and forth.
6. If the tennis ball goes off track, the partner must move the scooter board to the ball while remaining on his stomach.
7. It helps to position the children near a wall on one side and place an upright folded mat as the other side wall.

Adaptations:
1. For the child who has difficulty with strength in one hand, wrap the weaker hand onto the rolling pin with an Ace® or similar elastic bandage. Try a lighter-weight bat such as a heavy cardboard roll from wrapping paper, a wooden dowel, a tube made from foam pipe insulation, or a piece of PVC pipe.
2. For the child who has a visual impairment, add rice, dry beans or bells inside the balloon before blowing it up.
3. For the child using a wheelchair, place the balloon at chest height for the child in the chair. For the tennis ball game, place the child using a wheelchair at one end of a table and another child at the other end with dowels or rolling pins. Place table against the

wall with the other side blocked by a mat or chair backs. The child sitting in the wheelchair will be able to play the tennis ball volley game with another child.

Multilevel
Instruction:

1. Instead of scooter boards, use foam wedges or rolled up towels to help the children maintain prone (on stomach) position while batting at the tennis ball or the balloon.

2. Have the children hit the balloon while sitting on a T-stool,* large ball, therapy ball, or standing on one foot.

Letter to Parents
Balloon and Tennis Ball Games

This week we played balloon and tennis volleyball. We used a rolling pin and kept a balloon or tennis ball moving. While holding different postures such as lying on our stomachs, sitting on the floor, and kneeling, we tried to concentrate on hitting a balloon while holding rolling pins by their handles. Then, we played a tennis-type game with a partner. While lying on a scooter board, we hit a tennis ball back and forth to each other. If we missed the ball, we would propel ourselves on our scooter boards to get it.

Purpose of the Activity

This activity works on the child's ability to use both hands in a coordinated fashion, called "bilateral coordination." While hitting the balloon in different postures such as sitting, kneeling, and lying on their stomachs, the children maintained their posture and crossed the midline of their bodies. These activities helped to build your child's trunk strength as well as to improve his or her visual attention and tracking skills. The ability to cross the body's midline is a prerequisite for developing hand-dominance and smooth visual tracking. When your child cuts, colors, reads, or writes, his or her ability to visually track across the paper and maintain good postural alignment while working at his or her desk will help to improve the quality and decrease the effort of the school work.

Home Activities to Help Your Child Grow

Playing catch games at home with large balls (like basketballs, beach balls, and balloons) will help your child develop visual tracking skills, eye-hand coordination, and bilateral coordination. To encourage bilateral coordination and crossing his or her body's midline during these activities, try to have your child either sit with his or her legs folded like a pretzel on the floor, sit "cowboy" style in a chair (sitting backwards with legs around the back of the chair), half-kneel (kneeling tall on one leg with the other leg knee-up with the foot flat on the floor), sit in an arm chair, or sit on a T-stool* or a big ball. Throw the ball slightly off center so that your child must rotate his or her body while placing both hands to either side to catch the ball. Increase the distance your child must reach as he or she easily succeeds.

* A T-stool is a one-legged stool in the shape of the letter "T." A simple T-stool can be made from two one-foot-long pieces of 2"x4" wood, securely fastened in the shape of the letter "T" as shown in the drawing.

Learning in Motion

A Simple T-Stool

Securely fasten seat to leg using 2 - 3½" nails or construction screws

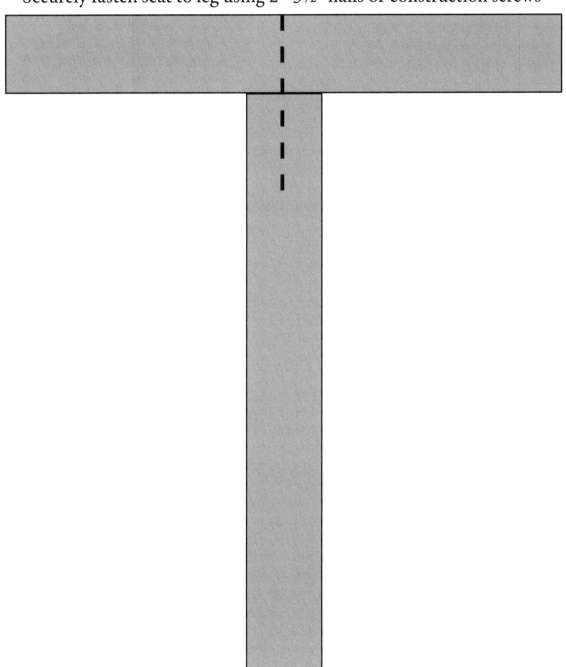

Big Ball Kick-Off I

Activity Goals: Bilateral Coordination Development

Strength and Endurance Improvement

Time: 20-to-30 minutes

Objectives: Upon successful completion of this activity, the child will be able to

1. Kick with both feet together
2. Pick up and bounce the large ball
3. Stand on one foot momentarily

Materials:
1. Twenty-four-inch ball
2. Masking tape
3. Rug squares
4. Gertie Ball or a slightly deflated beach ball.

Procedure:
1. Gather children in a circle. Have them sit on the floor with their hands placed on the floor behind their hips. In this position they are tilted slightly backward while sitting on the floor. Demonstrate how to kick the large ball with both feet together.
2. Have the children stay in the circle and try to kick it back and forth between themselves.
3. Have each child take a turn or several turns.
4. You can have the children call out the name of another child in the group and direct the ball to the child whose name is called.
5. Demonstrate to the children how to lie on their backs and pass the Gertie Ball from their feet to their hands and then to the next person's feet.
6. Have the children lie on their backs in the circle so that one child reaching his hands over his head touches the next child's feet.
7. Then start passing the Gertie Ball or a slightly deflated beach ball.
8. Go around the circle several times.
9. Group the children into pairs and show them how to pick up the large ball and bounce it to their partner, who is standing about 7 feet away. Use rug squares for standing places to keep the children at a consistent distance.
10. Continue the bounce and catch game with each pair of children.

Adaptations:
1. For children with weak legs or for wheelchair users, have them push the ball with their hands or wheelchair.
2. For children with poor sitting balance, have them sit against the wall and try to kick the ball with both feet.
3. For children with visual impairments, let them be the first ones to kick the ball or pass the ball. Give verbal cues to help them anticipate their turn.

Multilevel Instruction:
1. Have the children do the foot and hand passing game while lying on their backs but in a straight line. Make two lines and play the game like a relay race. Have the children pass the ball with their feet in one direction; then pass the ball back down the line with their hands.
2. Play the large ball kicking game while seated in a chair.

Letter to Parents
Big Ball Kick-Off I

This week, we sat in a circle and used our feet together to kick a big ball around to each other. Then we lay down and passed the ball around the circle with our feet and hands. After that, we stood across from our partner and bounced a big ball to each other.

Purpose of the Activity

These activities involved working with both hands or both feet together in a coordinated manner, called "bilateral coordination." Bilateral coordination is important for the young child because it first helps to develop strength and later reciprocal hand and foot skills. Examples of later skill development fostered by bilateral coordination are hopping on one foot, writing, and holding down the paper with the assisting hand, and cutting and moving paper with the assisting or helper hand.

Home Activities to Help Your Child Grow

Activities at home that help to develop bilateral coordination are riding a bike, climbing on playground equipment, swinging on a swing, walking on a balance beam or railroad tie, pushing a sled, wagon or a shopping cart, jumping rope, playing hopscotch, rolling out cookie dough, using a dust pan and brush, cutting meat, dressing, etc. As you can see there are many opportunities to develop coordination between the two sides of the body. You can also help your child develop this area by providing activities that require carrying or moving large objects, or motor activities such as wheelbarrow walking, bear walking, crab walking, tall-kneel walking, and hopping with feet together or on one foot.

Big Ball Kick-Off II

Activity Goals: Bilateral Coordination Development

Balance Improvement

Time: 30-to-40 minutes

Objectives: Upon successful completion of this activity, the child will be able to

1. Kick with both feet together
2. Pick up and bounce the large ball at a target and catch it
3. Stand on one foot for three-to-five seconds

Materials:
1. Twenty-four-inch ball
2. Masking tape
3. Rug square
4. Tennis ball

Procedure:
1. Gather children in a circle. Have them sit on the floor with their hands placed on the floor behind their hips. In this position they are tilted slightly backward while sitting on the floor. Demonstrate how to kick the large ball with both feet together.
2. Have the children stay in the circle and try to kick it back and forth between themselves.
3. Have each child take a turn or several turns.
4. Group the children into pairs and show them how to pick up the large ball and bounce it on a masking tape X on the floor. Using rug squares for standing places, keep the children at a consistent distance of approximately 5 feet from the X or 10 feet apart.
5. Continue the bounce and catch game with each pair of children.
6. Now demonstrate for the children how to roll and stop the tennis ball with their foot. Remind the children that the point of the game is not to kick the ball but to roll it. Have the children first practice stopping the ball with one foot on top of the ball.
7. Once the children are able to stop the ball with one foot on top of the ball increase the challenge. Have the children roll the ball in front of their stable foot and back before rolling it to their partner.
8. Continue to provide practice for the partners in this activity. Allow the children to have one or more turns.

Adaptations:
1. For the child with weak legs or using a wheelchair, have him push the ball with his hands or wheelchair.
2. For the child with poor standing balance, have them stand against the wall or hold onto the back of a chair as they try to lift their foot to stop or roll the ball.
3. For the child with visual impairments, let him roll the ball to other children with his feet. Don't be as concerned about catching.

Multilevel Instruction:
1. Have the children lie on their backs on the floor. Then have the children try to lift their legs to kick the ball across the circle.
2. Play the large ball kicking game while seated in a chair.
3. Play the ball rolling game with their foot. Before rolling the ball to their partner, the partner calls out a letter, number or a shape. The child with the ball must make the figure by tracing it with their foot on top of the ball.

Letter to Parents
Big Ball Kick-Off II

This week we sat in a circle and used our feet together to kick a big ball around to each other. Then we stood across from our partners and bounced the big ball to each other. Finally, we played a catch and roll game with a ball. Instead of catching it with our hands, we caught it and rolled it to our partner using our feet.

Purpose of the Activity

These activities involved working with both hands or feet together in a coordinated manner, which is called "bilateral coordination." Bilateral coordination is important for the young child because it helps to develop strength and, later, reciprocal hand and foot skills. In this activity, we used more advanced bilateral coordination skills to stop and roll the ball with one foot.

The ability to watch the ball and time the motor response needed to stop it requires good balance, eye-foot coordination and motor-planning skills. These activities helped to build trunk, hip, and shoulder strength needed for gross and fine-motor skills. One-footed skills like hopping, standing on one foot, and kicking a ball are a few of the higher level gross-motor skills that can be developed using these activities.

Home Activities to Help Your Child Grow

At home, you can try these activities to help your child develop bilateral coordination and eye-foot coordination. Start by using a small ball like a tennis ball. With your foot on top of the ball roll the ball slowly toward your child. Have your child place his or her foot on top of the ball to stop it. Once the ball has come to a complete stop, have your child roll it back to you with his or her foot on top of the ball (not kicking the ball).

To make this game more challenging, have your child place his or her foot on top of the ball and try to roll the ball in front of the stable foot and back before rolling it to you. Then increase the challenge by having your child roll it around the stable foot before rolling it to you. The longer the time required and more variations in the direction of the ball's path, the more balance is required. You can also increase the challenge of this activity by increasing the size of the ball to a softball-size and then to a small playground-size ball.

Edible Dirt

Activity Goals: Sensory Processing Improvement
Self-Help Skills Development

Objectives: Upon successful completion of this activity, the child will be able to

1. Use assist hand to hold the cup and dominant hand to scoop with a spoon.
2. Spread with a knife
3. Tolerate different textures on her hands
4. Follow two step verbal directions

Materials:

1. Plastic 7-oz. cups or other clear containers.
2. Chocolate round wafer vanilla cream sandwich cookies
3. Chocolate pudding
4. Gummy worms
5. Gummy bugs
6. Plastic knives

Procedure:

1. Explain the activity for the day. Have the children identify the ingredients they are going to place into their cups.
2. With the children at the table, demonstrate how to open the sandwich cookie. Once opened, demonstrate how to use the knife to scrape off all of the crème middle.
3. Hand each child a cookie and have them try step 2. Repeat for 2 to 3 more cookies.
4. After all the cookies are opened and crème is removed have the children use their fingers to crush the cookies into crumbs.
5. Have the children place half of the cookie crumbs into the clear cup. Then add half of the chocolate pudding followed by some gummy worms and bugs. Finish with the second half of the ingredients.
6. Now enjoy eating your special treat, "Dirt."

Adaptations:

1. For the child with decreased hand control, stabilize the cup or bowl on non-slip material and use an adapted spoon and/or dish to make it easier to scoop out the pudding.
2. For the child with visual impairment, arrange materials in a container and verbally explain the location of the ingredients. For example, place the object in a straight line in front of the child and arrange them in a left to right sequence.

Multilevel Instruction:

1. Have the group make instant chocolate pudding before starting this project.
2. Use a rolling pin or hammer to crush cookies inside of a plastic bag.
3. Have the student follow written instructions or icons to make the snack.

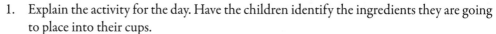

Letter to Parents
Edible Dirt

This week we made a special treat called "Dirt." We crushed chocolate cookies and added chocolate pudding, gummy worms and bugs to make this dessert. After we were finished making this "Dirt," we ate our creation.

Purpose of the Activity

This simple cooking activity involves multiple steps as well as important fine-motor and self-help skills. The first step in this cooking project was to take the crème-filled chocolate sandwich cookies and separate them. After they were separated, we took plastic knives and scraped all the crème off the cookies. Scraping with a knife is the same skill needed to spread jam, peanut butter or butter on a piece of bread or a cracker.

Next, we scooped out pudding and placed it in a container. This scooping involves using visual attention and eye-hand coordination with an appropriate grasp to hold and manipulate the spoon. Your child crushed the cookies into crumbs before adding them to the pudding. Crushing the cookies, placing the gummy worms and bugs into the mixture, helped to increase your child's pinch strength and tolerance for varied textures.

Home Activities to Help Your Child Grow

Children love to cook and bake. These activities can teach your child a wealth of information, greatly improve his or her vocabulary, reinforce the ability to follow directions, and develop self-help skills. Cooking and baking offer many opportunities for improving hand strength, pinch power, visual attention, and eye-hand coordination. They also provide elements that involve touching and working with different textures that can help to decrease tactile sensitivity.

Certain children become distracted or preoccupied with keeping their hands clean. This inability to tolerate "dirty hands" can inhibit the child's ability to learn to discriminate using his or her sense of touch. Allow your child to help you mix with a spoon, spoon out mix into cupcake tins, spread jelly on a cracker or bread, make meatballs, roll out cookies or knead dough. I am sure as you start to include your child in cooking or baking, you will find numerous ways to work on sensory exploration and strengthening activities.

Festive Boleros

Activity Goals: Scissor Skills Development
Pre-Writing Skills Development

Time: 30-to-40 minutes

Objectives: Upon successful completion of this activity, the child will be able to
1. Open and close scissors with one hand to snip paper
2. Use two hands together in a coordinated fashion to snip paper
3. Imitate simple visual patterns

Materials:
1. One large brown grocery bag per child
2. Scissors
3. Magic markers or bingo markers
4. Picture of a bullfighter or someone wearing a bolero

Procedure:
1. Prepare grocery bags for vests. Cut an opening from the top front center of the bag to the bottom of the bag. Make a circle cut in the bottom of the bag for the head. On each side cut a large armhole.
2. Gather children together and show them the picture of the person wearing a bolero. Explain that bullfighters and dancers in Spain, South America, and Mexico wear this fancy vest. Point out the elaborate designs of this piece of clothing.
3. Demonstrate snipping with scissors. Show children where to make fringes or snip with scissors.
4. Hand each child a paper bag and scissors.
5. After the bag is fringed, demonstrate how to decorate the vest with the markers. Show a completed vest with a simple pattern for the children to copy. Encourage the child to copy the same pattern on the right and left front side of the vest.
6. Have the children turn the vest to the back and make a design on the vest.
7. Let vest dry and wear vest for a party or special occasion.

Adaptations: For the child with visual impairment, glue yarn or Popsicle sticks about 3 inches from the fringed edge to make a tactile cue to help the child locate the area to be snipped and to stop the child from snipping the vest too far. This can also be helpful for a child with a problem in motor planning or poor scissor skills.

Multilevel Instruction:
1. Provide various materials such as ribbon, jewels, glitter, sequins, mirror pieces, beads, paints, etc., to decorate the vest.
2. Use bingo markers to decorate the vest.
3. Set up a bolero design pattern that each child must copy. Try using rulers to draw lines or measure placement of the design.

Learning in Motion

Letter to Parents
Festive Boleros

This week, we made festive boleros or vests that are worn by bullfighters and Spanish dancers. We practiced our cutting skills by fringing the bottom of our vest. Then we decorated our vests with markers. We are saving them for a special occasion or party.

Purpose of the Activity

For the young child, cutting with scissors is a skill that requires practice. Fringing the bolero helped the children practice the skill of holding the scissors properly and opening and closing the blades without the added demand of following a design as they cut. Just holding the scissors and opening and closing the blades requires hand strength and wrist, elbow, and shoulder stability. This is the same pattern of stability and strength needed for coloring and writing. As your child practices these skills, he or she is also developing the underlying strength for many other school-related fine-motor skills.

Home Activities to Help Your Child Grow

Other ways to develop the strength in your child's dominant hand and stability in her arm is to have your child work on activities on an easel, chalkboard wall, or other vertical surface. As your child colors, draws, or paints in this plane, she must use a "wrist-up" position (wrist extended), which develops the wrist strength needed for good pencil control. For the young child or a child who doesn't hold a crayon, pencil, or chalk correctly, try to use a bingo marker (found in the dollar stores), stamp with a stamp pad, sidewalk chalk, a large handled paintbrush, a thick marker, or chunk crayon to work in the vertical plane.

King Humpty Dumpty's Horses

Activity Goals: Bilateral Coordination Development
Body-Scheme and Motor-Planning Improvement

Time: 20-to-30 minutes

Objectives: Upon successful completion of this activity, the child will be able to
1. Assume and roll in a supine flexor position (snowball)
2. Gallop
3. Roll toward an object
4. Take turns in the group

Materials:
1. Large lightweight building blocks
2. Plastic eggs or yarn pompoms
3. Tongs
4. Children's music for galloping

Procedure:
1. Gather children together to tell them the nursery rhyme "Humpty Dumpty." Demonstrate how to assume and rock in a supine flexor position. The children should lie on their backs with their knees bent to their chest and arms wrapped around knees. Have the children try to rock forward and backward and side to side in this position while you retell the nursery rhyme. During the rhyme when Humpty Dumpty breaks, have the children straighten their bodies to imitate a broken egg.
2. Set up a wall of blocks then demonstrate how to roll and knock down the wall while in the log roll position.
3. After the child rolls and knocks down the wall, have her help you build it up again.
4. After each child has had a turn or several turns rolling, demonstrate how he will pick up the plastic eggs or pompom balls with a pair of tongs. Tell the children that this part is helping to pick up and put Humpty Dumpty back together again.
5. Next, demonstrate how to gallop. Place one foot in front of the other and skip with the back foot. Have the children practice galloping.
6. Play the galloping music and either have the children take turns or have the group gallop in a circle.

Adaptations: For the child using a wheelchair have her knock over the wall with her chair. Have the child push her chair in a line or in a circle while the other children gallop.

Multilevel Instruction:
1. Try changing from a log roll to an egg roll and back again while rolling down the wall.
2. Act out the nursery rhyme with one child being Humpty Dumpty and rest of the group divided between horses and men.
3. Practice horse kicks. Have the children get on their hands and knees and try to kick up both feet or alternate between feet.

Learning in Motion

Letter to Parents

King Humpty Dumpty's Horses

This week, we learned a new nursery rhyme, "Humpty Dumpty." We pretended to be eggs like Humpty Dumpty. We curled up our bodies and rolled to our pretend wall and knocked it over. After we knocked over the wall, we had a chance to try and pick up Humpty Dumpty eggs off the floor with tongs. Then we practiced galloping like horses to music.

Purpose of the Activity

Activities like rolling and galloping work on the coordination of the two sides of the body together (bilateral coordination) and body strength. As the child is rocking in the egg position he or she has to coordinate movements, and this requires good strength in his or her trunk and large joint muscles. These types of movement patterns also help the child develop body awareness, which is needed to motor plan more advanced motor skills like skipping, hopping, jumping rope, and climbing on playground equipment. The child who has better body awareness and strength learns motor skills easier and has the necessary stability to use his or her hands for fine-motor activities in school.

Home Activities to Help Your Child Grow

Activities such as riding a bike, playing on swings, climbing monkey bars, swimming, doing gymnastics, or playing basketball, soccer, volleyball, etc., are great ways to encourage your child to develop bilateral skills while outside in the nice weather. Children need gross-motor experiences to help build strength and endurance, as well as to experiment and learn motor skills. Provide weekly opportunities and challenges for your child to develop his motor skills.

Large Ball Pass

Activity Goals: Gross-Motor Skills Development
Group Development

Time: 20 minutes

Objectives: Upon successful completion of this activity, the child will be able to
1. Lift ball over head
2. Roll ball to another student
3. Attend to group activity and anticipate turn
4. Follow verbal directional commands with visual demonstration

Materials:
1. Large ball, 24-to-30-inch diameter
2. Rug squares

Procedure:
1. Gather children in a circle on rug squares. Explain the pass game. The children sit sideways, facing the same direction in the circle. The ball can be passed overhead, forward, backward, to the right side, or to the left side.
2. Have the children sit in the circle facing the middle of the circle. Try passing the ball to each other.
3. While facing forward in the circle, have the child call out a name of another child in the circle. Then roll the ball to that child. Continue until each child has had one or several turns.

Adaptations:
1. For the child with a visual impairment, have the teacher lend a hand to help with learning to follow verbal directions. Use verbal cues for the ball's direction and name the sequence of children as it approaches the child.
2. For the child who is using a wheelchair or has a physical impairment, have a physically able child as a partner to assist with rolling or passing the ball.

Multilevel Instruction:
1. Play a game like dodge-ball with some children standing between two lines of children sitting. The sitting students will roll the ball back and forth attempting to hit a student with the ball. The child who is hit sits with the children trying to roll the ball. When all the children are sitting down, the game is over.
2. Try the first and second passing games (see Procedure) with the children standing in two straight lines like a relay race.
3. Try the first and second passing games with the children lying on their backs and moving into sitting (sit-ups) to get the ball.

Learning in Motion

Letter to Parents
Large Ball Pass

This week, we played games with a big ball. First, we lifted the ball and passed it around to our friends in the circle. We had to lift it up over our heads and pass it forward and backward. Then we passed it side to side. We rolled the ball to other children in the circle, and they rolled it back.

Purpose of the Activity

Lifting and moving this large ball helps the child build strength, Balance Improvement skills, and work on attention and cooperation in the group setting. For children, the large ball is heavy and challenges their ability to maintain their balance as they try to pass it overhead, backward, or to the sides. They also need to watch the ball and anticipate their turn. The ability to sustain attention in the group used in this activity is a skill needed during classroom activities, too. While the teacher is asking questions of other students or demonstrating information in the front of the class, the child must be attentive in order to learn and be ready to participate when called upon. The strength and balance skills developed during this ball game also help your child in the classroom setting, where he needs to be able to maintain correct sitting posture in his seat during classwork, circle time, or fine-motor activities, such as cutting, coloring, and tracing.

Home Activities to Help Your Child Grow

If you have a large (24-to-30 inch diameter) ball at home, you can try these same activities. If not, try asking your child to carry or move a large box. Fill the box with some light objects and have him or her carry it from place to place. A suggestion might be to place all your child's toys in a box and carry them to the toy box to be put away. Your child can also help to carry the laundry basket, take out or empty the trash, put school bags away, carry groceries, or push in chairs at the table. Carrying large and slightly heavy objects will help your child increase his or her strength and Balance Improvement.

Moving Bugs

Activity Goals: Sensory Processing Improvement
Strength and Endurance Improvement

Time: 30-to-40 minutes

Objectives: Upon successful completion of this activity, the child will be able to
1.   Push arms and legs against resistive materials
2.   Imitate body postures on command
3.   Spread fingers against resistance
4.   Participate in a cooperative activity with another child

Materials:
1.   Large fabric tubes of Lycra or stretch knit
2.   Scooter boards
3.   Tissue paper
4.   Caterpillar story, gestural or fingerplay about caterpillars and butterflies

Procedure:
1.   Gather children together and demonstrate how to place themselves on the scooter board. Have the children lie on their stomachs and push forward with hands and feet. To pretend to be caterpillars and bugs on scooter boards, have them use either their hands or feet in this position.
2.   Give each child a turn being a bug and/or a caterpillar.
3.   Demonstrate how to use the fabric tube (Body Sox˘) or a 48-inch tubes of cotton stretch knit material. Have the children remove their shoes. Place one or two children at a time in the "Body Sox" and have them push with arms and legs against the material.
4.   Try having the children sit down and lie down while in the tube. If using the cotton knit tube, have the children try these postures one child at a time.
5.   Have the children sit in a circle and place their palms together. Take tissue paper or toilet paper and wrap their fingers together to make a "cocoon."
6.   Tell or read the story of "The Hungry Caterpillar," another bug story, or recite the finger play.
7.   After the story is over, have the children try and spread their finger to rip the paper off, pretending that the paper is the cocoon, and their hands are the butterflies breaking free.

Adaptations:
1.   For a child with limited mobility, dress her in the body sock and roll her on the floor.
2.   For the child using a wheelchair, have her place the tube over her upper body or lower body only and try to move her arms or legs.
3.   For the child with poor motor planning or a visual impairment, let him help you place the tube on and off his body.

Multilevel Instruction:
1.   Instead of using body tubes for a young group, you can use the cut-off legs from large-size adult sweat pants.
2.   Roll up the children into tubes in large beach towels and let them pretend to be moving caterpillars.
3.   Use finger paints or ink pads and have children use either their thumb or index finger to make pictures of caterpillars on a piece of paper.

Learning in Motion

Letter to Parents
Moving Bugs

This week we pretended to be caterpillars and bugs moving along the floor. We used scooter boards to push ourselves along the floor. Then, we got stretchy material tubes and put them on like our cocoons. While in the cocoons, we tried to stretch and push on the material and change positions inside this tube. We listened to a story and pretended our hands were butterflies in a cocoon. After the story, we stretched out our fingers and broke free of the tissue cocoon.

Purpose of the Activity

The activities we did today using resistive materials as cocoons helped the children learn to move and plan motor activities without being able to view their body parts. With the stretchy or resistive materials, the children received extra tactile and kinesthetic (muscle) input. These types of input reinforced body part awareness and the ability to execute motor activities using mental images of themselves. Refined motor tasks that involve speed often are performed without visually monitoring them. For example, activities such as typing, writing, buttoning collar buttons, or tying an apron bow are done without watching our hands move. The activities today helped to reinforce this ability, which is needed in school when handwriting, packing book bags, and dressing.

Home Activities to Help Your Child Grow

You can try some of the same type of tasks at home. Make a stretchy fabric tube from the leg of an adult pair of sweat pants, stretch pants, or a tube top—or, you can wrap your child in a beach towel. Then, have your child push and move inside this tube. You can have your child pull up and take off the slightly tight garment. This will help your child build hand strength needed for dressing.

To reinforce hand awareness and the ability to move without viewing his or her hands, you can play puppets with your child. Have your child move the puppets' bodies and talk while they act out a story. Playing in shaving cream, pudding, whipped cream, sand, dough, dry rice, or beans also will help your child become more aware of finger and hand movements without using vision. Depending on your child's ability, have him or her find letters, numbers or small hidden objects in these materials (rice, sand, beans, etc.).

Piñata

Activity Goals: Strength and Endurance Improvement
Scissor Skills Development

Time: 30-to-40 minutes

Objectives: Upon successful completion of this activity, the child will be able to
1. Form a paper ball with both hands
2. Snip with scissors
3. Pick up small objects off the floor
4. Cooperate with others and take turns
5. Demonstrate one-to-one correspondence

Materials:
1. Several large brown paper grocery bags
2. Newspaper
3. Scissors
4. Glue
5. String
6. Wrapped candies
7. Plastic bat
8. Picture of a piñata

Procedure:
1. Gather children together and explain the piñata game and use of piñata for parties. Describe how the group will first stuff the brown bag with newspaper then cover it with fur (brown paper bag strips snipped with scissors) to make the bull's body.
2. Have children sit in circle and squeeze newspaper into balls. Once each child has made three balls, have her place one ball with one piece of candy inside the bag.
3. Continue this process until the bag is full and close it with staples. Also, staple strings around the opening so the children can pull the piñata apart if it doesn't open.
4. Have the children sit at a table or work area. Demonstrate snipping along the edge of a brown paper bag strip approximately 3" wide the length of the bag.
5. Give each child strips and a pair of scissors. Make enough strips to cover the bag.
6. Once all the strips are snipped, have the children take turns gluing the strips to the bag.
7. The teacher then adds the bull's head and legs. Head: stuff a paper grocery bag with newspaper and tape on horns. Use small brown paper lunch bags stuffed with paper for the legs.
8. Suspend the bag from a string wrapped around the bull's body.
9. Give each child a chance or several chances to hit the bull with a plastic bat. If desired, let the children hold the strings and pull all at once to open up the piñata.
10. After the bull opens, have each child take a turn to pick up a candy or candies.

Adaptations:
1. For the child with one functional hand, have him make paper balls with smaller pieces of paper and use the floor or table to push the paper into a ball.
2. For the child with a visual impairment, have him stuff the head and legs of the bull while the other children work on the fur.

Multilevel Instruction:

1. Have the child use one hand to make a paper ball. Then switch hands for the second ball.
2. After snipping the strips of brown paper, show the children how to roll the paper around a pencil to curl it. Find a recording of *Woolly Bully* and play this while they work on the fur.
3. Have the children pick up the candy with a long-handled reacher toy or tongs.

May

May

Letter to Parents

Piñata

This wee, we made a piñata that looked like a bull. First, we stuffed it with newspaper and surprises. Then we added fur that we made by snipping strips from brown paper bags. After it was finished, we had an opportunity to hit it with a bat and try to break it open to get the prizes inside.

Purpose of the Activity

This activity helps the child develop hand strength and scissor skills. The ability to control pencils, crayons, and scissors is affected by the child's hand strength, so activities like this one help the children build strength and control in their hands to prepare for other tasks they will do in school.

Home Activities to Help Your Child Grow

Building hand strength and scissor skills can be accomplished at home with some of these games. Try having your child use tongs to pick up small toys, bean bags, cotton balls, and Koosh balls. You can have your child punch holes in stiff paper with a hole punch to make designs to lace with yarn. Also, in the bathtub, provide some squirt toys to build your child's hand strength. Place some soap on the side of the tub and have your child draw a shape in it and squirt it off.

If your child has good large-muscle strength but needs work on pinch strength, try having him or her make pictures or designs on coffee filters by using an eye dropper with food coloring in water. Hole punches, which make small design cutouts, tweezers, and "strawberry pickers", which are small tongs used to pull off the stems from strawberries, are a few other tools that will help your child build pinch strength.

Special Flowers

Activity Goals: Visual-Perceptual Development

Pre-Writing Skills Development

Time: 20-to-30 minutes

Objectives: Upon successful completion of this activity, the child will be able to

1. Pinch and release fluid from an eyedropper
2. Visually attend to a task for 2-3 minutes
3. Twist a pipe cleaner
4. Wait turn during group activity

Materials:
1. Automatic drip coffee filters
2. Eyedroppers
3. Food coloring
4. Vinegar
5. Pipe cleaners
6. Sample of the flower

Procedure:
1. Place 2-to-3 ounces of water, several drops of food coloring and a tablespoon of vinegar in a small cup or bowl.
2. Place one eyedropper in each color cup or bowl.
3. Gather children and show them the sample of the flower.
4. Give each child a coffee filter. Start to pass around the bowl and the eyedropper.
5. Each child places one or several colors on three different coffee filters.
6. Teacher hangs up filters to dry. Depending on the location, the coffee filters may take 15-30 minutes to dry. Have the children work on a gross-motor activity during this time.
7. When the coffee filters are dry, the children return to the work area. The teacher demonstrates how to place the pipe cleaner folded in half over the gathered middle of the three coffee filters.
8. Then the teacher demonstrates how to twist the pipe cleaner to make it tight around the three coffee filters.
9. After the children have completed steps 7 and 8, the teacher demonstrates how to fluff the coffee filters to make it look like a flower and the children imitate her demonstration.

Adaptations:
1. For the child with poor pinch strength, have him or her use a paint brush or paint sponge to dip into food coloring and place on coffee filter.
2. For the child with visual impairment, place the filter on a plate or pie tin to give the child tactile borders to work within.
3. For the child with use of one functional hand, have the pipe cleaner pre-folded in half. Then have the child try to stabilize the coffee filter with the assist hand and place the pipe cleaner on the coffee filters and twist it.

Multilevel Instruction:
1. Instead of using food coloring, use either magic markers or bingo markers to decorate the coffee filters.
2. Make a vase of flowers or make the flowers into a bouquet.
3. Make fringe along the edges of the dried coffee filters by snipping them with scissors. Make leaves on the flower stems with strips of green tissue paper.

Letter to Parents
Special Flowers

This week we made some beautiful flowers using coffee filters, eyedroppers, and pipe cleaners.

Purpose of the Activity

This activity involves using pinch strength and fine-motor control while using an eyedropper to place color on the flowers. It also involves visual attention and eye-hand coordination to place the color on the coffee filter. The children had to follow verbal directions from the teacher to gather and twist the pipe cleaner stems on the flowers. At the end, the child needed graded finger control to fluff the coffee filters (without tearing the paper) to make it look more like a flower. Pinch strength, graded finger control, and visual attention are important school-related skills. For example, to hold a pencil and write requires pinch strength and finger control to hold and move the pencil correctly, as well as attention to the written material.

Home Activities to Help Your Child Grow

At school and at home, pinch and grip strength are important because your child needs adequate pinch and grip strength to be able to dress; handle closures like buttons, snaps, and zippers; open packages; and turn on and off the faucet in the bathroom. Activities at home that can help improve pinch and grip strength are using a spray bottle with water to clean the table after meals, clipping clothespins around a plastic container, using salad tongs to pick up small objects, and placing pennies in a piggy bank. Some games and toys that are available at toy stores also help build hand and finger strength like Bed Bugs, Operation, Connect Four, and Play-Doh.

Wash Day

Activity Goals: Self-Help Skills Development
Visual-Perceptual Development

Time: 30-to-40 minutes

Objectives: Upon successful completion of this activity, the child will be able to
1.   Wring wet clothes with both hands
2.   Hang clothes on a clothesline
3.   Pinch clothespins to open them
4.   Fold clothing in half

Materials:
1.   Doll clothes, washcloths, and waterproof smocks
2.   Water
3.   Mild soap or detergent
4.   Clothesline or string
5.   Clip clothespins
6.   Play irons and ironing board

Procedure:
1.   Gather children together and recite the rhyme "This is the way we wash our clothes, etc." Imitate the motor play that accompanies the rhyme. Explain to the children that doing the wash is a job that their parents do every week for them. They are going to practice this skill like their moms and dads.
2.   Ask the group what they need to wash clothes.
3.   Demonstrate to the group how to wash out the clothes by hand. Use a basin, bucket or sink with mild soap or a bar of soap to wash the clothes.
4.   Have the children try to wash some clothes by hand. Make sure they wring the clothes well, rinse the clothes, and wring them again.
5.   Next, set up a clothesline. Demonstrate how to hold up the wash to the line, and then clip the clothespin on the clothes and the line together.
6.   Have the children practice opening and closing the clothespins first. Then practice placing the clips on the clothesline. Finally, have the children each take a turn to hang up a piece of clothing, clipping it on with two or more clothespins.
7.   When the clothes are dry, have each child take down a piece of clothing from the line. Demonstrate how to iron the clothing and fold it in half.
8.   Have the children practice these skills during playtime.

Adaptations:
1.   For the child with poor hand strength or limited arm movement, place the basin on the table. Allow the child to squeeze the water out of the clothes by rolling the clothes up into a ball, placing it on a towel, and then pressing down on the ball with both hands to release the water.
2.   For the child with a visual impairment, teach him to place one hand on the clothesline first and then place the other hand and clothes close to this hand. Give the child verbal cues to help him find the clothesline. Use high contrast, colored string for the clothesline.

Multilevel
Instruction:
1. Have the children undress a doll before washing the clothes and redress the doll after the clothes are dried, ironed, and folded.
2. Pretend to wash clothes without real soap and water then hang them to dry.

Letter to Parents
Wash Day

This week we pretended to do the wash like our moms and dads. We got some things to wash, and soap and water to wash them with. After we wrung out the clean clothes, we hung them up on our clothesline to dry. When they were completely dry, we ironed or folded the clothes.

Purpose of the Activity

This activity (doing the wash) had many different benefits for your child. First and most obvious, were the benefits of learning the task. Your child learned how to perform the functional life skills of hand-washing clothes, folding clothes, and hanging laundry on the line. Also, while performing this activity, your child practiced coordinating both hands together to wash, wring, hang, and fold the wash.

Working with his or her two hands together helped your child build bilateral coordination as well as improve his or her visual attention and develop eye-hand coordination. The areas noted above are important for the development of visual tracking, which your child will need for reading. He or she will need the eye-hand coordination, bilateral coordination, and upper body strength for writing, cutting with scissors, and coloring.

Home Activities to Help Your Child Grow

Young children are often present during some aspect of the laundry process. This can be a great opportunity to encourage learning and cooperation in a life skill. The first part of the laundry process is often sorting by color (light, white, or dark). This activity can be performed together with your child. Explain what you are doing and have your child help you with this task.

Next, after the clothes come down from the line or out of the dryer, they will need to be folded and the socks will need to be matched. Have your child help by matching pairs of socks, folding the towels, and folding wash cloths. In the summer months or after swimming, hang a low clothesline outside so your child can hang up his or her bathing suit. If needed, your child could rinse and squeeze out the water from the suit before hanging it out to dry.

Educational Goals by Activity

Attention Improvement	Balance Improvement	Bilateral Coordination Development	Body-Scheme and Motor-Planning Improvement	Cognitive Development	Fine-Motor Skills Development	Gross-Motor Skills Development	Group Development	Hand-Dominance Development	Pre-Writing Skills Development	Scissor Skills Development	Self-Help Skills Development	Sensory Processing Improvement	Strength and Endurance Improvement	Visual-Perceptual Development	Activity	Page
	✔		✔												Circus Tricks	256
									✔					✔	Clowning Around	259
										✔			✔		Cocoons and Butterflies	261
											✔	✔			Fruit Salad Fiesta	263
				✔									✔		Going on a Picnic	266
						✔							✔		Jumping Rope	269
	✔					✔									Mountain Goats	271
				✔										✔	Red, White, and Blue Flag Celebration	273
									✔			✔			Shaving Cream Fun	275
									✔					✔	Water and Ball Play	277
			✔						✔						Zoo Animals	279

June

Circus Tricks

Activity Goals: Balance Improvement

Body-Scheme and Motor-Planning Improvement

Time: 20-to-30 minutes

Objectives: Upon successful completion of this activity, the child will be able to

1. Walk forward 6 feet on a balance beam
2. Throw and catch a chiffon scarf
3. Catch a ball while standing on a balance beam
4. Wheelbarrow walk fifteen feet forward
5. Throw a beanbag through a Hula Hoop from a distance of five-to-seven feet
6. Perform a forward roll

Materials:
1. Chiffon scarves
2. Balloons
3. Mats
4. Balance beam
5. Beanbags
6. Hula hoop

Procedure:
1. Set up materials for stations: a balance beam and mat, suspend a Hula Hoop from a string at the children's eye level, mark a start and finish line for wheelbarrow walking and catching games; and provide a mat for forward rolling.
2. Gather children together and explain the tricks or activities they will try as part of this circus activity.
3. Either proceed with the activity visiting each station with the whole group, or provide adult supervision at each station and rotate the children in small groups through all activities.
4. Give each child multiple opportunities to try these skill areas.

Adaptations:
1. For a child with limited mobility, a child with Down's syndrome who is not cleared to do a forward roll, or a child who is afraid to do a forward roll, do a log roll.
2. Assist children who want to learn how to do a forward roll to bend forward and tuck their heads under so they won't try to roll starting on the tops of their heads (get an experienced teacher/therapist to show you how to do this safely).
3. Let a child who is a wheelchair user position his or her wheelchair across the balance beam, with 1 wheel on either side of the beam. Keeping the balance beam in between his wheels go the length of the beam.
4. If a child has limited upper body movement, adapt the ball and scarf throwing games. Allow the child to roll a ball or attach a ball, scarf, or balloon to a string and let him or her hit it.
5. Give some hands-on guidance when necessary for the child with a visual impairment. Refer to the section on adaptations for ideas on improving visibility for this child.

Multilevel

Instruction:
1. Change balance activities to make it easier or more difficult by altering the way the children walk on the beam, such as sideways, backward, or heel to toe.
2. Try to catch a chiffon scarf with one hand or use the beanbags for this activity.
3. Change the distance or the size of the target during beanbag toss game.
4. Conduct this activity outside, for added novelty. Add a water activity, such as tossing ping-pong balls into colored water or coins into bowls of water, as more challenging tasks.

June

Letter to Parents
Circus Tricks

This week we pretended to be circus performers. We performed tricks and feats to entertain ourselves and our classmates. We were encouraged to try different activities. We took turns being jugglers, acrobats, strong men or women, and skilled performers.

Purpose of the Activity

Activities such as walking and standing on a balance beam and walking like a wheelbarrow help to increase your child's strength and ability to maintain his or her balance. The ability to maintain a static (stationary) posture while seated in the classroom is important so that the child can attend to class instruction and perform fine-motor activities.

Other activities, such as juggling with chiffon scarves and throwing a beanbag at a target, involve visual attention and eye-hand coordination. Early in the educational process, children gather the majority of information in the classroom through visual demonstration. Visual attention and eye-hand coordination are very important for developing coloring, writing, and cutting skills.

Home Activities to Help Your Child Grow

Children enjoy showing off their special talents. These novel activities (juggling, wheelbarrow walking and balance beam walking) can be used at home to help your child develop better visual attention and eye-hand co-ordination. Ball skills work on visual attention as well as eye-hand coordination. For example, just as we did in our activities, you can have your child try throwing and catching a chiffon scarf. As your child succeeds, change this to a more difficult skill, such as catching a balloon, a beach ball, and then, a Nerf ball.

Wheelbarrow walking is a great activity for increasing your child's trunk and upper body strength. Initially, you may have to hold your child at his or her thighs while wheelbarrow walking. As your child's stability improves as he or she gains better strength in the trunk and upper body, you will be able to move your hands to his or her knees or ankles. As your child improves in this skill, gradually increase the distance or time for wheelbarrow walking.

June

Clowning Around

Activity Goals: Pre-Writing Skills Development
Visual-Perceptual Development

Time: 20-to-30 minutes

Objectives: Upon successful completion of this activity, the child will be able to
1.   Stamp color on a paper using a bingo marker
2.   Color on a chalkboard
3.   Accurately throw to a target three-to-five feet away
4.   Wait turn in a group

Materials:
1.   Sponges and water
2.   Different-colored bingo markers
3.   Folded paper towels
4.   Pipe cleaners
5.   Colored chalk
6.   Chalkboard or large vertical surface
7.   Streamers (optional)
8.   Bowl or bucket for water

Procedure:
1.   Draw the outline of two or three clowns on the chalkboard. Fill one or more containers with water and place sponges inside the containers. Make a sample of the clown bow tie.
2.   Gather the children together and show them the clown on the chalkboard. Tell them that after they color dots on the clown with chalk, they will get a chance to try to hit the clown with a wet sponge. Then, show the children the polka dot clown bow ties they are going to make.
3.   Have each child take a piece of chalk about two inches long and demonstrate how to make a large polka dot on the clown. Have each child make several dots on the blackboard clowns.
4.   After each child has had a turn making dots, set up the bucket and sponges. Before throwing the sponges, have each child squeeze out the sponges. Have the children aim for the clown on the chalkboard. Give each child two-to-three opportunities to hit the clown and try this several times. Remember to squeeze out the sponge well before throwing.
5.   Have the children return to the table and demonstrate how to spread out the folded paper towels and use the bingo markers to make dots on them. Let the children do this activity.
6.   Let the paper towels dry. When they dry, gather the paper towels in the middle and twist the pipe cleaner around them to make bow ties.
7.   Attach a streamer to the bow tie. This will go around the child's neck to hold the bow tie.

Adaptations: For the child with hand or arm weakness, wring sponge out well before throwing and move closer to the target. Instead of the clown on the chalkboard, try to put the child at a table with a clown picture on it. Then have the child toss or push the sponge onto the clown picture.

Multilevel Instruction:
1.   Try using sidewalk chalk instead of regular-sized colored chalk to color the clown.
2.   Place the paper towels on a vertical surface and have the children stamp them to make the bow tie.

Letter to Parents
Clowning Around

This week we made polka dots on chalkboard clowns, and then we threw wet sponges at them. After that, we made our own clown bow ties with big markers and paper towels.

Purpose of the Activity

This activity works on arm, hand, and finger strength needed to hold and use many school tools, such as scissors, crayons, pencils, and glue. For the first part of the activity, the children worked on a vertical surface—the chalkboard. Working on this surface while coloring helps to build shoulder and wrist strength needed for better hand control and coordination. While making clown ties, the children also held the bingo markers to make dots on ties. This task not only increases arm and hand strength, but it also improves eye-hand coordination and visual attention. Visual attention to the teacher and learning materials is important in school. If the child is visually inattentive, he or she will miss important information presented at the early educational level.

Home Activities to Help Your Child Grow

As stated above, changing the location or surface where the child is working can help increase his or her arm, wrist, and hand strength. Having your child work on an easel or the chalkboard will help improve his strength and skills in activities such as coloring, writing, and cutting. If you do not have an easel or chalkboard, you can place a coloring or painting activity on a wall with tape and encourage your child to work there. Another motivating activity that can be done on a vertical surface is to use stamps and stamp pads. Draw some circles, squares or lines on a large sheet of paper and have your child fill them in with stamps. Stamping on a vertical surface builds arm, hand, and wrist strength.

Cocoons and Butterflies

Activity Goals: Scissor Skills Development
Strength and Endurance Improvement

Time: 30 minutes

Objectives: Upon successful completion of this activity, the child will be able to
1. Move along floor on stomach using arms (commando crawl)
2. Cut along a line two inches long
3. Place small pieces of paper in a bag
4. Follow two-to-three step directions with visual demonstration

Materials:
1. Beach towels (colorful ones, if available)
2. Ziploc® bags
3. Strips of construction paper (bright colors)
4. Pipe cleaners
5. Picture of a caterpillar, a cocoon, and a butterfly

Procedure:
1. Gather the children in a group and show them the pictures of the caterpillar, cocoon, and butterfly. Explain how the larva eats to grow and then builds a cocoon. After growing inside a cocoon, it breaks out and becomes a butterfly.
2. Have the children roll up in beach towels and crawl on the floor using their arms to pretend they are caterpillars. Let them slide their knees up and then slide their hands forward like inchworms, too. Ask them to roll up into a cocoon, like a ball, when they are tired.
3. After a rest in their "cocoons," have them roll out of the beach towels and become butterflies. The child stretches out her arms, slowly flapping them up and down while using both hands to hold the large beach towel (butterfly wings).
4. Have the children come back to the table. Show them the sample of the butterfly. The butterfly is made of a Ziploc bag filled with different colored construction paper squares about 2" by 2." Then the bag is gathered at the middle and a pipe cleaner is placed there to hold it and act as the body and antennae for the butterfly.
5. Give the children scissors and strips of brightly colored construction paper approximately 2" wide and 8½" long. Have them cut these strips to make squares.
6. After they are all cut, place them in Ziploc bags.
7. Gather at the middle and hold with a dark pipe cleaner.

Adaptations:
1. For the child with functional use of one hand, have the one end of the paper strip taped to the top of a container and have the child snip at the paper. Stabilize the bag by taping the opened top to the outside of a large cup. This will also help the child with poor coordination or impaired vision.

Multilevel Instruction:
1. Have the children tear the strips of colored construction paper instead of cutting them.
2. Use clip clothespins instead of pipe cleaners to make the butterflies' bodies.
3. To simulate cocoons, wrap the children's hands, clasped together, with tissue. Let them break out of their "cocoons" and imitate butterflies using their hands with thumbs wrapped together.

June

Letter to Parents
Cocoons and Butterflies

This week we pretended to be caterpillars that turned into cocoons and then became beautiful butterflies. We rolled up in a beach towel to become a caterpillar, and moved around eating everything until we became a cocoon. After lying still, we broke out of our cocoon (beach towel) and became a lovely butterfly that gently flapped its wings (beach towel). After this, we made our own butterflies by cutting construction paper and placing it inside a Ziploc plastic bag to make wings with a pipe cleaner body and antennae.

Purpose of the Activity

This activity starts with heavy work movements such as commando crawling, breaking free from the beach towel, and holding the beach towel while flapping arms up and down. Activities where the child is working against resistance can have positive effects for your child in school. The first effect is that the exercise improves the child's strength in his or her arms and trunk. This will help your child maintain good sitting posture and have sufficient arm strength for fine-motor tasks like coloring, writing, and cutting. Second, this type of "heavy work" generally helps a child calm down so he can focus his attention more easily for fine-motor activities. Our activity this week also worked on scissor skills. Children enjoy cutting with scissors, especially if the stress is off them to follow lines exactly. Our activity encouraged practice in scissor use and improved your child's hand strength for cutting with scissors.

Home Activities to Help Your Child Grow

When a child is working on cutting, it is best to provide materials to cut that are stiff such as holiday cards, birthday cards, or playing cards. Children enjoy cutting out the pictures on the cards. Have your child cut out some large pictures from cards, then take a hole punch and punch holes along the border of the picture. With some yarn or thick string, have your child lace the edges. To make it easier for your child, use a piece of masking tape and wrap the tip of the yarn with it. This gives the child a lacing end that makes it easier to get the thread through the holes.

June

Learning in Motion

Fruit Salad Fiesta

Activity Goals:	Sensory Processing Improvement Self-Help Skills Development
Time:	45 minutes
Objectives:	Upon successful completion of this activity, the child will be able to

1. Use a plastic knife to cut five slices of a fruit like a melon or banana
2. Feed herself fruit using a spoon
3. Wash her hands independently
4. Work within a group to make a finished product

Materials:
1. A variety of fruit, such as bananas, apples, melon, and berries
2. A plastic knife for each child
3. A bowl for each child
4. Napkins
5. Pictures of the fruit you are using (if available)
6. Large bowl
7. Large spoon
8. Sharp knife (for adult use)
9. Small spoon for each child
10. Plate for each child

Procedure:
1. Children wash their hands and then sit at the table.
2. Show children the fruit that you have brought and ask them to identify it.
3. Show children the pictures of the fruit and ask them to identify them.
4. Partially cut the fruit for fruit salad. For example, core the apples and cut them in half, and cut the melon into slices and trim the rind.
5. Demonstrate how to peel a banana and allow each child to peel one-half of a banana.
6. Give each child a plate and a plastic knife and allow each to slice small pieces of the peeled banana.
7. Have children "dump" the sliced fruit into a bowl.
8. Let children slice remaining fruit and add it to the fruit salad.
9. Children throw their plates and plastic knives away and clean the table, if necessary.
10. Children take turns stirring contents of bowl with large spoon.
11. Each child is given a small bowl, plastic spoon, and napkin.
12. Adult distributes fruit salad.
13. Enjoy the treat!
14. Children wash hands and wipe mouths.
15. Children recall the events, in order, of making the fruit salad.

Adaptations:
1. Child with the use of one arm can stabilize her bowl on non-skid surface. Also, when she is slicing her fruit, it can be placed against the corner of a baking pan for stability.

2. When slicing the fruit with a knife, the child may need hand-over-hand assistance if he has poor coordination or limited impulse control.

Multilevel Instruction:

1. Children can read "fruit" words and match pictures of the fruit with the correct word.
2. Children can count the number of fruits, slices, stirs, etc., used in the activity.
3. Children can sequence pictures that represent the process of making fruit salad.

June

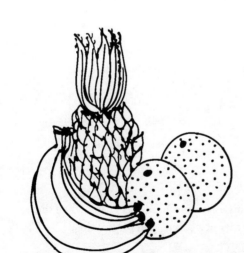

Letter to Parents
Fruit Salad Fiesta

This week we made fruit salad. We talked about the types of fruit that we would use, learned the names of the fruit, and practiced saying the correct names. The children peeled bananas and used plastic knives to cut pieces of a variety of fruits. They combined the fruit and learned how to stir and mix the fruit together. Finally, they got to eat their creation!

Purpose of the Activity

Through participation in the group, the children learned the labels for various fruits and how to categorize them. They practiced sequencing events in the correct order and used their memories to recall what happened in the group. Labeling, sequencing, and remembering are skills that are required in the classroom for completion of common educational tasks. They also practiced the self-help skills of cutting with a knife, stirring, serving food out of a bowl, and eating with utensils. Sometimes children will avoid eating different types of food but are more willing to try foods that they have had an active role in making. In the group, they were encouraged to try new flavors and textures of food.

Home Activities to Help Your Child Grow

When you are in the grocery store with your child, have him or her tell you different types of food in each food group. For example, "Tell me three types of vegetables" or "Tell me four kinds of fruit." When you go somewhere with your child, ask him to tell you the events of the outing, in the correct order, when you return from the trip. Your child can practice his scissor skills as well as his ability to categorize "like" items by cutting out pictures from a magazine that have the same theme; e.g., people, transportation, etc., and gluing them onto a piece of construction paper or into a book.

June

Going on a Picnic

Activity Goals: Cognitive Development
Strength and Endurance Improvement

Time: 30 minutes

Objectives: Upon successful completion of this activity, the child will be able to

1. Jump from one carpet square to another one
2. Walk forward six steps on a balance beam.
3. Remember a five-part sequence of events.
4. Maintain an extended posture (feet and arms off the floor) while lying on stomach on the floor for five seconds

Materials:
1. Tunnel
2. Balance beam
3. Carpet squares
4. Picnic basket or cooler
5. Mat
6. Picnic blanket

Procedure:
1. Beforehand, set up an obstacle course in the following order:
   a. Tunnel
   b. Carpet squares (stones)
   c. Mat (lake)
   d. Balance beam (bridge)
   e. Blanket with cooler or basket on it
2. The children sit in circle and adult tells them that they're going to go on a pretend field trip on the school bus. The bus is going to make a few stops. The story should be something like:
   a. "Let's all get on the bus." Children pretend to step onto bus, sit down, and buckle seat belts.
   b. "We're driving through a tunnel." Children crawl through a tunnel.
   c. "We're driving to the lake; let's get out for a swim." Children pretend to leave bus. First child steps on stone (carpet square) and jumps to next stone (square) which is about 2-feet away. The other children follow and stop at the lake (mat).
   d. "Let's take a swim." Children lie on their stomachs on mat and pretend to swim. Children should have arms and legs off of surface of mat for at least 5 seconds.
   e. "Back on the bus; we're going across the bridge." Children take turns walking across bridge (balance beam).
   f. "Let's get off the bus and go have a picnic." Children sit on blanket. Adult begins to pull imaginary items out of the cooler/basket and asks children what the picnic foods could be. Children make appropriate suggestions (watermelon, sandwiches, chips, etc.). Children use actions to pretend to eat the food.
   g. "Now it's time to climb back on the bus and return to school."
3. Children sit in circle and recall events of the field trip in order.

Adaptations: Child in wheelchair can wheel himself through the course. A pathway can be set up for him using cones or masking tape. He could pull himself across the lake by using his arms to pull on a rope.

**Multilevel
Instruction:**   If the group is higher-level, more activities can be included. If the group is lower-level, include fewer activities.

June

Letter to Parents

Going on a Picnic

This week we made a pretend trip on the school bus. We talked about getting in the bus and looking out the windows, and we made several stops. We stopped at the lake and took a swim. We walked across a bridge, climbed through a tunnel and, at the end, we made and ate a big pretend picnic lunch.

Purpose of the Activity

This activity worked on the ability to listen in a group and follow verbal directions. The children learned how to imitate body movements and to pretend to perform activities. They used strength and balance to successfully negotiate the obstacle course.

Home Activities to Help Your Child Grow

After going on a short trip together, to the store, beach, zoo, playground, etc., have your child make up a story using a sequence of movement patterns. If your child is too young to do this, you can demonstrate the movement pattern and have your child imitate it. For instance, if you were baking cookies, you would start by pretending to measure the ingredients, then stir and roll out the cookies, then place them in the oven, and then eat them after letting them cool. This fun exercise works on memory, sequencing, and storytelling skills, which is the beginning of whole language and reading/comprehension skills.

June

Jumping Rope

Activity Goals: Visual-Perceptual Development

Gross-Motor Skills Development

Time: 20-to-30 minutes

Objectives: Upon successful completion of this activity, the child will be able to

1. Jump over a rope which is two-to-four inches off the ground
2. Visually attend to a moving rope
3. Jump over a moving rope
4. Take turns in a group

Materials:
1. Rope (approximately ten-to-fifteen feet long)

Procedure:
1. Attach one end of the rope to a stable surface.
2. Gather children in a circle and demonstrate the jumping games.
3. Have the children stand in front of the still rope on the floor and try to jump over it.
4. Have the children stand in front of the rope two-to-four inches off the floor and try to jump over it.
5. Take the rope and shake it up and down to make waves. Have the children watch the rope then try to jump over it.
6. Take the rope and shake it side to side like a snake. Have the children watch the rope before they try to jump over it.
7. Now take the rope and swing it gently. Have the children try to watch the rope then jump over it.

Adaptations:
1. For the child with visual impairments use a thick piece of masking tape, bright orange or reflective tape on a dark or high contrast floor surface for a jumping line instead of a rope.
2. For the child using a wheelchair, have the child go under the rope while other students hold the rope up high. The child who is a wheelchair user can hold the rope and gently move it in various directions for his classmates.

Multilevel Instruction:
1. Vary the height or movement of the rope to increase or decrease jump rope skill level.
2. Have the children practice jumping rope by themselves with individual jump ropes.
3. For the group unable to jump and get feet off the floor, try using a trampoline and practice jumping from it to the floor. Encourage the children to jump as far as possible.
4. Instead of jumping over the rope, make this into a game of over-under. Place the rope low to the floor and ask the child to go over the rope. Place the rope up higher and ask the child to go under the rope.

Letter to Parents

Jumping Rope

This week we enjoyed practicing some jump rope games like high-low waters, waves, and snakes. We took turns jumping rope and watching our classmates try to get over the waves or not step on the snake.

Purpose of the Activity

Jumping over a stationery object and then a moving one involves planning movements with appropriate speed, direction, force, and timing. This complex task uses the coordination of visual perception for size, distance, and speed, as well as attention, prior movement experiences, and motor memory. All these areas help the child move with confidence in a new or unfamiliar setting or activity. It helps the child develop refinement in movement needed for skilled motor tasks, as well as reinforces spatial concepts such as next to, over, under, high, and low.

Home Activities to Help Your Child Grow

Any activity that requires your child to jump with direction and distance toward a target will help him or her develop visual perception and refined motor planning skills. I am sure many of us remember "Don't Step on the Crack," "High-Low Waters" (a rope game moving the rope gently up and down to make waves), and "Snake" (a rope game moving rope side to side). All of these activities were games we played to help us develop visual judgment for the direction and force needed to make appropriate body movements to jump over the line or rope. For your child, you can encourage jumping games with a rope or during familiar outings. For example, in the supermarket, have your child only jump on the dark tiles (or at home, place rug squares or other non-slip materials on the floor and have your child jump from one to the other). Outside, you can have your child jump over the cracks in the sidewalk, over puddles, or over leaves.

Mountain Goats

Activity Goals: Gross-Motor Skills Development

Balance Improvement

Time: 20 minutes

Objectives: Upon successful completion of this activity, the child will be able to

1. Jump across a six-to-eight-inch distance and remain upright
2. Jump forward and in a diagonal pattern with both feet
3. Jump with direction toward a target

Materials:
1. Rug squares with non-slip backing or "sit-upons"
2. Masking tape

Procedure:
1. Set up rug squares in a straight line six-to-eight inches apart.
2. Gather children in a circle and explain how goats love to jump. Demonstrate jumping from one rug square to another without falling.
3. Have children try this once or several times.
4. Place rug squares in a large circle and have the children practice jumping in a circle from one rug square to another.
5. Have children try this several times.
6. Place rug squares in a zigzag pattern and have the children practice this several times.

Adaptations:
1. For the child using a wheelchair, have him move his chair or mobility device from one rug square to another. Encourage the child to stop on the rug square before moving to the next.
2. For the child with a visual impairment, use high-contrast colored rugs or hold the child's hands as he attempts to jump forward.

Multilevel Instruction:
1. Change the distance between rug squares to make it easier or more difficult.
2. Vary the distance apart and direction of the rug squares to make it more of a motor planning task.
3. Practice jumping sideways and jumping on one foot.
4. Add a balance beam, and after practicing jumping from rug square to rug square, read the "The Three Billy Goats' Gruff" and have the children act out the story with the balance beam as the bridge.

June

Letter to Parents
Mountain Goats

This week we pretended to be mountain goats, jumping from one rock to another. Then we practiced jumping in different directions and tried not to fall off the rocks.

Purpose of the Activity

This activity worked on building leg strength, coordination, and the ability to maintain balance during a dynamic motor task. As the child jumps from one square to another, he or she must plan the direction and force of each jump. This requires adequate strength and the ability to use visual information to ready muscles and joints to jump toward the target (rug square). This is an important skill development area because it helps the child become more able to move around his or her environment without tripping over objects and uneven surfaces (or failing to negotiate steps). Acquisition of these skills also prepares the child for higher gross-motor skills such as bunny hopping, climbing a ladder, hopping on one foot, jumping rope, and riding a bike.

Home Activities to Help Your Child Grow

At home, a variety of different objects can be used to encourage your child to jump toward or over a target. Start with small objects such as empty paper towel rolls or rolled up newspaper sheets. Set up several in a row and have your child stop and jump over each one. Next, set up slightly larger objects to jump over such as rolled up bath towels, paperback books, or cardboard blocks. These objects are a little higher and larger than the newspaper or paper towel rolls. As your child easily succeeds at these tasks, vary the size of objects, their distance from each other and the direction in which your child needs to jump.

Red, White, and Blue Flag Celebration

Activity Goals: Visual-Perceptual Development
Cognitive Development

Time: 30-to-40 minutes

Objectives: Upon successful completion of this activity, the child will be able to
1. Hold a streamer and wave it across her midline
2. Perform gross-motor skills, such as jumping and crawling
3. Identify colors of red, white, and blue
4. Recall a sequence of two or three steps

Materials:
1. Red, white, and blue crepe paper streamers
2. Cones to tape streamers across
3. Masking tape
4. Pompoms in red, white, and blue
5. Tongs or strawberry pickers
6. Small cups or baskets
7. Marching music

Procedure:
1 Allow each child to choose a streamer of her choice. Start with one hand or have the child try one in each hand.
2. Play some children's marching music and have the children wave the streamers imitating your pattern. Call out a color and have the children with that color streamer move it while the other children wait. For example, "Let's move just the blue streamers."
3. Tape a streamer between two cones placed 6-8 feet apart. Use different colors for each pair of cones (one red, one white, etc.). Make up a simple sequence to start like "crawl under the white streamer and jump over the red one." As the children succeed easily, add additional steps.
4. Spread pompoms out on the floor and challenge the children to pick up all the blue ones, then the red, then the white.

Adaptations:
1. For the child with motor planning problems, try putting one-half-to-one pound wrist weights on her arms for the streamer activity. This weight will give some additional sensory feedback.
2. For the child with limited mobility, try using a scooter board or rolling during the gross-motor skills activity using the cones and streamers.

Multilevel Instruction:
1. Try marching and waving the streamers as the children walk in a line or in a large circle.
2. The group can play magician at the end. Have the children take the streamer with one hand. While the streamer is dangling down, have the child attempt to gather it up into palm of their hands using only their fingers of that one hand to make it disappear.
3. After marching, playing with streamers and jumping over streamers, collect streamers and have the children create a large flag using a piece of oak tag or other heavy paper with a flag pattern. Take the streamers and place the red and white ones on the stripes and the blue ones for the star field. Later, have the children add stars. This will make a flag for each child.

June

Letter to Parents
Red, White, and Blue Flag Celebration

This week we had a flag celebration. At first the children waved red, white, or blue streamers while listening to marching music. Then the children tried to make their streamers move like the teacher's. Then we played games with the streamers like crawling under and jumping over them. The teacher put red, white, and blue pompoms on the floor and the children practiced using special tongs to pick up the color the teacher called out.

Purpose of the Activity

Moving the streamers around in imitation of the teacher helps your child build arm and hand strength needed for self-care and school-related activities. Jumping and crawling activities not only help your child develop body strength and endurance, but also work on his or her listening skills. During this part of the activity, the teacher gave verbal directions such as "Jump over the blue streamer and climb under the red one." Your child needed to listen to those directions and plan how to carry them out without being distracted by the others in the group. In the classroom, directions are frequently given and the child needs to listen and carry them out.

Home Activities to Help Your Child Grow

At home you can make streamer toys for your child by taking a two-to-three foot long crepe paper streamer and attaching it to an empty paper towel roll. Play some marching tunes or children's music and have your child imitate your movements with the streamer. Move your arms at or above your shoulder height, which will help your child build his or her upper body and shoulder strength. You can also have your child move the streamer and march around the table at the same time.

June

Shaving Cream Fun

Activity Goals: Pre-Writing Skills Development

Sensory Processing Improvement

Time: 20-to-30 minutes

Objectives: Upon successful completion of this activity, the child will be able to

1. Squeeze a spray bottle with one or both hands
2. Aim water spray toward a target three feet away
3. Tolerate soap on his hands without behavioral overreaction
4. Manipulate a Popsicle stick to "shave" with good motor planning

Materials:
1. Shaving cream or Silly Foam
2. Small spray bottles filled with water
3. Beach balls or large balloons
4. Buckets or containers to hold the balloons
5. Popsicle sticks or tongue depressors
6. Old shower curtain or large piece of plain plastic to cover a table

Procedure:
1. If possible, conduct this activity outdoors. Set up beach balls or balloons inside buckets so the ball or balloon is just stable enough not to fall out of the bucket when sprayed. Make sure most of the balloon or ball is exposed.
2. Gather children in a circle and explain today's activity. Tell them that we are pretending to shave our dad, grandfather or other male adult caregiver. Show the children the ball or balloon. Have them watch you shake and spray shaving cream on the ball to make a beard and mustache.
3. Let the children each have a turn spraying off the shaving cream with the spray bottles.
4. Next, go to the table covered with the plastic cover. Give each child a washable marker to create a face or large circle on the plastic. Give each child a chance to spray shaving cream on his or her tabletop face.
5. Clean the face off (shave it) with the tongue depressor or Popsicle stick and then try this again.

Adaptations:
1. For the child with a visual impairment, use high-contrast materials. Help him aim the spray bottle and give verbal cues to encourage and report his progress.
2. For the child with a weak grasp, try a squirt ball instead of squeeze bottles. If using a spray bottle, place rubber bands on the handle to enlarge it, or decrease the distance of the spray handle from the bottle by placing rubber bands around the bottle and handle to partially depress it.

Multilevel Instruction:
1. You can do the same activity on finger paint paper and add food coloring to increase the visual interest to the task. The faces can be drawn ahead of time with a marker for the children.
2. Indoors, try having the children create a face on the chalkboard. They can use shaving cream for the beard and shave the beard using a Popsicle stick.
3. Have the children draw a face and add cotton balls, packing bubbles, or tissue paper balls on it as the mustache and beard.

June

Letter to Parents
Shaving Cream Fun

This week we pretended to shave someone. Our teacher took a big ball and placed a shaving cream beard and mustache on it. Then we each took a turn trying to spray off all the shaving cream (shaving the beard). We made our own face on a table and put a beard on with shaving cream. Then we used a Popsicle stick as our razor and shaved off the shaving cream beard.

Purpose of the Activity

This activity develops fine hand movements and tactile discrimination skills to get ready for writing. The first part of the activity involved aiming and spraying a spray bottle of water at the ball decorated with a shaving cream beard. This type of repetitive squeezing not only helped to build your child's hand strength but also provided deep pressure to his or her hands in order to desensitize them to touch. This desensitization was used prior to the second half of the activity, during which your child removed the shaving cream from a drawing of a face with a Popsicle stick. As the children worked on getting all of the shaving cream off the faces, they got some of the cream on their hands. The children needed to be able to tolerate this texture and continue to work on the activity. Some children become so distracted by things on their hands that they cannot concentrate. By preparing the children to be comfortable with touching different textures and materials during our motor activities, we are helping them be better able to tolerate using glue, paste, and other materials in their classroom work.

Home Activities to Help Your Child Grow

You can use Silly Foam or shaving cream with your child right before bath time. In the empty bathtub, let your child spray the foam on the tub wall. After the foam is spread around on the wall, you can have your child either paint with his fingers or spray it off with a spray bottle. You can give your child a Popsicle stick and let him or her "shave" the soapsuds off his or her hands. Another way to help your child build hand strength is to have your child use the spray bottle to help clean the table after dinner or to help clean the car.

Water and Ball Play

Activity Goals: Visual-Perceptual Development
Pre-Writing Skills Development

Time: 30-to-40 minutes

Objectives: Upon successful completion of this activity, the child will be able to
1. Aim a small ball at a target
2. Stand on a balance beam and toss a ball
3. Squeeze a sponge with both hands
4. Follow a two-step sequence for a relay race

Materials:
1. 12 Ping-Pong balls
2. Large plastic bowls of different sizes, filled with water
3. Food coloring
4. Balance beam
5. A beach ball for each child
6. 4 buckets
7. Large car wash sponges

Procedure:
1. Set up these activities outdoors. Line up different-sized bowls filled with colored water on a table. Place a balance beam several feet away, parallel to the table. In addition; fill two buckets with water and place sponges in each one. Set up the two empty buckets 15-to-20 feet away.
2. Explain the first game to the children. Demonstrate how to toss a Ping-Pong ball into colored water. Give each child an opportunity to toss some balls into the bowls of water, standing on the ground and then standing on the balance beam.
3. Group the children in pairs. Set up the children at one end and explain the game. Have the children take a sponge from the filled bucket, run to the empty bucket, squeeze the water out into it, and then run back to their line and sit down. Then, the next child begins.
4. Finally, have the children practice throwing and catching beach balls.

Adaptations:
1. For the child who has difficulty coordinating for throwing, try having her wear light weights around her wrists to enhance sensory feedback when throwing Ping-Pong balls.
2. For the child with a visual impairment or who has difficulty releasing objects, place the bowls of water low or on the ground and allow the child to drop or push the Ping-Pong ball along the table into the water.

Multilevel Instruction:
1. Instead of using sponges for the relay race, you can use small cups. Have the children fill the cups up with water from one bucket and pour into the other bucket.
2. Place Ping-Pong balls on the table and give the children spray bottles filled with water or squirt balls to shoot the Ping-Pong balls off the table.
3. Place Ping-Pong balls on the table and have the children blow them to the other side in order to improve the children's expiratory force, and chest muscles, too. Blowing the Ping-Pong balls across the table will help improve visual attention and, as an added benefit, may result in calming the children down.

Letter to Parents
Water and Ball Play

This week we played some fun games. We threw Ping-Pong balls into big bowls filled with pretty colored water. Then we tried this again standing on a "bridge" (balance beam). After that, we had a kind of relay race using sponges and buckets of water. We picked up the wet sponges to move the water from one bucket and filled up another one by wringing the sponges out. We ended our activities by chasing and catching beach balls.

Purpose of the Activity

Children are visually attracted to colors and love playing with water. The activity of tossing a Ping-Pong ball into a bowl of water used these two great motivators to encourage your child to visually attend and practice ball throwing at a target for accuracy. By adding the balance beam activity, we increased your child's balance skills and improved stability while she worked on eye-hand coordination. The bucket and sponge activity helped your child improve hand strength because carrying and squeezing the sponges required effort. The beach ball activity encouraged your child's visual tracking skills and eye-hand coordination. This kind of ball moved more slowly than a playground ball, allowing the children time to visually follow its path and catch it.

Home Activities to Help Your Child Grow

Children love playing with water in warm weather. You can encourage this play with activities similar to the one presented this week. Set up some bowls or containers filled with water and food coloring outside. Then have your child practice throwing Ping-Pong balls or even coins into the containers. Another activity that works on hand strength that your child needs for manipulative skills such as self-care, pre-writing, writing, and coloring, is painting with water. On the sidewalk or patio, give your child a bucket of water and an old paintbrush. The best size is a four-to-six inch wide brush. Have your child draw shapes, letters, words, roads for cars, designs or just paint the sidewalk with the water. It will soon dry and the painting can be repeated many times. Finally, let your child help you squeeze out the sponge when you do dishes by hand or wash the car to build up hand strength.

Zoo Animals

Activity Goals: Pre-Writing Skills Development
Body-Scheme and Motor-Planning Improvement

Time: 30 minutes

Objectives: Upon successful completion of this activity, the child will be able to
1. Tear off and squeeze brown paper into small peanut shapes
2. Move along the floor using just arm strength
3. Stand on one foot for one-to-ten seconds
4. Pick up small objects with a grabber toy

Materials:
1. Brown paper cut in strips
2. Several large towels
3. Long-handled toy grabbers (see appendix)
4. Wide paper cylinders or containers to act as the elephant's trunks
5. Zoo book with flamingo, elephant, snake, and alligator pictures
6. Music for elephant walking

Procedure:
1. Gather children together to talk about zoo animals. Show the pictures of the animals to them.
2. Start with the elephant. Have the children imitate an elephant walk swinging two hands together side to side and lifting them up to imitate the elephant moving his trunk.
3. Demonstrate how to tear off and squeeze pieces of brown paper to small balls or peanut shapes.
4. After squeezing 4-5 peanuts have children take turns throwing them into the elephant's trunks, standing 3-5 feet away. You can place the "trunks" on a large mat and tell the children to stay off the mat, as they "should not go into the elephants' pen."
5. Gather children together and demonstrate alligator and snake body movements. Take one child and have him roll up in a towel with his arms outside the towel. Show the child how to stretch his arms forward, open them wide, and clap them shut to imitate the alligator's mouth opening and closing. To be a snake, he can slide on his belly along the floor using his arms.
6. Give each child an opportunity to try both animal imitations.
7. Next, demonstrate how to stand still on one foot like a flamingo with hands on waist and elbows out to imitate wings. Encourage the children to stay still as long as possible. Try standing on either foot. See if the children can maintain their balance as they gently "flap" their wings.
8. Dump out peanuts on the floor and have children take turns picking them up with the long-handled grabber toys and placing them in elephant's trunk or other container.

Adaptations:
1. For the child with one functional hand, have him try to squeeze the paper into a peanut using one hand and pushing the paper against a surface to crush it into shape. Try using crepe paper for this child and have him manipulate it into a ball using just one hand.
2. For the child with a visual impairment, give verbal cues and physical assistance, as needed, to try different animal movement patterns.

June

3. For the child using a wheelchair or with limited mobility, have him try these postures in his chair or help him with hands-on assistance.

Multilevel Instruction:

1. Play a musical game by having the children freeze in the animal postures when the music stops.
2. Make animal shapes of snakes, alligators, etc., for the children to trace, color, and cut out.

June

Letter to Parents
Zoo Animals

This week we pretended to be zoo animals. We started by pretending to be elephants walking along and swinging our trunks. By crushing brown paper into small peanut shapes, we made peanuts to feed our pretend elephants. After we made the peanuts, we tossed them into their trunks. We had fun rolling up in towels to become snakes and alligators sliding along the floor. We practiced being flamingos and stood on one foot. We used a long-handled toy grabber to pick up small objects to feed to the elephants.

Purpose of the Activity

By sliding along the floor, your child worked on developing upper body and arm strength needed for fine-motor development. Also in this activity, we used crumbling, squeezing, and long-handled grabbers to build your child's hand strength. Working on upper body, arm, and hand strength will help your child develop the strength needed for fine-motor control when using scissors, coloring, and writing. Tossing objects into a container helped build your child's ability to visually attend and improved eye-hand coordination.

Home Activities to Help Your Child Grow

You can help your child continue to develop arm and upper body strength by playing snake and alligator games at home. Roll your child up in a large towel leaving his or her arms free. Have your child practice moving along the floor using his or her arms. Try it first on a tile or hardwood floor because it is easier to slide on these surfaces than on carpeted surfaces. You can also set up a peanut toss at home. Have your child tear up brown paper bags into small pieces and then squeeze them into small balls. Set up a large coffee can or small waste paper basket into which the peanuts can be tossed. As your child's throwing pattern and aim improves, move the container farther away.

June

Educational Goals by Activity

Attention Improvement	Balance Improvement	Bilateral Coordination Development	Body-Scheme and Motor-Planning Improvement	Cognitive Development	Fine-Motor Skills Development	Gross-Motor Skills Development	Group Development	Hand-Dominance Development	Pre-Writing Skills Development	Scissor Skills Development	Self-Help Skills Development	Sensory Processing Improvement	Strength and Endurance Improvement	Visual-Perceptual Development	Activity	Page
								✔		✔					The Aquarium	284
			✔				✔								Be a Bubble	286
			✔										✔		Boats and Bridges	288
✔	✔														Bubbles	290
			✔											✔	Bubbles Go Pop!	292
		✔								✔					Cornstalks	294
		✔											✔		A Corny Party	296
								✔				✔			Edible Sand	298
										✔			✔		Paper Roll Fireworks	300
			✔							✔					Pets	302
	✔												✔		Vegetable Garden	304

July

The Aquarium

Activity Goals: Hand-Dominance Development
Scissor Skills Development

Time: 45 minutes

Objectives: Upon successful completion of this activity, the child will be able to
1. Demonstrate preference for using one hand to dab paint on the mural paper and fish
2. Be able to paint in midline, making a vertical line
3. Cut along curved lines, using a dominant-assistive hand pattern while cutting accurately on the lines

Materials:
1. Large sheet of mural paper
2. Poster paint: blue for water, various colors for fish
3. Green and blue streamers
4. Sponges
5. Paper plates
6. Scissors

Procedure:
1. Hang mural paper on a wall. Set the children up to sponge on blue paint to make an ocean. Show them how to press the sponge on the paper, lift it up, and then press it down again, making a vertical line. This will give them lots of practice with developing eye-hand control in midline.
2. When dry, let the children help you hang green and blue streamers on the mural to simulate the ocean waves.
3. At the table, give each child scissors and a paper plate with three wedges drawn on it—one to make a mouth and two to make the tail for a fish. Show them how to cut out the fish.
4. Let the children use sponges and poster paint to paint their fish. When dry, hang them on the mural.

Adaptations:
1. Sit a child on a chair while painting on the mural if he or she has difficulty with balance, or lay the mural paper on the floor and have him or her paint on hands and knees.
2. Refer to the Appendix (on page 342) for suggestions on adapting types of scissors.

Multilevel Instruction:
1. For the child who may not have decided on a dominant hand for coloring, encourage him to use both hands on the sponge while making vertical lines and painting his fish.
2. Children who are beginning to cut may enjoy "fringing" a fish (by making short cuts along the edges of the fins and tail) if they cannot yet cut along curved lines.
3. Let the children use markers to add eyes and scales to the fish when they are dry.
4. Children can cut out round circles and glue them on the mural for bubbles coming out of the fishes' mouths.

July

Letter to Parents

The Aquarium

Our class made a giant picture of an aquarium this week. We painted the water, decorated it with streamers to make waves, and cut out fish, which we painted in lovely tropical colors.

Purpose of the Activity

This week's activity focused on helping the children develop good eye-hand coordination and cutting skills. We asked the children to paint on the water using sponges, pressing from the top to the bottom in a vertical line. This will help strengthen their ability to focus their eyes in midline while using their hands. Children need to be able to work in midline when they are writing. Our activity also helped children practice using their preferred hand in a simple, fine-motor activity to develop hand dominance.

The children also practiced using scissors to cut along lines. We used paper plates to make the fish. Using a heavier type of paper helps the children strengthen the muscles used for cutting and makes it easier to control the scissors.

Home Activities to Help Your Child Grow

You can continue helping your child improve his or her skill cutting with scissors at home with simple activities. For example, using brown paper bags for paper, have him or her cut out round "cookies," "hamburgers," or, perhaps, rectangular 'French fries." If your child cuts pretty well, try tracing designs with cookie cutters. Glue two together at the top, add a string, decorate, and your child has made a card or gift tag.

Some children seem to choose their dominant hand for cutting and writing later than others. If your child doesn't seem to have made up his or her mind and is four years old or more, consistently offer crayons, scissors, and finger food in the middle of the table. If he or she seems to start with the same hand most of the time, you will have a good indication of his or her dominant hand. Ask the occupational therapist at your child's school to check if this continues to be an area of concern for your child.

July

Be a Bubble

Activity Goals: Body-Scheme and Motor-Planning Improvement
Group Development

Time: 20 minutes

Objectives: Upon successful completion of this activity, the child will be able to
1. Move around the room imitating a bubble
2. Move showing good body awareness by maintaining space around himself
3. Be able to follow the rules for a group game

Materials:
1. Music suitable for "floating"
2. Carpet squares, placed in a circle
3. Bubble wand to blow through

Procedure:
1. Have the children each sit on a rug square, which you have placed in a large circle. Explain that they will "float" around the outside of the circle as the music plays. When you touch them, they will "pop" and sit down on a rug square. When you blow through the bubble wand toward them, they will stand up and float around some more.
2. Start the music and the game.
3. Finish by popping all the "bubbles."

Adaptations:
1. A child with a visual impairment may feel more comfortable floating around with a physical boundary to "insulate" him. Try having him wear a large inner tube.
2. Allow a child who is in a wheelchair to push himself around and wheel over to a rug square when "popped."

Multilevel Instruction:
1. Let children take turns being the leader who pops the other bubbles and blows them up again.
2. Let the children practice cutting large bubbles out of paper for cutting practice after doing this activity.

July

Learning in Motion

Letter to Parents

Be a Bubble

The children played a game pretending to be bubbles today. They floated around to music. When the leader touched them, they were "popped" and had to sit down. When the leader blew through a bubble wand towards them, they became bubbles again and could stand up and float.

Purpose of the Activity

This activity helped the children practice their skill at imitating a movement. They practiced cooperating in a group, learning how to move around carefully and leave some space around themselves. They had to follow the rules for a game, which helps them also learn how to cooperate in a group.

Home Activities to Help Your Child Grow

Following the rules for simple games is a good thing even for young children to start learning. At home, you can work on following the rules by playing simple games with your child. Preschoolers enjoy games like Hungry Hungry Hippos and Fleas on Fred, which require simple actions. Kindergartners and first graders can learn the rules for board games like Candyland®, picture lotto games, and card games like "Go Fish." These types of games are also important because the children use fine-motor coordination to play them as they pick up small objects and move them to the correct locations.

July

Boats and Bridges

Activity Goals: Body-Scheme and Motor-Planning Improvement
Strength and Endurance Improvement

Time: 20 minutes

Objectives: Upon successful completion of this activity, the child will be able to
1. Hold position on all fours while pretending to be a bridge
2. Scoot underneath the bridge

Materials: Mats

Procedure:
1. Line up the mats.
2. Show the children how to place their hands on the floor keeping their legs straight in order to make a bridge.
3. Line the children up single file at the end of the mats. Have them practice scooting on their stomachs, using their arms to push themselves, in a "commando crawl."
4. Have several children line up on the mats and bend over to form a bridge.
5. Let the rest of the children scoot underneath the bridge, doing a commando crawl.
6. After each child scoots under the bridge, have them replace one of the bridge members to give him a rest.
7. Repeat going under the bridges with the "boats" lying on their backs to push with their feet and scooting on their sides.

Adaptations:
1. Place a child who is non-ambulatory on a towel and pull her underneath the bridges.
2. Let children who have difficulty being a bridge member due to reduced strength and endurance make a bridge another way, such as balancing on their knees and joining hands.

Multilevel Instruction:
1. Make a tall bridge with the bridge members holding their arms up high holding a towel. This will help build strength and endurance in the arms and shoulders.
2. Use scooter boards as boats going underneath the bridges.

Letter to Parents

Boats and Bridges

We learned how to be boats and bridges this week using our bodies. We put our hands down on the floor, keeping our legs straight, to be a bridge. When it was our turn to be a boat, we slid under the bridges different ways: on our stomachs, backs, and sides. It was fun to see how long we could make the bridge and still go under it without touching.

Purpose of the Activity

The children used a lot of strength and endurance to maintain a bridge position while their classmates slid underneath. The longer we made the bridge, the longer each child had to hold the position!

Sliding under the bridge was also a learning experience in a different way. Moving underneath without touching the arms and legs of the children who were the bridges required good motor planning and body awareness. Children build a sense of their bodies by moving and getting feedback when they touch things. They need a good sense of their body shape and size in order to be able to imitate movements and remember movements, such as writing letters and numbers

Home Activities to Help Your Child Grow

Here are some activities to help your child develop good body awareness:

1. Try "Dot Spot"—touch or rub a place on your child while her eyes are closed. When your child opens her eyes, ask her to show you where you touched.

2. Have your child close her eyes. Move her arm or leg on one side in a pattern, such as up and down. Then ask your child to do it with the opposite arm or leg.

3. Write a shape or letter on the back of your child's hand and see if she can guess what you wrote.

July

Bubbles

Activity Goals: Bilateral Coordination Development

Attention Improvement

Time: 30 minutes

Objectives: Upon successful completion of this activity, the child will be able to
1. Coordinate both hands together to hold and move cup to make large bubbles
2. Demonstrate good tolerance to touching bubble solution
3. Show improved visual attention during activity
4. Blow through cup to make bubbles

Materials:
1. Baby shampoo
2. Glycerin (available at pharmacies)
3. Plastic tray for each child
4. Plastic cup with bottom cut out
5. Blender

Procedure:
1. Seat the children around a table. Show them how you are mixing up bubble foam in the blender using some shampoo, water, and glycerin.
2. Give each child a little of the foam in his or her tray and a cup. Show the children how to place both hands on the cup and pull upwards to make a bubble tower. Some children may get half spheres, which you can show them how to pop with one finger. (Try adding more water or more soap to get the effect you want.)
3. Show the children that they can lift up their cups and blow through them to make bubbles that float. While the children are still seated, blow some bubbles for them to reach up and pop.
4. Have the children rinse their hands and gather on the floor in a circle. Use rug squares, if desired, to establish boundaries. Tell them that they are not to leave their rugs, but, when you blow, they will get to pop as many bubbles as they can. Have each child take a turn blowing lots of bubbles for the group.

Adaptations:
1. If some children cannot seem to purse their lips to blow effectively, try having them practice before a mirror while they are blowing through the cup. If you use a large enough cup, they should be able to see their mouths through the opening.
2. If your group is very active, try laying terry towels down on the table or floor to help with spills.
3. Use a squeeze toy, such as a "bubble gun," if a child cannot blow bubbles due to a disability.

Multilevel Instruction: Let the group explore making different kinds of bubbles using different sizes of cups. Large bubble wands can be made out of bent wire hangers, dipped into a bucket of bubble solution, and waved around to make huge bubbles.

July

Learning in Motion

Letter to Parents
Bubbles

We made our own bubble mix using baby shampoo, water, and some glycerin (from the pharmacy). We explored using plastic cups to wave and blow through, making huge bubbles. We had fun taking turns blowing bubbles for the children to pop as many as they could.

Purpose of the Activity

Blowing the bubbles through a large cup gave the children practice using both hands together in an activity. The blowing also gave them practice learning to use their facial muscles and helped to strengthen the eye muscles for convergence, which they need for looking at close objects. Staying in one spot and watching bubbles in order to pop them helped the children develop visual attention and visual tracking skills, too. Finally, the activity required lots of deep breathing. This helps children (and adults) improve their level of attention.

Home Activities to Help Your Child Grow

Help your child play with bubbles at home, too. You can make a different type of bubble blower for your child by wetting a small washcloth, placing it over a plastic cup, and securing it with a rubber band. Make a little hole in the side of the cup and push a short plastic straw through it. Then put a few drops of shampoo or dish washing liquid on the washcloth. When your child blows, he or she will make lots of bubbles. If your child should suck by accident, he or she will get only air. Since it takes a lot of force to blow through the straw, your child will build up good strength in facial muscles and the muscles for respiration.

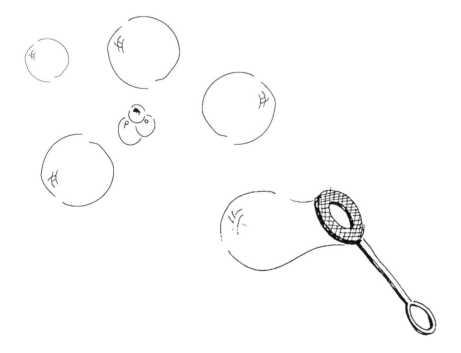

July

Bubbles Go Pop!

Activity Goals: Body-Scheme and Motor-Planning Improvement
Visual-Perceptual Development

Time: 30 minutes

Objectives: Upon successful completion of this activity, the child will be able to
1. Pop bubbles and hit balloon with different parts of the body
2. Coordinate eyes with hands to pop bubbles and catch balloons

Materials:
1. Bubbles
2. Non-latex balloons
3. Rug squares

Procedure:
1. Have the children stand or sit on a rug square. Review the parts of the body by having them touch the spot on their bodies when you name it.
2. Name a body part, such as "thumb," and have the children try to pop a bubble with it. Try giving each child a turn, one by one, and then blow a lot of bubbles and let the whole group try at the same time.
3. Try the same thing using a balloon. Let each child try to hit the balloon with the named part.
4. Finish with the children catching and throwing the balloon to each other.

Adaptations:
1. To help children who have difficulty with moving a body part, keep the bubble stuck to the bubble wand and hold it close to them.
2. Use a bright-colored balloon and have the group positioned so the light is behind them to make it easier to see for a child with a visual impairment.

Multilevel Instruction:
1. Increase the physical demands of this activity by positioning the children on their stomachs, so they have to raise their arms up to pop bubbles or hit a balloon. You can provide them with towel rolls or wedges to make it easier.
2. Try suspending the balloons on strings to control them more easily when asking the children to hit it with a body part.

Letter to Parents

Bubbles Go Pop!

We worked on popping bubbles in a new way this week. First we took turns trying to pop a bubble with one part of our bodies: an elbow, a foot, even our heads! Then we tried to do the same thing with a balloon. We practiced catching and throwing the balloon to each other, too.

Purpose of the Activity

Popping bubbles with different parts of the body helps the children develop awareness of how to move their bodies and improves their sense of distance between themselves and an object. Practicing catching and throwing with a balloon instead of balls is often easier. The balloon moves more slowly, giving the children time to get ready to catch it.

Catching and throwing balls and other objects helps children develop their eye muscles, too. They learn to focus their eyes for a longer time when they watch a slowly moving object. This helps improve their ability to maintain visual attention, which they will need when they watch their teacher demonstrate how to write letters.

Home Activities to Help Your Child Grow

Eye-hand coordination activities are fun to do at home. Your child would enjoy playing ball with you. You can play with a balloon, as we did, and then move on to other objects such as a scarf, a beach ball, a beanbag, or a large playground ball. You can make a beanbag by putting rice in a sock and knotting it.

If your child is afraid of being hit by the ball, be sure to use only light objects until he or she has gained confidence catching them. Then try a heavier ball to help develop accuracy for throwing, as the lighter ball is harder to throw. If you're using a beanbag to improve accuracy, throw it back gently from a short distance so your child will not become afraid of being hit. Lots of practice and confidence will help your child develop a good level of skill in throwing and catching.

July

Cornstalks

Activity Goals: Bilateral Coordination Development
Scissor Skills Development

Time: 30 minutes

Objectives: Upon successful completion of this activity, the child will be able to
1. Fold paper in half
2. Cut four-to-five-inch straight lines
3. Make colored dots on ears of corn
4. Roll up corn stalks
5. Glue on ears of corn

Materials:
1. 11-by-17-inch construction paper in green, yellow, or brown, or paper bags cut in large pieces
2. Scissors
3. Pre-cut paper ears of corn
4. Glue
5. Tape
6. Cotton swabs
7. Small dishes of paint

Procedure:
1. Demonstrate and have the children fold and crease a sheet of paper lengthwise and then open it up.
2. Have them cut from the long edge up to the crease in the middle, repeating this along the length of the paper to make a fringe.
3. Roll up the paper from the narrow side, so that the fringe makes a corn tassel. Put a piece of tape on to hold.
4. If desired, the "tassel" can be pulled gently in the center to make a more realistic shape.
5. Have the children roll sheets of construction paper into tubes about 1" in diameter to make corn stalks.
6. Have the children dot the paper ears of corn with colored circles using cotton swabs and poster paint.
7. When the ears are dry, let the children glue the tassels to the top of the ears and glue the bottom of the ears to the cornstalks.

Adaptations:
1. Add lines with crayon or felt-tipped pen to help the children see where to cut the fringe.
2. Pre-cut the fringe and let the beginning cutter snip the edges to make it fancier.

Multilevel Instruction:
1. Let the children who are more advanced with cutting cut out their own ears of corn. You can provide lines for them to follow or ask them to draw their own, following a model.
2. Let the children turn the ears of corn into Indian corn by dotting them after dipping their index fingers in various colors of paint.

Letter to Parents

Cornstalks

July

This week we made cornstalks. We folded paper, cut long fringes, and rolled them up. Then we glued on ears of corn, which we painted first to show the kernels.

Purpose of the Activity

The children had a chance to practice cutting this week. Since they had to stop in the middle of the page each time they cut, it helped them develop good eye-hand coordination, spatial sense, and visual attention while cutting with scissors.

Folding, cutting, and rolling the paper required using both hands together, which is called "bilateral coordination." Children need to learn to use both hands together in activities that don't require a lot of precision in order to be able to coordinate them for more precise activities when they are older. An example of a bilateral coordination activity that requires a lot of precision would be threading a needle.

Home Activities to Help Your Child Grow

Folding and rolling up paper are skills you can help your child practice at home. Try using newspapers. Let your child fold them up and put them in a pile or bag for recycling. Help your child practice rolling up a few half sheets. You can put rubber bands around them to keep them rolled up and use them for markers to practice jumping over. To practice counting skills, let your child see how many newspaper rolls he or she can jump over. Newspaper rolls can be used to practice forming letters and numbers, too,

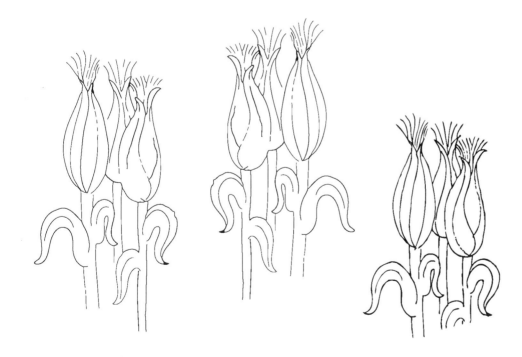

July

A Corny Party

Activity Goals: Strength and Endurance Improvement
Bilateral Coordination Development

Time: 30-to-45 minutes

Objectives: Upon successful completion of this activity, the child will be able to
1. Peel an ear of corn independently
2. Hold a cooked ear with both hands and rub over the butter stick or hold the ear with one hand and rub the butter on with the other

Materials:
1. An ear of fresh corn for each child
2. Microwave dish and oven; or, cook in a pot of boiling water in an area safe from the children's reach
3. Butter in a stick form

Procedure:
1. Give each child an ear of corn. Show her how to strip off the husk and pick off the tassel and silk threads.
2. Cook the ears and let them cool until just warm.
3. Show the children how to butter the corn: they could use a special holder and rub the butter on or they could hold the ear of corn with a hand at each end and rub it on the stick of butter.
4. Eat and enjoy!

Adaptations: If there are children who cannot eat the whole kernels off the cob, try cutting some of the raw corn off and letting the children have some fun grinding it in a food processor. Then try cooking the corn, adding some whole milk and butter to make a sauce. Or provide some corn bread on the side.

Multilevel Instruction:
1. While the corn is cooking and cooling, do the "Cornstalks" (on page 294) activity or "Vegetable Garden" (on page 304) activity.
2. Have the children roll ears of corn in poster paint and roll them on paper bags to make prints.

July

Learning in Motion

Letter to Parents
A Corny Party

We prepared and cooked corn on the cob today. The children learned how to pull off the husk and silk threads. When it was all cooked, they rubbed butter over the corn and ate it. We had a great party!

Purpose of the Activity

Our activity today helped the children build strength and coordination in their hands. Pulling off the husks builds strength and coordination between the two hands because it takes effort. Pulling off the little silk threads required a good pinch. The children had to use both hands together to butter their corn, too.

Home Activities to Help Your Child Grow

Preparing food at home helps children learn valuable skills for independence. Young children love to "help," and even though they may seem to make the task longer, it's a good idea to take advantage of their willingness! Giving your child small jobs such as spooning food onto dishes for the family or washing potatoes will make him or her feel important to the family, too.

The other benefit in letting your child help you prepare meals is that so many of the chores require using both hands together. Stirring, tearing lettuce, holding a glass while pouring milk, and drying off the utensils after they are washed will help your child develop good bilateral coordination.

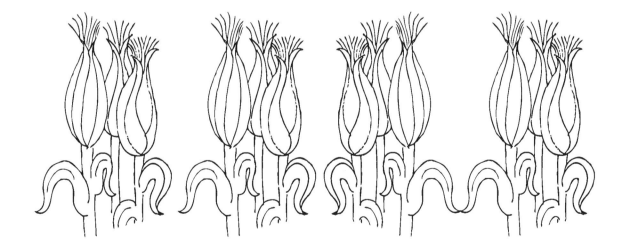

July

Edible Sand

Activity Goals: Sensory Processing Improvement
Hand-Dominance Development

Time: 30 minutes

Objectives: Upon successful completion of this activity, the child will be able to

1. Touch and manipulate food ingredients without discomfort
2. Motor plan to crush vanilla wafers and construct dessert as demonstrated by the teacher, using a dominant-assistive hand pattern as needed

Materials:

1. Vanilla pudding: pre-made or mix plus ingredients
2. Cup or bowl for each child
3. Jelly fish candy
4. Vanilla wafers
5. Rolling pin or toy hammers
6. Plastic bags
7. Pretzel sticks

Procedure:

1. Set up materials and seat children around a table. Let them help you make the vanilla pudding, following the directions. Give each child a turn to stir.
2. Help the children crush the vanilla wafers to make "sand." Put the cookies in either one large, strong, clear, plastic bag to share or smaller bags, one for each child. Let the children crush the cookies either rolling with a rolling pin or pounding with the toy hammers.
3. Let the children spoon vanilla pudding, "the ocean," into their cups.
4. Give them all some fish to mix in to "swim in the ocean." Use a pretzel stick for a stirrer.
5. Let them sprinkle on some of the vanilla wafer crumbs, the "sand."
6. Give them the pretzel sticks. These can be broken into small pieces and represent stones, seaweed, or whatever they imagine.

Adaptations:

1. Have the children stand up so they can put more force into crushing the cookies if they are having trouble when using the rolling pin.
2. Precede this activity with one that provides "heavy work" (see "Sensory Processing Improvement" on page 5) to prepare a child who is sensitive to touch. If you find that a student will not eat the dessert because the different textures are mixed together but will eat the foods when they are separate, consult a speech or occupational therapist, as this may indicate difficulty with sensory tolerance or oral-motor control.

Multilevel Instruction: Encourage more advanced students to open and close the plastic bags themselves, using either a wire closure or a zipper bag.

Letter to Parents
Edible Sand

We love to make things to eat! This week, we made a treat that reminded us of going to the beach. We mixed up vanilla pudding for our "ocean," sprinkled on crushed vanilla wafers for sand, added some jelly fish and pretzel sticks and had a feast!

Purpose of the Activity

Our activities helped the children develop their senses of touch and taste, and practice using both hands together. For example, they used both hands to crush the cookies, snap the pretzel sticks in pieces, and spoon pudding into their cups.

Home Activities to Help Your Child Grow

If your child is a "picky" eater, you might find that he or she is more likely to try to eat something he or she has helped make. You are also teaching your child important skills for independence when you let him or her spread his or her own peanut butter on crackers or bread, pour milk, and find plates and silverware.

Playing in the sand is a good activity at home for developing fine-motor coordination, the sense of touch in the hands, and thinking skills, such as measuring. You don't need a big sandbox—try using a large plastic box. Give your child a set of cups of different sizes, plastic bottles with different openings, a funnel, water, strainer, and any other small toys that he or she would enjoy; and he or she most likely will be entertained and learning for some time!

July

Paper Roll Fireworks

Activity Goals: Visual-Perceptual Development
Scissor Skills Development

Time: 20 minutes

Objectives: Upon successful completion of this activity, the child will be able to
1. Hold paper roll using a full palmar grasp (using the whole hand)
2. Cut four two-to-three-inch slits in cardboard
3. Use a pincer grasp to pick up and sprinkle glitter on paper
4. Put on smock independently

Materials:
1. 3 paper rolls per child, each approximately 6" tall
2. Scissors
3. Paper for the picture: black or white
4. Red, gold, and blue paint
5. Glitter, placed in a small cup
6. Paper plates
7. Newspaper
8. Smocks (optional)

Procedure:
1. Gather enough paper rolls for the class. Long rolls from wrapping paper or paper towels can be cut to 6" lengths. Draw four or five 2"-long lines lengthwise on the bottom of each roll. Cover a table with newspaper to prepare for painting.
2. Have children sit at the table. Discuss why we celebrate the 4th of July. See if they remember fireworks.
3. Demonstrate cutting the lines on the paper rolls to the children. Pass out scissors and 3 paper rolls to each child. Let them cut the lines, stopping at the end of each line.
4. Demonstrate holding the paper rolls with the cut ends against the table top and pressing down on them to spread the cut ends out. Have the children do this to their paper rolls.
5. Have the children put on their smocks. Give each one a large sheet of paper and take one paper roll. Give them a paper plate with paint on it and cups of glitter.
6. Show the children how to press the spread out end of their paper rolls into the paint and stamp them on the paper. They will then sprinkle glitter on while the paint is still wet.
7. Let the children begin stamping and sprinkling. Have them use a different roll for each color paint.

Adaptations:
1. Children with poor hand strength may need to have their paper rolls pre-cut.
2. Mix sand in the poster paint. When it is dry, a child with a visual impairment can "feel" the fireworks.

Multilevel Instruction: Instead of making individual pictures, have the children use one large sheet of mural paper, and add pictures of people, grass, dogs, etc.

July

Letter to Parents

Paper Roll Fireworks

We celebrated the 4th of July this week by using paper rolls to make fireworks. The children cut slits in the ends of paper rolls. Then they fanned out the bottoms by pressing them down on the table. They dipped the ends in blue, red, and gold paint and stamped their paper. The last step was sprinkling the fireworks with glitter, just like the real fireworks. How colorful!

Purpose of the Activity

This activity gave your child the opportunity to practice cutting with scissors, an important classroom skill for the young child to learn. Also, pressing down when preparing the paper rolls and stamping with them gave the children lots of pressure into their hands. This type of stimulation is needed by children to develop a sense of position and how one part of their body is connected to the other. The actual nerve cells are located in muscles and joints, and react specifically to pressure. The children also practiced using their thumb and index fingers to pinch and sprinkle the glitter. This type of grasp is important for your child to be able to take care of his or her own clothing fasteners, pick up coins, string beads, and eat finger foods.

Home Activities to Help Your Child Grow

Activities that involve pressure are sometimes called "heavy work" activities because they involve using large muscles in tasks that offer resistance. Other activities you could try are playing tug of war, pushing a heavy box across the floor, jumping, carrying groceries, pushing a vacuum cleaner, pulling a wagon, and pushing a grocery cart. These types of activities help your child develop body awareness, an inner picture of how his or her body is assembled, and how it is positioned at any given moment. Children who have poor body awareness tend to look clumsy, bump into others, or misjudge how quickly they are moving.

To help your child develop a good pincer grasp, encourage him or her to play with small objects. Of course, you would want to supervise his or her play if there is a chance that a small inedible object could be eaten by your child or another in your home. You could make up a box which contained a selection of padlocks with keys, beads to string, Perler beads to put on templates, decorative hole punches, a container with a slit in the top to push coins through, and lacing cards. Playing with these toys will help your child develop better pincer grasp and finger dexterity.

Pets

Activity Goals: Body-Scheme and Motor-Planning Improvement
Scissor Skills Development

Time: 30 minutes

Objectives: Upon successful completion of this activity, the child will be able to

1. Guide scooter board to a target area, carrying a toy animal
2. Imitate animal gestures using the whole body
3. Cut accurately along a straight line

Materials:

1. Stuffed pet animals hidden in a large bag
2. Pictures cut from magazine and pasted into strips of the same types of pet animals hidden in the bag.
3. Scooter boards
4. Scissors

Procedure:

1. Sit the children in a circle around the bag full of animals. Show them some pictures of animals representing those in the bag. Then ask them to put their hands in, guess which animal they have chosen, and then pull it out.
2. Show the children how to place the animals on the scooter boards and give them a ride to their "homes." The children could try giving their animals a ride on the scooter boards in various ways, such as lying down with the animals on their backs or sitting and pushing with their feet.
3. Let the children cut apart the pictures of the animals and place them in an envelope to bring home. Tell them to show their parents how to do the animal gestures using the pictures to remind them.

Adaptations:

1. A child who uses a wheelchair can use her wheelchair instead of a scooter board.
2. Use hands-on assistance to teach a child with a visual impairment the gestures for the animals. Help her review the gestures by orally naming the animals and demonstrating them before she takes home her pictures. Use light weights on her arms and legs to increase sensory feedback to improve memory for the motor patterns.
3. Refer to the *Appendix* (on page 342) for scissor adaptations.

Multilevel Instruction:

1. Provide pre-cut pictures for the children to take home to simplify this activity.
2. Prepare the picture strips by trimming the long edges so that the children will only have to cut apart the animals along the short lines.
3. To increase the difficulty of the cutting task, prepare the animal pictures using different shapes for the children to cut out, rather than a strip.

July

Letter to Parents

Pets

We had fun playing games with pets today. We took turns giving stuffed animals a ride on our scooter boards. Once we were familiar with them, we took turns finding one in a bag and guessing which one it was before we pulled it out.

We also pretended to be some pets and other animals. We tried jumping like a fish, scratching like a monkey, shaking our feathers like a bird, stamping like an elephant, and stretching like a cat. Finally, we practiced cutting pictures with scissors so we could bring them home to show you.

Purpose of the Activity

Gross-motor activities today worked on improving the children's strength and coordination. Practicing moving like various animals also helped the children develop imitative skills. Imitation is used to learn to write letters and numbers and to follow the teacher's directions for activities. We also practiced cutting with scissors along straight lines in order to develop more skill.

Home Activities to Help Your Child Grow

Using the pictures your child brought home, see if he or she can remember the gestures learned in school. The ability to remember a movement pattern is called "motor memory." Children need good "motor memory" when they learn to write in order to remember how to make the letters.

Help your child develop better motor memory by learning to copy gestures. An easy way to do this is during your child's bath. Squirt some shaving cream on the wall, let him or her spread it out, and then practice drawing. Try moving both hands together in circles, horizontal, and vertical lines, to improve his or her coordination. Try spreading shaving cream on your child's back, and see if he or she can guess what you drew!

Vegetable Garden

Activity Goals: Strength and Endurance Improvement
Balance Improvement

Time: 30 minutes

Objectives: Upon successful completion of this activity, the child will be able to
1. Maintain wheelbarrow position to walk on hands for 15 feet
2. Balance self on a scooter board holding on to a Hula hoop while being pulled

Materials:
1. Scooter boards
2. Hula hoops
3. Beanbags
4. Helmets, if desired

Procedure:
1. Talk about how farmers might use wheelbarrows to carry their vegetables back from the garden. Explain to the children that they will pretend to be "farmers" and "wheelbarrows" and will carry "vegetables," which are the beanbags, back to the barn.
2. Spread out the beanbag "vegetables" in the "vegetable patch." Use a Hula Hoop or rug square approximately 15 feet away to represent the barn.
3. Group the children in pairs. Have the "wheelbarrow" get on his hands and knees. Have the "farmer" put a "vegetable" on the "wheelbarrow," pick up the child's legs at the ankles, and help him carry the "vegetable" to the "barn." When they arrive, the wheelbarrow child can go down on his hands and knees and tip forwards or sideways to dump the beanbag off. The "farmer" then takes the "wheelbarrow" back to the beginning, and the pair change places.
4. When all the "vegetables" have been picked and taken to the barn, show the children how to ride on scooter boards. Have one child on a scooter board with a partner pulling him with a Hula Hoop. The children can try this either lying on their stomachs or sitting, although if sitting, they would be safest if using a helmet in case of a fall. Explain that the children on the scooter boards will be the "farmers" riding on the wagons and the children pulling them will be the "horses," helping the farmers take their vegetables to market.
5. Designate a marketplace. This could be quite a distance away, even down a hallway.
6. Let the pairs of children carry the "vegetables" to market, changing places so each has a chance to be a farmer and a horse.

Adaptations:
1. Use a scooter board to substitute for wheelbarrow walking for a child who is not able to do it.
2. Substitute a picture and tape it on if the child has difficulty keeping a beanbag on his back.
3. Use a wagon instead of a scooter board if a child cannot ride on it.
4. A child who must stay in his wheelchair could play a role being the farmer who picks the vegetable using a reacher. Later, he could be the person at the market to whom the children deliver the vegetables.

July

Multilevel

Instruction:
1. Let the children's ages, mobility levels, and skill levels help you determine how far away to place the target areas for wheelbarrow walking and riding on the scooter boards.
2. Expand this activity by having the children color and cut out paper vegetables first. They could be as simple as round "potatoes" cut from paper bags.

Letter to Parents

Vegetable Garden

We had fun pretending to pick vegetables on our farm this week. We took turns being wheelbarrows, carrying vegetables from the field to the market. The "farmers" held our legs, while we walked on our hands. We also pretended to ride wagons to market. We took turns riding on our wagons while some of us pretended to be the horses that pulled us. We found out that farming vegetables is hard work!

Purpose of the Activity

This week's activity worked on building the children's strength, balance, and coordination between both sides of their bodies. Wheelbarrow walking not only builds up the children's arms and shoulders, but also their wrists and fingers. This helps them be able to hold pencils and crayons with good control while writing or coloring.

Our activity also required good balance. The children used their balance as wheelbarrows, as they leaned over like real wheelbarrows to tip the vegetables off their backs. They also used balance riding on the scooter board "wagons."

Home Activities to Help Your Child Grow

You can find activities at home to help your child build strength and endurance, such as helping to move furniture when you are vacuuming, using a watering can to water the garden, putting away food when you come home from the grocery store, and helping to push a stroller or shopping cart.

An added benefit to doing more strenuous activities is to help your child develop more control over his or her attention and activity level. Just as we adults often find a workout or a vigorous activity helps us feel better, children do, too. Try giving your child an activity that requires force for five-to-ten 15 minutes before you ask him or her to practice a fine-motor skill, such as cutting with scissors. This will help your child if he or she has difficulty paying attention.

July

Educational Goals by Activity

August

Attention Improvement	Balance Improvement	Bilateral Coordination Development	Body-Scheme and Motor-Planning Improvement	Cognitive Development	Fine-Motor Skills Development	Gross-Motor Skills Development	Group Development	Hand-Dominance Development	Pre-Writing Skills Development	Scissor Skills Development	Self-Help Skills Development	Sensory Processing Improvement	Strength and Endurance Improvement	Visual-Perceptual Development	Activity	Page
									✔				✔		Delivering the Mail	308
			✔			✔									Farm Animals	311
				✔										✔	Grocery Store	313
						✔								✔	In and Out the Shapes	315
		✔	✔												More Farm Animals	317
✔						✔									Musical Circles	320
									✔				✔		Ocean in a Bag	322
	✔						✔								Parachute Games	324
			✔										✔		Plowing the Farm	327
	✔											✔			Swinging in a Hammock	329
			✔										✔		Transportation Play	331

Delivering the Mail

Activity Goals: Strength and Endurance Improvement
Pre-Writing Skills Development

Time: 25-to-35 minutes

Objectives: Upon successful completion of this activity, the child will be able to
1. Fold paper precisely in half
2. Write or trace name (part or whole) on front of envelope
3. Propel himself forward a distance of six feet on scooter board

Materials:
1. 1 or 2 business-size envelopes per child
2. 1 or 2 pieces of 8½-by-11 inch paper per child
3. Pencils or crayons
4. Scooter boards for half the class
5. Pretend mailbox or mailbag
6. Picture of mail carrier

Procedure:
1. Discuss the role of a mail carrier as a community helper. Show picture and tell children that they are going to pretend to deliver mail today.
2. Children should be seated at the table and find the paper with their name on it.
3. Each child is given a piece of 8½" by 11" paper.
4. Demonstrate how to fold paper lengthwise by matching edges, holding the paper down with one hand and creasing the fold of the paper with the index finger of the other hand.
5. Children turn and fold the "letter" in half again to make ¼-page, and place it in an envelope that has been given to them.
6. Children seal the envelope and write or trace their name on the envelope.
7. Children place their letters in the mailbox/bag.
8. Children sit along wall on one side of the room—mailbag/box is placed on the other side of the room.
9. Mail can be "delivered" one of three ways:
   a. By Air: Child plays airplane by lying on stomach on scooter board.
   b. By Sea: Child sits on scooter board and pretends to row scooter board like a boat, using her legs to propel herself.
   c. By Land: Child sits on scooter board and pretends to use steering wheel to steer truck.
10. First child tells how she is going to deliver mail and goes to mailbox/bag that way.
11. She takes a letter out of box/bag, propels herself back, and "delivers" the letter to the appropriate person.
12. Repeat steps 10 and 11 until all children have had a turn. Children may then take another turn, pretending the scooter board is another form of transportation.

Adaptations:
1. Children in wheelchairs can flap their arms like airplanes, pretend to row or pretend to use a steering wheel as someone pushes them.

2. Child in wheelchair can hold mail bag/box and play "postmaster," giving out the letters.

Multilevel Instruction:

1. Depending on writing ability, children may trace, stamp, or copy their names or they may write all (first and last) or part (first letter) of their names on the envelopes.
2. For children who do not yet recognize their printed names, a picture can be used for identification.
3. Children can decorate their letters with stickers, stars, or they can stamp them using stamps and an ink pad.
4. Children can stamp their letters before they place them in the mail bag/box.

Letter to Parents
Delivering the Mail

This week we pretended to be mail carriers, familiar community helpers. We sat down in a chair in front of a paper with our name on it and then we folded the paper in half so that the edges were even. We folded the paper again and put it into an envelope. Then, we wrote our names on the front of the envelope and put it into a mailbag. During the next part of the activity, we delivered the mail by air (playing airplane on a scooter board), by ship (using our legs to propel a scooter board) and by land (sitting on a scooter board and pretending to steer a truck). We had to use our visual discrimination and beginning reading skills to deliver the mail to the correct person.

Purpose of the Activity

Name recognition and being able to reproduce the letters of their name are two very important lessons for the young child. Folding paper in half involves visual-perceptual motor skills, as well as finger strength. Children need this skill when tearing off computer paper, doing paper projects in art and sending letters to their pen pals. The second part of the activity encouraged the children to use their large body muscles in a number of ways to propel themselves forward. They were building strength and endurance in many of the muscles that are needed in order to maintain a good sitting posture in the classroom.

Home Activities to Help Your Child Grow

Your child will enjoy sending letters to other members of the family, such as grandparents, aunts, and uncles. They can draw a picture on the paper or glue special cut-outs to it, sign it, fold the paper twice, place it in an envelope, put a stamp on it, and put it in the mailbox (after you've addressed it properly). Hopefully, they'll receive mail in return.

You can promote visual matching and discrimination by cutting out pictures of food items, bringing them to the grocery store, and encouraging your child to match the food item to the corresponding picture. You can also play this game at home by having your child match pictures to food items in your pantry.

Farm Animals

Activity Goals: Gross-Motor Skills Development
Body-Scheme and Motor-Planning Improvement

Time: 30 minutes

Objectives: Upon successful completion of this activity, the child will be able to
1. Gallop a distance of twenty feet
2. Jump (starting and standing with both feet together) a distance of eighteen inches
3. Hop three times on one foot

Materials:
1. Carpet squares
2. Music for "The Chicken Dance"

Procedure:
1. Children sit in a circle. Teacher asks them to name a variety of animals that might be found on a farm.
2. Children pretend they are horses by galloping around the room, neighing, and switching directions.
3. Children pretend they are cows by crawling around the room and mooing.
4. Place carpet squares around the room, approximately 18" apart. Children pretend they are goats and jump from square to square.
5. Children form a circle (standing).
6. Put tape of "The Chicken Dance" in tape player. Adult demonstrates movements that go with song (e.g., opening and closing hands beside head, flapping wings, wiggling hips, clapping 3 times). During chorus, 2 children can link arms and turn around or each child can twirl independently.
7. Children sit down in circle and recall each animal they pretended to be.

Adaptations:
1. Child in wheelchair can practice propelling himself around room while making animal noise and carrying appropriate stuffed animal.
2. A child with visual impairment could have a partner with him.

Multilevel Instruction:
1. Child, rather than teacher, names farm animal and demonstrates how to move like it.
2. Teacher whispers in child's ear and tells him which farm animal to pretend to be. After child acts like the animal, classmates guess which one it is supposed to be (animal charades).
3. After an adult has demonstrated the movements, children try making animal movements with their eyes closed.

Letter to Parents
Farm Animals

This week the children had fun pretending to be farm animals. They were horses galloping around the room, cows crawling on the floor, goats jumping from place to place and chickens flapping their wings. It was an active and noisy barnyard!

Purpose of the Activity

This week, your child imitated many motor activities. This required the use of balance, strength, and endurance, which are necessary components of good postural stability in the classroom. Without postural stability, it is very difficult for the child to use his or her hands for fine-motor tasks such as cutting, manipulating clothing fasteners, or handwriting. In order to imitate the animal actions, your child had to plan motor sequences as well as pay close attention to the adult that was demonstrating the movements. This attention to demonstration is often required in the classroom in order to learn new skills from the teacher.

Home Activities to Help Your Child Grow

Imitation of gross-motor skills is an activity that children and their siblings can have fun doing. Try having them hop like a frog, gallop like a horse, swim like a fish, climb like a monkey, or slither like a snake. You can play animal charades by having one person act out an animal's movements and having the other players guess which animal they are portraying. Holding positions for 15 seconds or longer is a good way for your child to build stability. You can encourage your child to stand like a statue, freeze in one position, or stand on one foot. Play a game using music in which your child moves around the room like a certain animal and then freezes and holds that position when the music stops.

Grocery Store

Activity Goals: Cognitive Development
Visual-Perceptual Development

Time: 30 minutes

Objectives: Upon successful completion of this activity, the child will be able to
1. Identify common food items
2. Place items in bag in an organized way with regard to size and shape
3. Carry filled bag a distance of twelve-to-fifteen feet

Materials:
1. Grocery bags, 1 per child
2. Empty food packages/containers
3. Play money
4. Cash register, if available

Procedure:
1. Before group begins, gather empty food containers of all types, set up grocery store and checkout areas.
2. Give each child an empty grocery bag and some pretend money.
3. Send the children to the grocery area and ask them to pick out a certain number (approximately six) of food items.
4. Children pack their bags with the food they've chosen.
5. Children who have completed the shopping task carry their full grocery bag to the checkout area and pay their bill.
6. Children sit in a circle with their grocery bags.
7. Each child shows and tells the group what groceries he purchased.

Adaptations:
1. Children in wheelchairs may need a long set of tongs to pick items from a shelf.
2. Children with poor balance may need to push "grocery cart" with grocery bag in it rather than carrying bag.
3. Children who have limited strength and/or endurance can use "grocery carts" to carry the bags of groceries.
4. Children who are easily distracted may need an adult to go shopping with them or may need to go shopping without other people in store.

Multilevel Instruction:
1. Children can be instructed to pick out different food items from a variety of food groups.
2. Beginning readers can be given a short written list of items to gather.
3. Children can be given a list with pictures on it. They need to find the items (by matching pictures to packages) that are on their list.
4. Children can count out the money in order to pay their bill.

Letter to Parents
Grocery Store

This week, we learned about community helpers by playing grocery store. The grocery area of the room was filled with empty food containers and there was also a checkout counter. The children filled grocery bags with different food items. Then, they paid for the groceries at the checkout area and walked "out" of the store.

Purpose of the Activity

Working on food vocabulary, auditory memory, and visual recognition of food items were all parts of this activity. While packing the bags, the children worked on spatial relationships and motor planning. While carrying the filled grocery bags, the children performed heavy work, which helped to strengthen their large muscles. All of these tasks are important for school and life-skill development. In the classroom, the child will receive multi-step directions and need good visual memory to help learn spelling, reading, etc. When packing a bag in the grocery store, a child uses the same skills as when packing a school bag.

Home Activities to Help Your Child Grow

For the younger child, a short trip to the grocery store can be a great learning experience. There are many things you can teach your child there, such as colors and shapes. You can ask, "How many rectangles can you see in the cereal aisle? What is the shape of the cracker, cereal or cookie in the box? What is the color of the juice in the bottle or the color of the apple in the bin?" For the older child, you can save the labels from the items that you use commonly and make a list of items for your child to shop for while in the grocery store. As he gets better at distinguishing words, you can write the words on a list and have him find the product. You can also discuss classification in the store. For example, "What things do you find in the dairy department? Name three types of fruit. What types of vegetables do you see?"

In and Out the Shapes

Activity Goals: Visual-Perceptual Development
Gross-Motor Skills Development

Time: 30 minutes

Objectives: Upon successful completion of this activity, the child will be able to
1. Identify shapes
2. Perform motor sequences to follow a path, an obstacle course, and go in and out a specified way
3. Wait for her turn

Materials:
1. Refrigerator box or other structure for a playhouse, with windows and doors cut out as shapes
2. Cardboard shapes taped onto the floor for a path to the house, or equipment to make an obstacle course

Procedure:
1. Demonstrate to the children that there are windows and doors in the "house" through which to go in and out.
2. Call out a shape and let the child go on the shape path, stepping on the correct shape to the house, and then in and out of the house, and then back to the start.
3. Alternately, call out two shapes, have the child go over the obstacle course and then go in and out the two shapes.

Adaptations:
1. For young children who may not yet know their shapes or be able to recognize them easily, use an additional cue such as color. For example, all circles are red and the circle window is outlined in red.
2. Make cards with the shapes on them. Let each child choose one to see what shape she will be following.

Multilevel Instruction:
1. Increase the difficulty of the obstacle course by changing the types of motor skills with which the children navigate it. For example, they could use wheelbarrow walking in pairs, hopping backwards, or crab walking.
2. Instead of making doors, make just windows in the house. Fill the house with something to crawl through, such as pieces of foam or newspaper balls.
3. Link this activity to stories such as *The Three Bears* or *The Three Pigs*.
4. Follow-up this activity by teaching the children the song and game for "In and Out the Windows."

Letter to Parents
In and Out the Shapes

The children used a playhouse today to work on recognizing basic shapes. They followed a path to the house and went in and out of the house through the differently shaped doors and window.

Purpose of the Activity

Learning to recognize shapes is sometimes easier for children when they have a chance to "test out" how the shape feels. We used openings in the playhouse that they fit themselves through to get an idea of the shape.

The children also practiced many motor skills. They practiced gross-motor skills such as jumping with two feet together, hopping, and walking backwards.

Home Activities to Help Your Child Grow

You can help your child learn shapes at home by using activities which help him or her to play with them. Blocks of different shapes, puzzles, and Colorforms® help children experiment with how the shapes fit together and feel. You can play with these toys, naming the shapes, so that he or she will associate the name with the form.

Children need to be able to copy shapes, an ability that they develop as a pre-writing skill. For fun, you can help your child learn to copy shapes by using Play-Doh to make the shapes; or he or she can spread shaving cream on a tabletop and draw the shapes.

More Farm Animals

Activity Goals: Body-Scheme and Motor-Planning Improvement
Bilateral Coordination Development

Time: 30-to-40 minutes

Objectives: Upon successful completion of this activity, the child will be able to

1. Balance himself for one minute while straddling bolster (feet not touching the ground)
2. Use cardboard tube with both hands to push yarn ball and beanbag in straight line
3. Maintain balance for three-to-five minutes while bouncing on a therapy ball or an inner tube

Materials:
1. Bolster swing, if available
2. Barrel or bolster (1 per child)
3. Inner tube, large therapy ball, or hippity-hop toy
4. Yarn ball
5. Bean bag
6. Playground ball
7. Long cardboard tube (from wrapping paper)
8. Masking tape

Procedure:
1. Before the group begins, designate part of the room as the barnyard. Use masking tape to outline a space approximately 8' by 8'.
2. Place a beanbag pile, a yarn ball pile, a playground ball pile and the bolsters on the other side of the room.
3. Discuss types of farm animals with children and explain that the problem today is that some of the animals have escaped from the barn. The children need to help put them back into the corral.

Activity I

This activity should be done over a mat. Children pretend to ride a horse into the barnyard one or two at a time.
1. Children straddle bolster swing, teacher swings bolster gently and child tries to maintain sitting balance for at least one minute.
2. If bolster swing is not available, children can practice balancing on stationery bolsters that have been elevated on chair seats so that child's feet are not on the ground.

Activity II—Children herd sheep into barnyard.
1. Children line up beside each other.
2. Each child is given a long cardboard tube.
3. (White) yarn ball is placed in front of each child.
4. Child, using tube like croquet mallet, pushes yarn ball across room and into barnyard.
5. Children can make sheep noises ("Baaaa") while herding sheep.

Activity III—Children herd pigs into barnyard.

Same as above, except beanbags are used and children make pig noises ("Oink! Oink!").

Activity IV—Children Butt objects like goats

1. Explain how goats sometimes "butt" objects.
2. Demonstrate butting a ball with your head while on hands and knees.
3. First child gets on hands and knees.
4. Playground ball is placed in front of child.
5. Child uses head and butts the playground ball into the barnyard (like a goat would).
6. Other children take their turns. If enough adults are available, more than one child can "butt like a goat" at a time.

Activity V—Children Sit on the tractor

1. Explain that tractor rides are often bumpy.
2. If hippity-hop bounce toy is available, have first child sit on it and bounce into barnyard. Each child in class takes a turn using the hippity-hop to go to the barnyard.
3. If therapy ball is to be used, first child sits on ball and adult bounces them on top of the ball. Classmates can count how many bounces are made. Each child takes a turn.
4. If inner tubes are used, first child can bounce or rock on theon inner tube. Classmates can take turns.

Adaptations:

1. Child in wheelchair can use paper tube to push bean bags and yarn balls across table.
2. Child with visual impairment can be paired with another child in class. If available, ball with beeping sound or ball with bells inside can be used.
3. Child who is unable to use tool to move bean bags or yarn balls can use his hands (clasped in midline) together.
4. Child with decreased balance or a fear of bouncing may gently rock on tilt board to simulate wagon ride.

Multilevel Instruction:

1. Children can match name of animal, printed on index card, with picture of animal mounted on poster board.
2. Pathway to barnyard can be made of masking tape placed on the ground in zigzag pattern rather than a straight pathway.
3. Children can "herd" animals using a specific number of hits.

Letter to Parents
More Farm Animals

This week, the children had fun playing games having to do with farm animals. The children had a chance to ride a "pony" using a bolster or bolster swing, round up the "sheep" and "pigs" by pushing them (yarn balls and beanbags) into their pens and play "hayride" by bouncing on inner tubes. They also pretended to be "goats," pushing a ball around by butting it with their heads.

Purpose of the Activity

Our activities this week stressed building muscle strength, especially in the postural muscles. Holding onto the bolster, flexing and extending to bounce in tire tubes and on therapy balls, and twisting to push the beanbags worked on developing the stomach, back and side muscles. Arm strength was improved through the use of a variety of activities that the children had to do on their hands and knees, such as pretending to be goats.

Home Activities to Help Your Child Grow

If you're thinking of buying an outdoor playset or other types of outdoor toys, you might want to consider how many ways and what muscles your child would be using to play on the toy. Can he or she use arms as well as legs? Also, be sure not only to check the recommended age range for the toy, but also to think about whether it is safe for your child, as not all age ranges are realistic for every child. Frequent trips to the local playground or park will help your child develop strength and endurance as well as motor planning skills.

Musical Circles

Activity Goals: Attention Improvement
Gross-Motor Skills Development

Time: 15-to-20 minutes

Objectives: Upon successful completion of this activity, the child will be able to

1. Attend to the music, starting and stopping at the correct times
2. Perform motor skills such as hopping, jumping, tiptoeing, and walking backwards

Materials:
1. Large circles cut from cardboard and taped to the floor
2. Music* to play to signal the children to start and stop

Procedure:
1. Explain to the children that they will be walking around the outside of the circles until the music stops, and that they will then stand on a circle. Let them try out the activity using walking as the motor skill.
2. Try other motor skills when the music is playing. See if the children can think of some of them.
3. Try removing some of the circles to see if the children can share space.

Adaptations:
1. Sometimes younger children do not understand where they are supposed to walk. If they are having trouble walking around the shapes, try making a boundary more defined using a rope.
2. Make the music less distracting by using some that is only instrumental.
3. For the child who will be moving around in a wheelchair, make sure each shape is large and that there is room around the shapes so that he can maneuver his wheelchair.
4. For a child with a visual impairment, see the *Appendix* (on page 339) for adaptations.

Multilevel Instruction:
1. You can use just one shape, but vary the colors for a color recognition game. Hold up an example of the color at first if some of the children might have difficulty processing and following through on the directions.
2. Try putting more than one shape down. Tell the children which shape they should stand on when the music stops. See whether they can remember the directions and recognize the correct shape when the music stops.

* *Songames for Sensory Integration*, a 2-CD collection of children's music that includes "Musical Chairs," is available from www.SensoryResources.com

Letter to Parents
Musical Circles

We played a version of musical chairs today that we called "Musical Circles." The children walked around circles on the floor while the music played and stepped on one when the music stopped. They also practiced motor skills, such as jumping, hopping, and tiptoeing while the music played. At the end of the game, we took away some of the circles. When the music stopped, the children practiced sharing space on the circles so that everyone would be on one.

Purpose of the Activity

The children worked on their ability to listen and follow directions today by listening to the music and then moving to a circle when it stopped. This is an activity to help them practice a skill that they will use all through school: being able to listen to the teacher's directions and then beginning the task.

Another important skill your child practiced was paying attention to the other children in the class and being helpful. Walking around the circles and then trying to get on one quickly meant that some children had to walk around others to find one. Playing our last game, where there were fewer circles, helped the children reach out and help each other, which reinforces kind behavior that we want to see from them in other school activities. We also practiced motor skills such as hopping and jumping. This was a fun way to do it and helped to build strength, too.

Home Activities to Help Your Child Grow

Being able to listen to directions and follow through is a skill that children need to work on at home, too! You can help your child by making sure that he or she follows through on simple requests. For example, instead of getting your child's coat for him, ask him to get it. If your child has trouble following through on verbal requests, it might be because he is having difficulty remembering the motor sequences. Try making your words simple and brief, and ask him to do just one thing. If your child doesn't follow through within a minute or so, help him, repeating the instructions while you lead your child through the steps of the activity. Then give lots of praise!

Ocean in a Bag

Activity Goals:	Pre-Writing Skills Development
	Sensory Processing Improvement
Time:	20-to-30 minutes
Objectives:	Upon successful completion of this activity, the child will be able to

1. Pick up small objects using a pincer grasp
2. Use two hands to squeeze a resistive liquid
3. Tolerate different sensory texture on her hands

Materials:
1. Pint-sized, zipper-lock, food storage bags
2. Hair gel, either blue or green, approximately 4 ounces per child
3. Glitter
4. Fish stickers
5. Small plastic sea plants or animals, frog men, or submarines
6. Small seashells
7. Duct tape
8. Picture of the ocean and completed sample of the project

Procedure:
1. Gather children in a group and show them a picture of the ocean and the completed project.
2. Have the children identify the different things in the bag, like seashells, fish, and water.
3. Give each child a bag and demonstrate how to open it. Reinforce the fact that the bag needs to stay closed when the project is finished.
4. Have the children take off the fish, whale, shark, etc., stickers and place inside their bag.
5. Have the children place three or four small seashells in their bag.
6. Have the children place a few sea animals or other small plastic figures in the bag.
7. Have the children either use their hands or a shaker to place glitter inside the bag.
8. Demonstrate to the children how to hold the hair gel, squeeze bottle upside down, and squeeze in the hair gel. The teacher may need to help the young child.
9. After the gel is in the bag the teacher will push out all the air and make sure that the bag is closed. It is a good idea to place a piece of duct tape over the plastic zipper on the bag.
10. After closing the bag, demonstrate how to squeeze and mix the gel with the other contents.

Adaptations:
1. For the child with poor pinch, loosen the sticker from the page and allow the child to pull it the rest of the way. You can also have the child take it from your hand and place in the bag.
2. For the child with a visual impairment or poor motor coordination, place the bag open with top edges folded over a large mouthed cup placed on a non-slip surface for added stability.

Multilevel Instruction:
1. After the project is completed, have the children use their pointer finger to try to push the plastic figures from one side to another and from the top to the bottom of the bag.
2. Fill a large box or container with sand. Place different shape seashells in it and let children reach in sand, with eyes closed, and try to find them. Try this with their feet, too.

Letter to Parents

Ocean in a Bag

This week we made a special bag filled with sea shells, sparkles, little sea creatures and fish stickers. After putting everything in the bag with our fingers, we added green or blue hair gel and closed the bag. Then we mixed the stuff in the bag together with our fingers to create our "ocean in a bag."

Purpose of the Activity

This activity works on fine-motor skills such as picking up and manipulating small objects. It also incorporates gross hand and arm strength as needed to squeeze the gel out of the bottle into the bag. Once everything was placed inside and the bag was closed, the children had fun squeezing and moving the objects in the bag. This part works on hand strength, but also, because of the visual attractiveness of the activity, encourages visual attention and visual tracking skills. The children can move the shells and the small sea creatures around in the bag with their fingers. This helps to build finger strength, visual tracking, and visual attention as needed for writing and reading activities.

Home Activities to Help Your Child Grow

This activity worked on building hand strength in two ways. One was squeezing thick liquid from a squeeze-type, plastic bottle. Your child can continue to work on his or her arm and hand strength by playing with squeeze bottles in the bathtub, sink, or pool. Save empty plastic ketchup, shampoo, and salad dressing bottles. Leave the squeeze top on and let your child fill and empty them in the water. Place a boat or floating toy in the tub and try to sink it with the spray from the squeeze bottle. Also, you can make a fun writing or drawing material in a bag. Take a Ziploc bag and place corn starch, food coloring and a little water inside. Mix it until it becomes a thick paste. Close the Ziploc bag and place duct tape on the open edge to prevent leakage. Your child can trace or draw shapes, letters, or pictures on the bag with her fingers.

August

Parachute Games

Activity Goals: Bilateral Coordination Development
Group Development

Time: 20-to-25 minutes

Objectives: Upon successful completion of this activity, the child will be able to
1. Work with others in the group to accomplish a common goal using the parachute
2. Demonstrate the grip and arm strength to maintain a grasp on the parachute while it is going up and down five times
3. Hop on both feet holding onto parachute
4. Gallop holding onto parachute
5. Skip holding onto parachute

Materials:
1. Large parachute
2. Music, if desired
3. Foam balls or yarn balls

Procedure:
1. Explain to children that they are going to play a few games using the parachute.
2. Bring out parachute and lay it on the floor. Have children stand in circle around parachute, hold onto an edge with both hands, and lift it up.

Activity I
1. Pull parachute up from your toes—have children extend both arms above their heads.
2. Pull parachute back down quickly and crouch on floor.
3. Parachute should fill with air and make a bubble.

Activity II
1. Children hold parachute at waist level.
2. Children extend their arms overhead.
3. Children pull parachute down by reaching behind themselves so that they are inside bubble/dome created by parachute.
4. Try to maintain bubble as long as possible.

Activity III
1. Children hold parachute at waist level.
2. Foam balls or yarn balls are placed in center of parachute.
3. Children and adults begin waving arms up and down so that ball/balloon in center bounces around on parachute.
4. Try to keep ball on parachute by coordinating group efforts, e.g., not waving too vigorously.

Activity IV
1. Hold parachute at waist using one hand. Everyone in group needs to hold with same hand.
2. Instruct children to hop around in circle while maintaining hold on parachute.
3. Instruct children to gallop around in circle while holding onto parachute.
4. Children hold parachute with opposite hand and walk backwards while maintaining grasp on parachute.

Activity V

1. Give two children the same number or color.
2. Children hold parachute with both hands extended over their heads.
3. Adult calls number or color and children with that number run under parachute and exchange places around parachute.
4. Repeat until everyone has a chance to switch positions around parachute.

Adaptations:

1. Children with use of only one hand will be able to perform activities using one hand.
2. Use balls that have a bell inside them for child with visual impairment.
3. Handle of parachute can be looped around child's hand or parachute can be adapted with Velcro handles that can be placed over child's hands.

Multilevel Instruction:

1. When shaking the parachute up and down, follow a pattern. For example, follow 2 soft shakes with 2 vigorous shakes.
2. An adult can call children by name—one, two, or three at a time—to run under the parachute.
3. Children can play "Ring Around the Rosie" while holding onto parachute.
4. To make it easier to grasp, a tennis ball can be placed under the parachute. Place a rubber band at the base of the ball to make it easier to grasp.

Letter to Parents
Parachute Games

This week, we played many games using a large nylon parachute. Working together as a group, the children raised the parachute over their heads and brought it down quickly, which made a huge bubble. They again raised the parachute, but this time they brought it down behind them so that they were inside the bubble. They bounced balls up and down on the parachute, walked and hopped around it, and even ran or crawled under it.

Purpose of the Activity

Children love groups that involve using the parachute because it is generally a new and different kind of activity for them. Using a large parachute fosters group cooperation because everyone must do his or her share to make the parachute activities successful. Bilateral coordination, as well as arm, hand and grip strength, are needed to hold and wave the parachute. These skills carry over into educational activities such as using scissors, writing activities, and carrying books and lunch trays. The children also needed to listen carefully to directions and imitate the movements of others.

Activities to Help Your Child Grow

At home, you can use a large beach towel or old sheet to replicate some of the effects of the parachute. Family members can hold the sides of the sheet, place balls in the center and pop them up and down without letting them fall to the ground. The sheet can be raised to allow someone to run or crawl underneath it. Another arm strengthening and bilateral coordination activity would be waving scarves or flags in the air with both hands. Your child could imitate your motions or pretend to be a traffic police person or part of a drill team.

Plowing the Farm

Activity Goals: Strength and Endurance Improvement
Body-Scheme and Motor-Planning Improvement

Time: 20-to-30 minutes

Objectives: Upon successful completion of this activity, the child will be able to
1. Wheelbarrow-walk (held at knees) for a distance of five feet
2. Maintain an "airplane" position on a scooter board for ten seconds

Materials:
1. Scooter boards for half the class
2. Hula hoops for half the class

Procedure:
1. Adult explains to class what plowing the fields means. The children will take turns being the plow and being the horse that pushes or pulls the plow.
2. Teach the following song (to the tune of "The Farmer in the Dell"): "We're digging up the dirt; We're digging up the dirt; Hi Ho a Dario, we're plowing on the farm."

Activity I
1. Each child in class gets a partner and one child gets on hands and knees.
2. Partner lifts legs of child by holding onto knees or ankles.
3. Child, pretending to be plow, moves her hands and "plows" her way across the "field" (classroom), supporting her weight on her hands (wheelbarrow walk).
4. Children switch roles.

Activity II
1. Each child in class gets a partner and one child lies on stomach on scooter board.
2. Partner holds Hula Hoop, and child on scooter board holds onto Hula Hoop (with legs off the floor).
3. Child holding Hula Hoop pretends to be horse pulling plow (child on scooter board).
4. Horse and plow move across the room, the children switch rolls.
5. Children gather in a circle and sing the song that they learned.

Adaptations:
1. Children with decreased strength and endurance may have to be supported at hip level, or be given additional support at the abdominal level when wheelbarrow walking.
2. Children with decreased strength should be expected to sustain the airplane or wheelbarrow position for only a few seconds.

Multilevel Instruction:
1. Cones can be set up so that the fields have to be plowed in a certain pattern.
2. The plows can move backward and sideways as well as forward.

Letter to Parents
Plowing the Farm

This week we took turns pretending to be plows and plow horses. First, we got on our hands and knees and our partners lifted our legs so that we were in the wheelbarrow position. We walked across the room on our hands, pretending to be the plow while our partners pretended to be the horses. Then, using a scooter board and Hula Hoop, we took turns pulling each other around the room. The person on the scooter board pretended to be the plow, and the child pulling the plow pretended to be the farm horse.

Purpose of the Activity

This was really a workout, especially for the large muscles in your child's arms, trunk, and legs. These muscle groups are very important as they provide the body with a stable base of support. This stable base allows children to use their arms and hands to perform more refined tasks, as well as enabling them to use their legs and feet for skilled motor work. With a stable base of support, children are able to successfully hop, skip, kick a ball, jump rope, write on a chalkboard, catch a ball, and play with small toys (among other things.)

Home Activities to Help Your Child Grow

You can find many opportunities at home to allow your child to further develop strength in his or her large muscle groups. Outdoor play is one of the best ways to help build your child's strength and endurance. Encourage your child to play on swings, seesaws, monkey bars, jungle gyms, and sliding boards. Your child can help you push the grocery cart, carry the laundry basket, vacuum or mop the floor, or shovel snow off the sidewalk. Not only do you get some assistance with chores, but your child also develops further strength and endurance and, in addition, feels good about helping you.

Swinging in a Hammock

Activity Goal: Sensory Processing Improvement

                        Balance Improvement

Time: 15-to-20 minutes

Objective: Upon successful completion of this activity, the child will be able to tolerate vestibular input to her body

Materials:
1. Flannel sheet or blanket
2. Mat

Procedure:
1. Describe what a hammock is. Discuss the fact that people like to relax in hammocks.
2. Two adults hold either side of sheet or blanket, so that it is still touching mat, which is placed under it.
3. Child lies in hammock, and adults lift blanket off ground approximately one foot and swing it gently from side to side.
4. The rest of the class sing while the hammock is swinging.
5. Adults lower hammock to the ground and child gets off and sits with group.
6. Repeat steps 2 through 5 until all children get a turn.

Adaptations: For child who is fearful, gently rock her in rocking chair, on tilt board, on large toy boat, or on platform swing (if available). The child is generally less fearful if an adult swings with her initially.

Letter to Parents
Swinging on a Hammock

This week, we made a hammock in the classroom by having two adults suspend a blanket between them. Each child had a chance to lie in the hammock while the adults swung the hammock slowly, back and forth.

Purpose of the Activity

This activity stimulates the vestibular system, which has receptors in the inner ear and is concerned with giving a person information about where he or she is in space, the direction in which he is moving, and whether or not objects are in motion around him. It also influences the general activity level of the brain, the muscles of the eyes, and the postural muscles. The vestibular system is very influential, especially during early development.

Home Activities to Help Your Child Grow

Activities that provide movement, such as swinging, seesawing, sledding, sliding, rolling, tumbling, and many amusement park rides all stimulate this system. Since this system is very influential and very powerful, caution should be used. If your child becomes flushed, uncomfortable, very dizzy, pale, or clammy, immediately stop the activity.

Transportation Play

Activity Goals: Strength and Endurance Improvement
Body-Scheme and Motor-Planning Improvement

Time: 30 minutes

Objectives: Child will be able to
1. Push box, containing another child, a distance of five feet
2. Raise her arms and legs for ten seconds while on stomach on scooter board
3. Use a Hula Hoop to pull another child on a scooter board a distance of ten feet

Materials:
1. Boxes for half the class, large enough for a child to sit in
2. Scooter boards for half the class
3. Hula Hoops for half the class

Procedure: **Activity 1**

Review different modes of transportation that have been discussed in class (e.g., trucks, buses, airplanes, boats, cars, etc.)
1. Each child gets a partner.
2. One child gets into large box and pretends to steer.
3. Her partner pushes box across room pretending to drive a car, bus, or truck.
4. Children switch roles.

Activity II
1. Each child gets a partner.
2. One child lies on stomach on scooter board pretending to be an airplane.
3. Her partner uses Hula Hoop to pull child along on scooter board.
4. "Airplane" child is pulled across room.

Activity III
1. Half the class sits on scooter boards and half the class sits on one side of classroom.
2. Teacher demonstrates how to "row" scooter board across the room.
3. As children "row" across the room pretending to be boats, the other half of the class sings "Row, Row, Row Your Boat."
4. Children switch roles.

Adaptations:
1. Children in wheelchairs can propel their chair along a "road" outlined in masking tape on the ground. Children can hold arms out to sides like the wings of an airplane while wheelchair is being pushed.
2. Children in wheelchairs can be pulled using Hula Hoops. Children in class can push child in wheelchair rather than having child get into box.

Multilevel Instruction:
1. Pathways across room can be made to curve or zigzag.
2. Distance to be traveled can be lengthened or shortened depending on child's strength and endurance.

Letter to Parents

Transportation Play

This week, your child pretended to be different types of vehicles. He pushed (and was pushed) in a box (truck), rode on a scooter board (airplane) with his or her arms and legs held off the ground, and rowed a scooter board (boat) across the room. Afterwards, we discussed which form of transportation was the most fun!

Purpose of the Activity

While pretending to be vehicles, the children did a lot of pushing, pulling, and moving their body weight, either to climb in and out of boxes or to move themselves along on scooter boards. These activities required a lot of effort and helped your child build muscle strength and endurance. Pushing, pulling, and steering the vehicles required that your child has a good idea of where his body was in space and to plan motor actions to accomplish a task successfully.

Home Activities to Help Your Child Grow

You can replicate this activity at home by getting a large, sturdy box and having your child place some stuffed animals in it. He can pretend to be a train engine, pushing the train along and dropping off passengers (stuffed animals). Your child can play airplane by lying on his stomach and lifting his chest, arms, and legs off of the ground. By the age of five years, children should be able to hold this position (prone extension) for about twenty seconds. By playing airplane, your child will be strengthening the muscles in the back of his neck, trunk, buttocks, and legs.

This list is arranged alphabetically and then by month as a guide to activities that may be helpful in learning the letters of the alphabet.

A

September	Hide-and-Seek Apple Rubbings
	Apple Butter and People Sandwiches
	Apples on a Fence
December	Cinnamon and Applesauce People
March	Paper Airplanes
June	Zoo Animals
July	The Aquarium
August	Farm Animals
	More Farm Animals

B

September	Balloons and Body Parts
	Riding on a School Bus
	We Go to School on a Bus
	Body Tracing
October	Flying Bats and Ghosts
December	Bird Feeders
January	Bears
	Polar Bears
February	Boats and Bridges
	Ferry Boat Rides
April	Baseball and Softball Practice
	Boats, Bridges and Kites
	Butterflies
	Jump Rope and Baseball
May	Balloon Tennis
	Balloon and Tennis Ball Games
	Big Ball Kickoff I
	Big Ball Kickoff II
	Festive Boleros
	Large Ball Pass
	Moving Bugs
	Piñata (Bull)
July	Be a Bubble
	Bubbles
	Bubbles Go Pop

C

October	Crow, Crow, Scarecrow!
November	Celebrating Corn
	Corn and Popcorn Play I
	Corn and Popcorn Play II
December	Cinnamon and Applesauce People
	Holiday Wreath Cookies
January	Color Hunt
	Color Toss
February	Candy Clay
	Candy Hearts
March	Dr. Seuss Day (The Cat in the Hat)
April	The Nimble Cow
June	Circus Tricks
	Clowning Around
	Cocoons and Butterflies
July	Cornstalks
	A Corny Party

D

October	Dalmatians
November	Drums and Turkey Hunt
	Friends Sandwich and Dance
	Football Workout
May	Balloon Games (Donkey Kick)
	Edible Dirt

E

April	Egg and Log Rolling
	Silly Spring Eggs
May	Edible Dirt
	King Humpty Dumpty's Horses
June	Zoo Animals (Elephant)
July	Edible Sand
	Pets (Elephant)

F

September	Textured Finger Paints
October	Fall Leaves
	Flying Bats and Ghosts

	Stop, Drop, & Roll (Fire Prevention)
November	Football Workout
	Friends Sandwich and Dance
February	Ferry Boat Rides
March	Fan Folding
	Forsythia Branches
	Paper Plate Puppet Faces
May	Special Flowers
June	Fruit Salad Fiesta
	Red, White, and Blue Flag Celebration
	Zoo Animals (Flamingo)
July	The Aquarium (Fish)
	Paper Roll Fireworks
August	Farm Animals
	More Farm Animals
	Ocean in a Bag (Fish)

G

October	Flying Bats and Ghosts
	Flying Ghosts
	Ghost, Ghost, Witch!
December	Gingerbread Boys and Girls I
	Gingerbread Boys and Girls II
February	Gak
June	Mountain Goats
July	Vegetable Garden
August	Grocery Store

H

September	Hide-and-Seek Apple Rubbings
October	Pumpkin Hide and Seek
December	Hat Pass
	Holiday Wreath Cookies
March	Dr. Seuss Day (Hop on Pop)
May	King Humpty Dumpty's Horses
August	Farm Animals (Hayride)
	Plowing the Farm (Horses)
	Swinging on a Hammock

I

January	Fun in the Ice and Snow
	Sliding Seals and Penguins
February	I Love You
April	"Tisket a Tasket" and "In and Out the Windows"
August	In and Out the Shapes

J

October	Jack-o'-Lanterns
	October Party
November	Jumping Over the Creek
	Native American Jewelry
April	Jump Rope and Baseball
	The Nimble Cow
June	Jumping Rope
July	Edible Sand (Jellyfish)

K

January	The Three Little Kittens
May	Big Ball Kickoff I
	Big Ball Kickoff II
	King Humpty Dumpty's Horses

L

October	Fall Leaves
February	I Love You
March	Lion with a Linguini Mane
April	Egg and Log Rolling
	"This Old Man" at "London Bridge"
May	Large Ball Pass

M

December	Marching
February	Money
	Post Office
March	March Goes Out Like a Lamb
April	"This Old Man" at "London Bridge"
June	Mountain Goats
August	Delivering the Mail Musical Circles

N

| November | Native American Jewelry |
| December | Toy Workshop (Nails) |

O

October	October Party
December	Pine Cone Bird Feeders (Fruit "Os")
August	Ocean in a Bag

P

October	Pumpkin Hide-and-Seek
	Rolling Pumpkins
November	Corn and Popcorn Play I
	Corn and Popcorn Play II
	Making Pottery
	Pudding Painting
	Turkey Finger Painting
December	Pine Cone Bird Feeders
January	Peter and the Wolf
	Polar Bears
	Sliding Seals and Penguins
February	Post Office
	Trains and Planes
March	Making Irish Potato Candy
	Moving Potatoes
	Paper Airplanes
	Paper Plate Puppet Faces
	Potato Play
May	Piñata
June	Going on a Picnic
July	Pets
August	Parachute Games Plowing the Farm

Q

| March | Rainbow Mural (Q-tips) |

R

September	Riding on the School Bus
	Hide-and-Seek Apple Rubbings
October	Rolling Pumpkins

	Stop, Drop, and Roll
February	Valentine's Day Rubbing
March	Rainbow Day
	Rainbow Mural
April	Egg and Log Rolling
	Stars and Rolling

S

September	Guess Which Shape?
	Scrub-a-Dub-Dub
	Sensory Stations
October	Creepy, Wiggly Spiders
	Crow, Crow, Scarecrow!
	Scarecrows
	Stop, Drop, and Roll
November	Friends Sandwich and Dance
December	Newspaper Ball Snowman
	Sleigh Ride
January	Fun in the Ice and Snow
	Getting Ready for Snow
	Sliding Seals and Penguins
	Snow Painting
March	Dr. Seuss Day
April	Baseball and Softball Practice
	Silly Spring Eggs
	Stars and Rolling
June	Fruit Salad Fiesta
July	Edible Sand
August	In and Out the Shapes
	Swinging on a Hammock

T

September	Body Tracings
November	Drums and Turkey Hunt
	Story of Thanksgiving
	Turkey Day
	Turkey Finger Painting
December	Toy Workshop
February	Trains
	Trains and Planes

April	"A Tisket a Tasket" and 'In and Out the Windows"
May	Balloon Tennis
	Balloon and Tennis Ball Games

U

February	I Love You
March	Rainbow Day (Under the Rainbow)

V

February	Valentine's Day Rubbing
July	Vegetable Garden

W

September	Weather Ways
October	Ghost, Ghost, Witch!
January	Peter and the Wolf
March	Windsocks
May	Edible Dirt (Worms)
	Wash Day
June	Water and Ball Play

X

May	Big Ball Kickoff II (Target is an "X")

Y

January	The Three Little Kittens (Yarn Balls)

Z

June	Zoo Animals

Activities Alphabetically

This section discusses methods of adapting the environment so that the differently-abled child can actively participate in group lessons. The activities included in *Learning in Motion* contain adaptations specific to the activity. However, this section describes general modifications for seating, balance, wheelchair use, and fine-motor activities, including scissor usage. Further adaptations are included to assist children who have either functional use of one hand or visual impairment.

Adaptations for Seating

1. Place Dycem, non-slip bathtub appliqués, or non-slip materials on the seat of the chair so that the child can maintain an upright posture.
2. Use an arm chair or a cube chair to give the child with decreased trunk strength more support. These types of chairs will also help the active child stay on his chair.
3. Place a mat, with a rubber or non-slip surface, under the child's feet to keep his feet still.
4. Use a Move n' Sit™ wedge or a Sit 'n Fit™ disc for the child who needs to move frequently in his chair.
5. Have the child sit on a small therapy ball that permits him to place his feet on the floor. To prevent the ball from moving, place the therapy ball in a ball stand or in a carton.
6. Have the child straddle a large bolster with most of the bolster pushed under the desk.
7. Have the child sit on a T-stool or a large wooden block (hollow block square 11" x 11" x 5-½").
8. Have the child with poor posture or difficulty staying in a chair, sit on a piece of an egg crate mattress pad for added sensory feedback.
9. Use a lap or saddle-type sand bag across the child's lap (thighs) when he is sitting as a non-verbal sensory cue to remain sitting.
10. Try having the child turn the chair around to sit with his legs straddling the back of the chair and his chest leaning against it (cowboy sitting). This can aid the child with decreased trunk strength maintain an upright posture.
11. If you cannot lower the table and chairs, place a block covered with non-slip material under the child's feet. Straps can be added to attach to the legs of the chair so that the block remains in the correct place.
12. If a child frequently pushes back or rocks the chair, attach or nail it onto a piece of ¾-to-1-inch-thick plywood in order to make a base for the chair. Make sure that the plywood is narrow enough to be able to fit the chair under the desk, but large enough to prevent rocking. This will also prevent the child from pushing the chair away from the desk.
13. Provide breaks from seated activities by allowing the child to perform the same tasks in different positions such as kneel standing, lying on his stomach, using a rocking chair, etc. For example, if the child is reading a book or coloring, try having him read while he is on his stomach, propped on his forearms.
14. For the child who frequently moves his chair away from the desk at inappropriate times, consider having him use a desk with a chair attached.

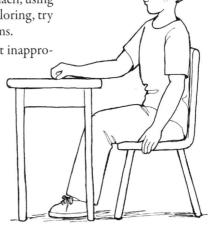

Illustration of correct sitting posture adapted from *The Sensory Connection* by Nancy Kashman and Janet Mora, published by Future Horizons, Inc. Used with permission.

Adaptations for the Child with Impaired Balance

1. Try the following adaptations to help children maintain their balance while they are standing.

   a. Provide support to the child by standing behind him and holding on to his waist while moving.

   b. Station the child near a wall or a stationary object to lean against or reach out and hold onto if needed.

   c. Encourage the child to perform the movement slowly, to give his or her balance system and muscles time to adapt to the movement.

   d. Try to keep the environment around the child free from distractions. If you are using music, try keeping the volume low.

   e. See if you can adapt the child's position. Could he or she perform the activity sitting on the floor, sitting in a comer, kneeling, or sitting on a chair?

   f. Provide a stationary object for the child to look at while performing the movement.

   g. Some children have difficulty with stationary balance as their muscle tone is slightly low. Try providing several minutes of warm-up activities before the stationary ones. Jumping games are very effective.

2. Try the following adaptations to help children maintain their balance sitting on the floor during story time or other activities:

   a. Sit the child on a wedge with the slope going downwards towards his or her knees. One type is inflatable, which allows the child to wiggle a little to keep up muscle tone.

   b. Have the child straddle a bolster, as if riding a horse.

   c. Have the child wear a weighted vest, which should be donned about five minutes before needed.

   d. Lap weights are also available and can be placed across the child's lap.

   e. Use a "back jack" chair to give added support.

   f. Let the children sit on folded mats or individual foam cushions rather than directly on the floor. This will help any child who has tight muscles in his or her legs from conditions such as cerebral palsy.

3. To make sure the child maintains his or her balance during dynamic activities such as jumping, running, and hopping, try the following:

   a. Have the child perform the activity within a defined space. If possible, provide a line to run, hop, or jump along.

   b. Try providing some light weight around the child's waist, to give him or her more sensory feedback when moving.

   c. Try slowing down the activity, if possible.

   d. Have the children perform the activity closer to the floor. For example, instead of running, have the children crawl or walk on their knees.

   e. Give the child external support for jumping or hopping, such as having him or her follow a wall, sliding his or her hand along.

Adaptations for the Wheelchair User

1. If the child is using a power chair or can self-propel the wheelchair, have him use a lapboard, wheelchair tray, side-mounted basket, or his lap as a placement for an object when moving around in the wheelchair.

2. Place objects at the height where the child can safely reach them, for example, at desk height, on a shelf, chair, etc.

3. Long-handled reachers can be purchased for children using wheelchairs. Encourage the child's parent to purchase one for school and one for home. Some models are equipped so that they can be attached to the wheelchair for ease of access.

4. The wheelchair leg rests could prevent the child from getting close to some objects. Encourage the child to approach the object that is to be retrieved from the side of the wheelchair. Have the student drive the wheelchair parallel to the object and reach out to the side.

5. During jumping activities, try to get the student out of the wheelchair to sit on a large ball (therapy ball). With your assistance, the child can get the feeling of jumping by moving or bouncing on the ball.

6. During obstacle courses, have the child drive around the obstacles. You can also make a separate wheelchair obstacle course.

7. Instead of creating a separate wheelchair obstacle course, make all the physically capable students use a scooter board to navigate the obstacle course.

8. Pair a physically capable child with a child using a wheelchair for movement activities if the wheelchair user is unable to maneuver it independently.

9. If the child is unable to propel the chair, have him verbally direct a physically capable child. For example, he might instruct her to turn to the right, go forward, stop, etc.

10. During jump rope activities, have the child hold a rope or have him ride over a rope on the floor in a slalom pattern.

11. If the wheelchair user needs to place an object on the floor, he can either push it off the tray, use the reachers to lower it, or place a rope or string on the object to lower it.

12. For physical activities, such as body imitation or exercises, have the child do the upper and/or lower body activities as best he can from the chair.

13. For kicking activities, the child can throw the ball, push a large therapy ball with the wheelchair, or choose a partner to be his designated kicker.

14. During balance beam activities, have the child move his chair between two strips of masking tape on the floor slightly wider than the wheelchair and 6 feet long.

15. To facilitate activities involving moving in a circle, use the type of Hula Hoops that can be joined together. This will permit all the children, including those using a wheelchair, to participate. Have the children stand in the circle and move the large ring (multiple linked Hula Hoops) around instead of moving in a circle. You can do the same thing with a large ring made of rope.

Adaptations for the Child with Visual Impairment

1. If possible, encourage the child to handle the materials to be used in the group before the group begins.

2. Allow the child to assist in demonstrating the group activity.

3. The child will probably require additional time and/or assistance to actively participate in activities.

4. Visually impaired children benefit from multi-sensory cues, e.g., tactile, auditory, olfactory, to help guide their movements during activities.

5. In general, using larger manipulatives, e.g., beads, blocks, will help the child succeed during projects.

6. Directions for the group should be clear and concise. Reference to previously experienced activities should be given whenever possible.

7. Consistent organization and arrangement of materials, using numbers on a clock as reference points if possible, is important to assist the child in completing activities independently.

8. Assist the child with visual impairment in being independent in parts of a task, if a task cannot be completed with total independence.

9. Steps of an activity should be done in a logical, predictable way so that the child is not confused.

10. Use of a slant board, inclined desk top, or bookstand during reading and fine-motor activities, will bring the fine-motor work closer to the child's eyes.

Adaptations

11. During drawing or painting activities, masking tape borders can be formed around paper in order to provide tactile cues about the boundaries.

12. When "painting" with pudding, hair gel, etc., sand or other grainy materials can be added to provide additional texture to the "paint."

13. Elmer's glue can be used to create raised boundaries. For example, if the child is to color within a circle, the circle can be outlined the day before using a thin line of the glue. Once the glue hardens, in about 6 hours, the outline of the shape will be raised and provide tactile cues to the child.

14. When appropriate, bright, neon, or contrasting colored materials should be used during activities for the child.

15. Staff members need to be aware of visual field cuts in children and place activity materials accordingly.

16. Using containers to hold materials for individual activities will assist the child to be more independent.

17. During cutting activities, the lines can be marked with glue, yarn or punched holes to give the child additional tactile cues.

18. During cutting activities, the child can cut on a thick-lined, contrasting circle or square drawn around the desired picture rather than on more complex, less visible lines.

19. Bright-colored tape can be placed on the edges of the balance beam to assist the child in using this equipment.

20. Bright-colored tape can be placed on the floor to assist the child in following a path while using a scooter board.

21. The child can be paired with a sighted child when appropriate.

22. Some gym equipment, such as balls and goals, are equipped with beepers and provide the child with auditory feedback regarding location. They can be ordered from specific companies that are listed in the appendix of this book.

23. Because children who are blind or severely visually impaired from infancy may not have experienced positional concepts, it may be necessary to reinforce spatial concepts (e.g., below, above, behind) through movement.

24. During dressing activities, use simple clothing. The fewer fasteners to manipulate, the easier it will be for the child to get dressed. Fasteners can be adapted by using elastic or Velcro®.

25. Classroom lighting should be behind the child whenever possible. This cuts down on glare for the child. Also, if the desk or table top is providing too much glare, dark, non-reflective paper can be placed under the child's work.

26. When doing writing or pre-writing work, contrasting visual symbols can be used for stop and start points. For example, children can "start at the star and end at the stop sign," or "begin at the green line and stop at the red line."

27. During food spreading activities, sandwich boxes can be used to provide specific borders for the food. In other words, a piece of bread to be spread with jelly can be placed inside a small, open, square plastic container.

28. Fine sandpaper or quick point sheets can be placed under paper to provide additional tactile cues while coloring or writing.

29. When making overlays for the overhead projector, black marker can be used with yellow acetate to provide contrast.

30. To make it easier for the child to copy from the blackboard, an extra chair and desk can be set up close to the board.

31. Grid sheets can be used when copying designs.

32. When using letters for activities, magnetic letters can be placed on cookie sheets. This provides a boundary for the letters as well as giving additional tactile cues as to letter shape.

33. When writing letters, the child can use chalk to write on a dark-colored carpet square. Erasing the letters using her hands (or feet) provides additional tactile input to the child.

Adaptations for Fine-Motor Skills

1. To facilitate a tripod grasp on a crayon while coloring or writing
   a. Provide larger diameter crayons, for example, Crayola So Big® crayons. This helps the child keep a "C" shape between the thumb and index finger.
   b. Try crayons that are shaped differently in order to facilitate grasp
      1. Jumbo anti-roll crayons: show the child how to place his or her thumb on the flat side.
      2. Ball shaped crayons or "animal markers", which the child can use with the ball end placed in his palm. The child also can insert his or her thumb inside the ball crayon and grasp it with the other fingers on the outside.
      3. Triangular-shaped or Hand Hugger® crayons.
      4. Rectangular-shaped crayons, such as "Rainbow Crayons."
   c. Try using smaller pieces: break up larger, fatter crayons to 3" lengths, or use "Chubbi Stumps."
2. To facilitate better pencil control and a tripod grasp while drawing, tracing, or writing
   a. Use shorter pencils, about four inches long
   b. Use pencils of a different diameter: either larger diameter, such as a "Big Dipper" or smaller such as the tiny pencils used for miniature golf, "Skinney Minney" pencils, and "Thick-Leaded Thin" pencils.
   c. Use pencils of different shapes:
      1. Triangular shaped: Hand Huggers® or "Try Rex"
      2. Mechanical pencils with built in shapes: "Grip Tec," "Zaner Bloser," or Finger Fitting Pencil®
   d. Add a pencil grip: "The Pencil Grip," a triangular grip, a "Stetro" grip, or a spongy grip: traditional round, smooth satin finish, ripple bumpy finish, or baseball-bat shaped.
   e. Try a weighted pencil grip.
   f. Add more "feel" to the fingers holding the writing implement using a vibrating pen such as the "Squiggle Wiggle Writer."
3. To improve the child's visual attention to the writing or coloring task and to improve motor control by making the task multisensory
   a. Add more "feel" by placing paper on a bumpy surface: sand paper, concrete sidewalk, piece of fluorescent lighting cover, or piece of plastic embroidery canvas.
   b. Use "magic slates" (plastic-covered waxed tablets) which give a little resistance when you write on them and add novelty to the task.
   c. Rather than paper, use more resistive writing surfaces such as individual chalkboards, boxes with colored sand, or trays spread with a thin layer of plasticine.
4. To adapt fine-motor materials when the child has poor finger control or does not have a refined grasp
   a. Insert pushpins into small rubber stamps or other toys to make holders.
   b. Purchase and glue on knobs or short pieces of dowels to adapt wooden toys and puzzles.
   c. Build up push buttons with a dab of hot glue.
   d. Clip on a clothespin to sponges for sponge painting so the child can hold it in a gross grasp.

Adaptations

e. Build up handles on paintbrushes or other tools with commercial foam handles, foam from hair curlers, or pieces of narrow diameter foam pipe insulation.

f. Special adaptive equipment may be prescribed by an OT to help adapt fine-motor materials such as a Grip-mate holder or universal cuff. The OT may also make a hand splint or recommend a prefabricated one to help the child hold on to tools.

g. Use Velcro® hook and loop to substitute for more difficult holders and fasteners.

Adaptations for Cutting with Scissors

1. Mary Benbow Scissors™ are specially designed for small hands. These are great beginning scissors to start with for the young child or the child with small hands.

2. Wind rubber bands around the scissor loops to pad and reduce the size of the loops. This will promote better scissor positioning and grasp.

3. Enlarge the line width or provide maximum contrast for the lines to be cut. Lines can be as wide as a one-half inch.

4. Glue yarn along the edge of a shape before cutting. Allow to dry. This will act as a visual cue and also provide tactile feedback when cutting.

5. Glue a Popsicle stick on either side of a straight line to practice cutting. This provides a physical barrier and sensory cues.

6. Encourage the child to use his non-dominant hand in a thumbs up position when holding the paper for cutting.

7. Use heavier weight paper when starting to cut. Try oak tag, grocery bags, index cards and other heavy-weight paper.

8. If you must use copied materials for cutting, glue the copied paper to oak tag or other heavier papers. Try using glue spray as it works quickly and easily to hold the paper together.

9. If the child has increased tone in one hand (hand gets tight when trying to use it), have the child try to cut with both hands on the desk. This provides support for the arms and will help to keep the paper down during cutting.

10. Try taping the paper to be cut on a vertical surface like an easel, wall or the back of a chair.

11. Sharp vs. dull scissors: typical school-issued scissors tend to be dull, making cutting more difficult for the inexperienced cutters. Provide sharp scissors for the young students to decrease frustration and increase quality of their work.

12. Adaptive scissors available in catalogs:
    a. Electric scissors: The child still needs fine-motor control to use these. They can be noisy in the classroom.
    b. Cutting wheel: These tools are used by quilters to cut squares and other shapes. The child still needs fine-motor control but cutting can be done one handed. The cutting wheel is sharp and requires use of its cutting board.
    c. Loop scissors: There are small and large sizes available. The child still needs hand strength and the ability to open and close his hand while using these scissors.
    d. Double loop teaching scissors.

e. Left handers should use scissors specifically designed for them although the Fiskar® children's scissors seem to be ambidextrous.

Adaptations for the Child Who Has Functional Use of Only One Hand

1. For additional stabilization during writing and fine-motor tasks, non-slip material can be placed under papers, books, and materials to prevent sliding. Using slant boards with clips, or taping down the paper to the table or desk, will also assist in stabilization.

2. When dressing, the weaker or more involved side of the child goes into garments first. Also, the weaker side comes out last during undressing.

3. During cutting activities, an adult can hold the paper so that the student is able to cut; or tape one end or side of the paper to the desk or table, or clip it to a slant board to provide stability.

4. If a child has functional use of only one hand because of too much uncontrolled movement in the non-dominant hand, it may be helpful to assist the child in stabilizing her hand on a dowel equipped with a suction cup that has been placed on the desk or table.

5. During cooking activities, non-slip material can be placed under the bowl while stirring. Also, when spreading jelly, butter, etc., on muffins, bread, etc., the child with controlled use of one arm can place the bread or muffin in a plastic container so that it is stabilized against two sides.

Adaptations

Irish Potato Candy

2 cups confectioner's 10X sugar

1 cup coconut

1-to-4 tsp. half-and-half

½ tsp. vanilla extract

cinnamon

Mix sugar, coconut, and vanilla with enough half-and-half to make a paste. Knead and break off a small piece (about 1 tsp.). Roll to form a ball or potato shape. Roll the "potatoes" in cinnamon. Eat and enjoy!

Candy Clay

¼ lb. softened butter or margarine

½ cup light corn syrup

½ tsp. salt

1 tsp. vanilla extract

4 cups confectioner's sugar

In a bowl, blend together softened butter and corn syrup. Add salt, vanilla extract and confectioner's sugar and mix well using hands as necessary. Divide the candy clay. Makes about 4 cups.

Corn Flake Holiday Wreaths

½ cup margarine

10 oz. package (about 40) regular marshmallows

1 tsp. green food coloring

6 cups corn flakes cereal

red cinnamon candies

vegetable cooking spray

In large saucepan, melt margarine over low heat. Add marshmallows and stir until completely melted. Remove from heat. Stir in food coloring. Add corn flakes. Stir until well coated. Using a ¼ cup dry measure coated with cooking spray, evenly portion warm cereal mixture. Using buttered fingers, quickly shape into individual wreaths. Dot with cinnamon candies. Makes 16 wreaths.

Colored Sand

1 cup of sand

2 tsp. dry tempera paint

1 tsp. water

Add the dry tempera paint to the sand; mix well with a fork. Stir in water. Allow the sand to dry for several hours before using.

Fruity Putty

0.3 oz. package of sugar-free, fruit-flavored gelatin

2 cups flour

1 cup salt

4 tbsp. cream of tartar

2 cups boiling water

2 tbsp. cooking oil

Mix the dry ingredients in a pan. Add the boiling water and cooking oil. Stir over medium-high heat until mixture forms a ball. Place the ball on waxed paper to cool. Store in an airtight container. Cut the fruit picture from the gelatin box and paste to the lid. Use different flavors to make all different colors and smells.

Finger Paint Mixture #1

1 cup liquid starch

½ cup soap chips

6 cups warm water

dry tempera or food coloring

Dissolve soap chips with enough water and stir until all lumps have disappeared. Add to starch and remaining water. Keep covered in plastic jar. Color may be added into the mix, or as children paint. A few drops of oil of clove prevent bad odors. Be sure to keep mixtures in covered jars in a cool location.

Recipes

Play Clay #1

1 cup flour
½ cup salt
1 tsp. cream of tartar
1 cup water
1 tbsp. oil
food coloring

Put all ingredients in a saucepan and cook over medium heat until dough pulls away from the sides of the pan and forms a ball. Remove from heat and cool. Knead until smooth. Store in reclosable sandwich bags or an airtight container. This makes a soft dough that is great to play with.

Play Clay #2

3 cups flour
½ cups salt
3 tbsp. oil
2 tbsp. cream of tartar
3 cups water
food coloring (optional)

Mix and cook over very low heat until not sticky to touch. Cool and store in airtight container.

Goop

2 cups salt
1 cup water
1 cup corn starch
food coloring (optional)

Cook salt and ½ cup water for 4-5 minutes. Remove from heat. Add cornstarch and ½ cup water. Return to heat. Stir until mixture thickens. Let cook. Store in plastic bag.

Kool-Aid® Finger Paint

2 cups flour
2 packs unsweetened Kool-Aid™
½ cup salt
3 cups boiling water
3 tbsp. oil

Mix wet ingredients into dry. The kids love the color change. Finger paint away.

Puffy Paint

flour
salt
water
tempera paint

Mix equal amounts of flour, salt, and water. Add liquid tempera paint for color. Pour mixture into squeeze bottles and paint. Mixture will harden into a puffy shape.

Nutty Butter Play Clay

1 cup peanut butter
1 cup powdered milk
1 cup honey
1 cup oatmeal

Mix all ingredients together and play—or eat!

Beluga Bubbles

1 cup warm water
¼ cup blue dishwashing liquid
1 tsp. salt

Combine all ingredients. Mix well until salt dissolves.

Soap Crayons

1-¾ cups Ivory Snow® (powder)
50 drops food coloring
¼ cup water

Mix water and soap flakes together. Add food coloring and put mixture into an ice cube tray. Allow to harden. Break or cut into pieces. Fun to write with on the tub (and face and hands) when bathing!

Rainbow Stew

¼ cup sugar
1 cup cornstarch
4 cups cold water
food coloring

Cook ingredients until thick. Put in bowls and add food coloring. Put in reclosable sandwich bags. Let the kids

Recipes

play with it while it is in the bags for a neat sensory experience.

Goop/Slime

1 part liquid starch
2 parts Elmer's® glue
food coloring (optional)

Mix and enjoy. It's supposed to be like slime.

Cinnamon Applesauce Dough

1 part cinnamon
2 parts applesauce

Put applesauce into a bowl. Add cinnamon, a little at a time, and mix ingredients together until the consistency of the mixture is like moist play clay. Dough is now ready to be molded. Place finished product on wax paper. The dough will dry in approximately three days.

Salt Dough #1

1 cup salt
½ cup cornstarch
¾ cup cold water

Stir together over a low heat until too thick to stir, about 2 to 3 minutes. Put on waxed paper until cool and then knead until smooth. Can be rolled or shaped. Air dry.

Salt Dough #2

2-½ cups boiling water
2 cups salt
4 cups of flour

Add salt to water and then stir into flour. Knead on a flour-covered surface. Shape objects and then bake at 250° for two to three hours, checking frequently after 2 hours. Paint after it cools.

Best Bubble Solution

1 cup water
2 tbsp. light corn syrup or 2 tbsp. glycerin

4 tbsp. dishwashing liquid
Mix ingredients together and have fun!

Silly Putty #1

½ cup Elmer's glue
½ cup starch (liquid)
food coloring

DO NOT substitute any other glue for Elmer's glue! Slowly add starch to glue and knead with fingers. The more you work with it, the better it gels. Add food coloring, if desired,

Recipes

Additional Reading

The following sources can give further information about topics discussed in the activities and parent letters:

Fine-motor Dysfunction by Kristin Johnson Levine, M.S.Ed., O.T.R., Therapy Skill Builders, a division of the Psychological Corporation, 555 Academic Court, San Antonio, Texas, 78204-2498, 1-800-211-8378; Fax 1-800-232-1223.

Willard and Spackman's Occupational Therapy, 7ᵗʰ Ed. Helen L. Hopkins and Helen D. Smith, ed. Copyright 1988, J.B. Lippincott Co., Philadelphia, PA.

A Parents Guide to Understanding Sensory Integration, Southpaw Enterprises, P.O. Box 1047, Dayton, OH 45401-1047, 1-800-228-1698

Out of the Mouths of Babes by Sheila Frick, Ron Frick, Patricia Oetter, and Eileen Richter, Southpaw Enterprises.

Pre-Dressing Skills, Pre-Writing Skills (Revised), and Pre-Scissor Skills (3ʳᵈ Ed.) by Marsha Dunn Klein, M.Ed., OTR/L, Therapy Skill Builders.

Prepare, An Interdisciplinary Approach to Perceptual-Motor Readiness by Beth Witt, M.A. and Marsha Dunn Klein, M.Ed., OTR/L, Therapy Skill Builders.

Sensory Integration: A Foundation for Development by Charlotte Brasic Royeen, Ph.D., Isabel Garriton, OT and Betsy A. Slavik, M.A., O.T.R., Southpaw Enterprises.

When You Have a Visually Handicapped Child in Your Classroom, 2ⁿᵈ ed.

Suggestions for Teachers by Iris Torres & Anne L. Corn, American Foundation for the Blind, Copyright 1990, New York, NY.

Evaluations:
    Brigance
    HELP
    Peabody Developmental Motor Scales

About the Authors

Patricia Angermeier, OTR, BCP

Pat graduated from Temple University in Philadelphia, Pennsylvania in 1976 with a Bachelor of Science degree in occupational therapy. In 1995, she became board certified in pediatrics by the American Occupational Therapy Association. Since her graduation, Pat has worked in the field of occupational therapy in private and public school settings, in early intervention centers, as a home-based therapist, and in clinical settings. She currently resides in Shamong, New Jersey, with her husband and two sons.

Joan Krzyzanowski, M.S., OTR, BCP

Joan received a Bachelor of Science degree in elementary education from Skidmore College in Saratoga Springs, New York in 1969. She taught kindergarten and first-grade classes for the Compton Unified School District in Compton, California for two years. Joan was certified as an occupational therapist in 1990 and earned a Master of Science degree in occupational therapy from Temple University in 1995. She was board certified in pediatrics in 1996. Joan has worked in public and private school settings as an occupational therapist since 1990 and has also worked in pediatric home healthcare. She resides near Boston, Massachusetts with her husband and two daughters

Kristina Keller Moir, OTR, BCP

Kriss received a Bachelor of Arts degree in biology from Lafayette College in Easton, Pennsylvania, in 1978. In 1981, she earned a Bachelor of Science degree in occupational therapy from Temple University in Philadelphia, Pennsylvania. Kriss was certified in neurodevelopmental treatment techniques in 1991 and board certified in pediatrics in 1995. She has worked in early intervention centers and public and private school settings since 1981. She resides in Mount Laurel, New Jersey with her husband and three daughters.

About the Authors